WADSWORTH GUIDES TO LITERARY STUDY
Maurice Beebe, General Editor

APPROACHES TO *MACBETH*
edited by Jay L. Halio, University of California, Davis

APPROACHES TO *WALDEN*
edited by Lauriat Lane, Jr., University of New Brunswick

A *BENITO CERENO* HANDBOOK
edited by Seymour L. Gross, University of Notre Dame

CONRAD'S *HEART OF DARKNESS* AND THE CRITICS
edited by Bruce Harkness, University of Illinois

CONRAD'S *SECRET SHARER* AND THE CRITICS
edited by Bruce Harkness, University of Illinois

STEPHEN CRANE'S *MAGGIE:* Text and Context
edited by Maurice Bassan, San Francisco State College

CRIME AND PUNISHMENT* AND THE CRITICS
edited by Edward Wasiolek, University of Chicago

THE *KING LEAR* PERPLEX
edited by Helmut Bonheim, University of California, Santa Barbara

LITERARY CENSORSHIP: Principles, Cases, Problems
edited by Kingsley Widmer, San Diego State College, and Eleanor Widmer

LITERARY SYMBOLISM: An Introduction to the Interpretation of Literature
edited by Maurice Beebe, Purdue University

MELVILLE'S *BILLY BUDD* AND THE CRITICS
edited by William T. Stafford, Purdue University

OEDIPUS REX:* A MIRROR FOR GREEK DRAMA
edited by Albert Cook, Western Reserve University

THE RIME OF THE ANCIENT MARINER:* A HANDBOOK
edited by Royal A. Gettmann, University of Illinois

J. D. SALINGER AND THE CRITICS
edited by William F. Belcher and James W. Lee, North Texas State University

SATIRE: THEORY AND PRACTICE
edited by Charles A. Allen and George D. Stephens, California State College at Long Beach

A *SCARLET LETTER* HANDBOOK
edited by Seymour L. Gross, University of Notre Dame

SUCCESS IN AMERICA
edited by Robert H. Woodward and James J. Clark, San Jose State College

VOLTAIRE'S *CANDIDE* AND THE CRITICS
edited by Milton P. Foster, Eastern Michigan University

ROBERT PENN WARREN'S *ALL THE KING'S MEN:* A Critical Handbook
edited by Maurice Beebe and Leslie Field, Purdue University

WHITMAN THE POET: MATERIALS FOR STUDY
edited by John C. Broderick, Lake Forest College

ROBERT PENN WARREN'S

ALL THE KING'S MEN

A Critical Handbook

edited by

MAURICE BEEBE

and

LESLIE A. FIELD

Purdue University

WADSWORTH PUBLISHING COMPANY
Belmont, California

PREFACE

Robert Penn Warren's *All the King's Men* (1946) has established itself as a classic of modern American fiction. To say of any single novel that it could provide a liberal education in itself would be to exaggerate, but when one considers the numerous subjects touched on by Warren in this novel—history, philosophy, sociology, political science, religion, law, medicine, psychology, literature, even football and brain surgery!—it probably comes as close to providing materials for a liberal education as any American novel published in the twentieth century. *All the King's Men* has been read as a social document, a tragedy, a novel of ideas, a melodrama, a manifesto of the New Criticism, and so on. A novel seen so variously may well be called a modern epic.

No wonder, then, that *All the King's Men* is still widely read, taught, and studied. For the general reader, much of the book's appeal derives from its exciting story, its ironic variation of the rags-to-riches theme so common in American fiction, its realistic depiction of politics, and its frankly romantic treatment of love and sex. The thoughtful reader is attracted also to the way in which the novel offers no simple answers to the crucial questions it raises. Thus, *All the King's Men* has been called both conservative and liberal, nihilistic and Christian, pragmatic and idealistic. If the novel fails to provide simple answers to vital issues, it is largely because Warren is a modern intellectual committed to the stance of "irony." A well-educated, articulate literary critic and teacher, he knows that it is not only easier to ask questions than to answer them, but that final answers may be deadly. When Jack Burden, the narrator of *All the King's Men,* says that "the end of man is knowledge . . . the end of man is to know," we can be quite sure that Warren the critic is fully aware of the implications of the statement. "End" may well be equivalent to "purpose" or "goal": whatever distinguishes man from animals puts him on a search for truth. Read thus, the statement seems as affirmative as something a dean might say to a convocation of freshmen. Yet when Jack Burden undertakes a search for truth and finds it, his discovery leads to destruction. Humpty Dumpty falls from the wall, and if all the king's men can't put him together again, it is because they too have tumbled. Therefore, "to know" is literally "the end of man."

Or take one additional example—and what could be more immediate than the title? Because the phrase "all the king's men" obviously derives from the nursery rhyme, critics have speculated at length on whether Willie Stark is the Humpty who fell from the wall or the king who couldn't put him together again. Willie is obviously "king" of the unnamed state which serves as setting of the novel, but he also obviously "falls." If Willie is king, then the minor characters are his men. The novel does indeed appear to be structured on that assumption. But if Willie is Humpty, who is the king who fails to put him together again? It could be God, but it may also be Jack Burden, whose narration of the story is an attempt to reconstruct Willie Stark. Since it is Robert Penn Warren who is putting Jack's words on paper, is he telling us that he could not put Humpty together again? Or is he too modest, too ironic to think of himself as the king? The critics who speculate on the relevance to the novel of the nursery rhyme fail to note that Warren had another source in mind for his title. He has admitted that whereas Willie Stark is not to be equated with Huey Long, the novel could not have been written if Senator Long had not existed. Long used "every man a king" as his campaign slogan, composing a song with that title and using it also as the title of his autobiography. But if we hope to find a clincher to the Humpty-King question in this historical fact, we are taken aback when we realize that it is literally *Everyman a King*, that the terms are reversible, that therefore any man may be both Humpty Dumpty and the King. But why did Long choose that phrase as his slogan? Was it because he was popularly known as the Kingfish? And if so, how did he derive that nickname? The ingenious critic may be tempted to find the source in the Fisher King that has become so celebrated in myth, T. S. Eliot, and modern criticism. But could it also have something to do with the kingfisher bird, alluded to at least once in *All the King's Men*? Or could the source have been simply the Kingfish of the old Amos and Andy radio show, that wizard of the lodge whose ultimate origins are lost in primeval myth and ritual?

These are the kinds of questions which we find ourselves asking as we read *All the King's Men*. One can pull out almost any thread from the fabric and find that it leads on and on. We have tried to assemble materials that make the search for the end of the thread a challenging task, but an interesting one. *All the King's Men* is especially well adapted to controlled research because its plot hinges on a research project. Epic, tragedy, and social document, it is also a mystery story constructed in such a way that the reader, like Jack Burden, must assume the role of a detective in a quest for truth. Warren himself underwent much the same process in writing his novel.

To the extent that space permits, we have attempted to provide, in the first part of this book, materials that will give the student a view of what Warren had to work with: first, his *object*—the Huey Long analogy and several of the literary influences that Warren has acknowledged; then a representative view of the equipment which he as *subject* brought to that object—a selection from his literary criticism, a statement of his personal creed, and a scholar's description of Warren's several attempts to tell the story of Willie Stark in the form of drama. The second main part of this casebook is devoted to critical interpretations of the novel. In arranging these selections, we have attempted a progression that combines the chronological with the logical. The first section offers the first three full-scale analyses of *All the King's Men,* each introducing a different basic critical approach that may be found also in later discussions of the novel. The second section presents attempts to find a key to the meaning of the novel in such things as the Populist movement, nihilism, hedonism versus Puritanism, teleology, romanticism versus reality, and Hegelian conservatism. The final section of this second main part offers three recent assessments of the novel; the last of these selections presents a synthesis of the main themes evident in the novel and its criticism. The ultimate synthesis, however, is perhaps an A+ paper by an ideal student with unlimited time and total recall. To help such a student and others, we have provided in the appendices a chronology of Robert Penn Warren's career, topics for discussion and research, and a selected bibliography of additional criticism.

So that students may document their papers as if they had read the original materials, we have provided exact bibliographical references for each selection, and the original pagination is indicated by means of small raised numerals in the text. Although the selections are generally reprinted as they first appeared, we have made certain changes in the interest of clarity and consistency. We have taken the liberty of adding descriptive titles to some of the selections, though in all such instances the original titles are provided in the bibliographical references. We have followed the *MLA Style Book* in most matters of form, such as italicizing titles of books and incorporating short prose quotations into the text. Rather than perpetuate errors, we have unobtrusively corrected certain misspellings and mistakes of fact, and we have changed footnote numbers as required. In addition, we have added or standardized page references for quotations from the novel. Quotations of some length or importance are identified thus: (46, *41*)— the first number referring to the Harcourt, Brace original edition, the Grosset and Dunlap reprint, and the Modern Library edition; the italicized number, to the paperbound Bantam Books edition.

We hope that we have provided adequately challenging materials and sufficiently useful aids to enable the intelligent student to write an essay which could well be described in Jack Burden's words—"It was a perfect research job, marred in its technical perfection by only one thing: it meant something."

CONTENTS

PART TWO: THE CRITICS' RESPONSE

First Analyses

Varied Approaches

Three Recent Assessments

The Huey Long Analogy

HUEY LONG'S LOUISIANA HAYRIDE

Hodding Carter

For newspapermen, those were gargantuan, memorable days. You stood beside his hotel dining table, as he slopped up great tablespoonsful of cereal with a sidewinding sweep or tore broiled chicken to pieces with his fingers, and you jotted down the incessant harangues against the lying newspapers, the city machine and the battered enemy politicians, while the bodyguards glowered protectively nearby. You didn't like him if only because the slugging of newspapermen didn't seem justifiable even for vote-getting, and especially when the strong-arming became personal. You were chased by militiamen across the parade grounds of Jackson Barracks in New Orleans and held a prisoner after you had sneaked in to discover whether the governor was calling out the troops on the eve of the Senatorial election—in which the governor was a candidate.

In a corridor of the garish Roosevelt Hotel, managed by an oily former shoe clerk who was now his paymaster and treasurer, you watched a fellow-reporter being hustled out of the governor's suite. Inside the suite the reporter had struck the governor in retaliation for being cursed, and the governor had struck back, but only after his bodyguards had pinioned his attacker.

You interviewed him after he had precipitated a silly international incident by receiving a German admiral in disheveled green pajamas, and you laughed in spite of yourself at his shrewdly appealing account of his gaucherie. You heard a pale-faced man, thrust before a microphone, identify himself as Sam Irby, who had been kidnapped by state police on the eve of an election because he had threatened to tell what he knew about his daughter and the governor, who employed

Hodding Carter, "Huey Long's Louisiana Hayride," *The American Mercury*, LXVIII (April 1949), 435–447. Reprinted by permission of the author and the publisher.

1

her as his secretary. And after Irby had told who he was, in front of the microphone in the hotel headquarters, you marveled at his exoneration of the governor, and speculated upon the reasons therefor.

Afterwards, in the corridor, a fellow-reporter was to have a gun thrust into his stomach as he sought to enter[435] the elevator on which the mysterious Mr. Irby was being whisked away.

By the spring of 1935, Senator Huey Long owned Louisiana. And in that spring another and lesser man, except for his honesty, gave a fey, lonely warning.

His name was Mason Spencer. Young, big-boned, unafraid, he was relatively unimportant, almost the last member of the state legislature not to acquiesce in profitably, or accept silently, the final substitution of government by personal dictatorship for government by ballot. The Louisiana legislature had granted Senator Long, through his administrative and judicial proxies, incontestable control of all elections, including the appointment of commissioners, the power to disqualify unfriendly voters and the privilege of padding the voting lists wherever and whenever necessary. Already he possessed the courts, the municipal police forces, the school teachers, the taxing authorities, the governor, the state government, even the banks. Finally, he had the vote itself.

And Mason Spencer, an unimportant, honest man, rose in the legislature and said this:

When this ugly thing is boiled down in its own juices, it disenfranchises the white people of Louisiana. I am not gifted with second sight. Nor did I see a spot of blood on the moon last night. But I can see blood on the polished floor of this Capitol. For if you ride this thing through, you will travel with the white horse of death. White men have ever made poor slaves.

Representative Spencer was a better prophet than historian. In September of that year, the Capitol's marble floors were soiled with blood. Huey Long's blood, and the blood of the quiet, studious young doctor who shot him.

But the prophet of tragedy had overlooked the history of his state. Most Louisianians, for two hundred years, had been docile political slaves. Few knew enough about their state to recognize this almost uninterrupted and hitherto gently managed servitude. Nor was it something which those who did know wanted to be bruited about.

This historical truth must first be comprehended if the success of fascism in one American state is to be understood. Its colonists were a sad conglomerate, successively the vassals of two decadent and dying monarchies: Canadian *coureurs de bois* and their Indian women; professional soldiers of short life expectancy; a few adventurous or disappointed members of the French aristocracy; and a pitiful succession of peasants and artisans, sewer-scourings and exiled whores, having in common only poverty, hopelessness and neglect.

Among such settlers there was little thought of self-government. They were monstrously exploited. From the first, government was directed by the entrenched few. Creole gentry and American merchant and planter perpetuated a basic agreement. Only gentlemen and politicians managed by gentlemen should direct the backwoodsmen[436] who spilled over into the new territory and the descendants of the French and Spanish riffraff.

So, almost uninterruptedly, Louisiana politics from the Purchase until the Civil War was a story of genteel corruption, of steady political degeneration, of venality, of a studied neglect of civic advancement. Reconstruction further debilitated self-government; and where Reconstruction ended, rule under the gold-directed manipulation of the Louisiana Lottery began. At the beginning of the twentieth century, Louisianians could count on the fingers of one hand those major public servants who in all Louisiana history had been honest and progressive, active in behalf of the small people, and given to implementing campaign promises with administrative performance.

The political leaders were, for the most part, conservative stereotypes; and even in New Orleans the machine politicians were guided in the things that mattered. They cooperated with the bankers, the large merchants, the oil and sugar and cotton interests, the affluent votaries of the status quo. A wise statesman didn't antagonize the railroads, the banks, the refiners, the lumbermen, the enterprising developers—or exploiters—of the great and noble state of Louisiana. He orated, with elocutionary fire, about the glories of the past and the wonders of the future, about the dark days of Reconstruction, about white supremacy and black threats, God's mercy and the rightness of the established order. This is not to say that all were politically immoral or amoral, though most of them actually were. They resembled atavistic mastadons, towering above and unknowingly becoming trapped in a surging human slough. In this they were not unlike their fellow-politicians elsewhere. The difference was that for two hundred years Louisiana had been so very safe for the mastadons.

I I

Such was the political Louisiana in which Huey Pierce Long was born in 1893, in impoverished Winn parish in north Louisiana, a breeding ground of economic and political dissenters. His background was tailor-made for a politician. A log cabin, albeit a substantial one, was his birthplace. His father was a farmer of small means but with considerable ambition, who managed to send six of his nine children—but not Huey—to college.

Young Huey hated both farm work and conformity. In high

school he discovered his talent for spell-binding oratory, and the power of a vocabulary enriched by Biblical allusion and directness, acquired naturally in a devout Baptist home.

The years between his graduation and his becoming a member of the Louisiana bar at twenty-one tested to the limit his extraordinary physical energy and driving mental discipline—the only discipline which he ever perfected in himself. Marrying before he reached voting age, he supported himself and his wife by peddling Cottolene,[437] a cooking compound, throughout north Louisiana, meeting thereby and making friends of many farm folk who were to become the core of his political organization. He attended Oklahoma University Law School for one tempestuous term. Then, incredibly, he completed the three-year law course at Tulane University, in eight months; and, securing a special examination from the Louisiana Supreme Court, became a lawyer at twenty-one. No other student at Tulane has ever matched this record.

He hung out his shingle in Winnfield, county seat of Winn parish. His first benefactor in Winnfield was a state senator named Harper, a prosperous man for the locality, but a "radical" who proposed a redistribution of national income as the cure-all for the country's ills. During the first World War, Harper published a pamphlet calling for conscription of the nation's wealth as well as its manpower. A Federal grand jury indicted him. He was defended by his young disciple, Huey, who was deferred in the draft because he had a wife and child. (Huey also tried to gain exemption as a public official. He was a notary public. Through questionable stategy, Huey won Harper's acquittal.

At 24, Huey sought the one state office open to one of his age, a state railroad commissionership. The Railroad Commission was Louisiana's three-man utilities regulating body. He won. In the campaign he gained another ally, an older Winnfield man named O.K. Allen, who lent him $500 to help finance his campaign. Later, when Long was elected United States Senator, he rewarded O.K. by making him his governor, stooge and errand boy.

As railroad commissioner, Huey was something uncomfortably new and strange. Some regarded him as a radical menace, others saw only a coarse publicity-seeking clown, a thick, comical-looking youngster with a face that was a puffy caricature of a cherub, with its dimpled chin, snub nose and unruly, curling reddish hair. But among the masses there were multiplying thousands who saw a champion, a new Great Commoner, who damned and insulted Bigness in all its Louisiana manifestations.

In 1920 he supported for governor John M. Parker, one-time Bull Moose Vice-Presidential running mate of Theodore Roosevelt, because he believed the comparatively liberal Parker would deal strongly with Standard Oil. But Parker, to Huey's thinking, was too lenient after he became governor. Huey broke with him, was indicted and convicted of

libeling the governor, and was fined a dollar and given a 30-day suspended sentence. He refused to pay the fine, so the judge and opposing
counsel made up the dollar themselves.

But he was winning friends and influencing voters. In 1924, at the
height of the bitter Klan fight in Louisiana, Huey Long, now 30, announced for governor. He tried to go down the middle on the Klan
issue. He almost[438] succeeded. Before election day he predicted that
he would win if rain didn't keep the mud-farmers away from the polls.
It rained, and he lost. But already the uneasy feeling had arisen among
his opponents that he would be unbeatable the next time.

III

From 1925 to 1928 Huey mended political fences, kept himself in
the headlines, and built up a large and lucrative practice as attorney
for some of the vested interests against which he ranted.

The 1928 campaign was more like a cyclonic disturbance than
another three-way race for the governorship. Huey was probably the
most indefatigable campaigner and best catch-as-catch-can stumper
the demagogically fertile South has yet produced. He belabored and
promised and defamed, speaking in the harsh, bitter language of the
poor man, eighteen and twenty hours a day. Beneath the erroneously
named Evangeline oak, he drove his program home to open-mouthed,
whooping Cajuns:

And it is here that Evangeline waited for her lover Gabriel who never
came. This oak is an immortal spot, made so by Longfellow's poem. But
Evangeline is not the only one who has waited here in disappointment. Where
are the schools that you have waited for your children to have that have never
come? Where are the roads and the highways that you spent your money to
build, that are no nearer now than ever before? Where are the institutions to
care for the sick and disabled? Evangeline wept bitter tears in her disappointment. But they lasted through only one lifetime. Your tears in this country,
around this oak, have lasted for generations. Give me the chance to dry the
tears of those who still weep here.

No rain fell on Election Day this time. The evil city again rejected him, but Catholic and Protestant farmers united to give him a
lead, though not a clear majority. His two opponents wouldn't join
forces; and at 35 Huey Long sat in the governor's chair that he was to
transform into a throne. Louisiana's poor whites had come into their
own.

Long summarily discharged every state job-holder under executive
control who had not actively supported him. Lacking a majority at the
first session of the legislature, he swapped patronage for concessions,
and in both House and Senate placed his own men in the chair. The
legislature approved his proposal for a $30 million bond issue to pro-

vide farm roads, increased hospital and other institutional support, and free school books, levying a severance tax and higher gasoline taxes to pay for the program. Behind Huey were the people, and the people wanted these things.

And with the people behind him, Huey expanded ominously. Defying rule and convention, he personally directed strategy from the floors of the House and Senate. Once he bragged that he was the state constitution now, and again that he had bought a legislator like a sack of potatoes. He coerced banks which hesitated to make the state a tide-over loan. The legality of his free textbook[439] law challenged because it included parochial schools among the recipients, he argued his own case before the United States Supreme Court and won brilliantly. Without constitutional authority, he ordered the state militia into the unfriendly, wide-open parishes adjoining New Orleans, and closed the casinos until the gamblers cooperated.

All this was shocking enough to those Louisianians who favorably recalled less troublesome days and ways. But when Huey summoned the legislature into special session to enact a five-cent occupational tax on oil to aid "the sick, the halt, the blind and the children," all Hell broke loose. A barrel-house free-for-all took place on the floor of the House when Long's speaker, smelling impeachment in the air, declared the House adjourned *sine die*. Bloody-faced legislators groped blindly for assailants who had struck them from behind. Men were felled by inkwells, canes, bare fists.

The next day the speaker decided that the House had not adjourned, and the House proceeded to impeach Huey Long. The charges ranged from the grave to the ridiculous. Huey had sought to bribe legislators. He had plotted the murder of an opposition senator. He had misused, misapplied and misappropriated state funds. He had squandered monies allocated to a national governors' conference in New Orleans on a riotous, bosomy party, testimony concerning which left some governors red-faced. He had acted unbecomingly in public places, even to the extent of getting cockeyed drunk.

Huey fought back with promises, intimidation and circulars, distributed by the hundreds of thousands by state employees to the faithful. Again he barnstormed Louisiana. His primary targets, not altogether without justification, were Standard Oil, the newspapers—particularly the New Orleans newspapers—and the old political guard.

To most of the state it looked as if Huey were finished. Then, dramatically, he produced a round robin, signed by fifteen senators, who declared that no matter what evidence was submitted to the Senate they would not vote to convict the governor because they believed the charges against him were invalid. Their number was one more than enough to prevent a two-thirds majority necessary for conviction. The deserving fifteen reaped earthly rewards, and never again was Huey in dire political danger.

From this fiasco emerged the dictator, vindictive and intent upon a domination that could not again be challenged.

I V

Louisiana's frightened, vengeful governor surrounded himself with a half-dozen gun-ready, slugging bodyguards. He established a weekly newspaper, the *Louisiana Progress*, staffed it principally with skillful, conscienceless young newspapermen, and sicked it on his enemies. State employees[440] found it good insurance to subscribe to the *Progress*, the number of subscriptions depending upon the size of their salaries, but with a minimum of ten to be sold, eaten, or used as wallpaper. No opponent big enough to be worthy of notice escaped its libeling. The voters of the nation's most illiterate state could understand its cartoon obscenities even when they couldn't spell out the text.

The public-works program went into high gear. The depression was rocking Louisiana. Public works meant needed jobs. And the administration could count on at least five votes for each employee. The first program was followed by a second and more ambitious one: a $68 million highway construction project, a $5 million skyscraper capitol, and another $20 million in assorted projects, all to be financed by an additional three-cent hike in the gasoline tax. With a year and a half yet to serve as governor, and with the opposition organizing against the program, Huey decided to run for the United States Senate with the state program as his platform.

The use of the sound truck and the financial strangulation of the enemy city of New Orleans were the principal innovations of the campaign. Conservative, goateed, 70-year-old Joseph Ransdall, the incumbent whom Huey dubbed "Feather Duster," burbled unavailingly. Huey won hands down. He designated his old benefactor, O.K. Allen of Winnfield, as governor for the next full term.

Meanwhile he concocted what might have been a good if desperate expedient for the cotton South. With Biblical precedent to back him up, he proposed that in protest against ruinous five-cent cotton, the South should let its cotton crops lie fallow for a year. But Huey managed to insult Texas, the South's principal cotton producer, and the Texas legislature, thumbing its nose at "the arrogant jackass who brays from Louisiana ... ignoramus, buffoon, meddler, and liar," would have none of the plan. So it died.

In January, 1932, the Kingfish from Louisiana breezed into Washington. For the next three and one half years he performed simultaneously in two rings of a dazzling political circus, the capital of Louisiana and the capital of the nation. He soon broke with President Roosevelt, each sensing in the other a challenge, and from the Senate floor ridiculed "Prince Franklin, Knight of the Nourmahal," and his New Deal, unconcernedly violating the Senate's rule of personal decorum by lampooning administration stalwarts. Day after day Huey made news. Sometimes amusing news, as in the controversy over whether cornbread should be dunked or crumbled in turnip greens potlikker. Sometimes bad news for Huey, as when an unidentified guest at a Sands Point, Long Island, club resented with hammering fists the Kingfish's impatient attempt to make use of a urinal before the other had moved aside.

In 1934, Long formalized the program[441] which he hoped would eventually win him the Presidency. The hazy concept of a national redistribution of wealth, presented fifteen years before by the obscure state senator from Winn Parish, took definable shape in a national "Share Our Wealth" organization. No dues were necessary. Huey produced the expense money as easily as the nation disgorged the followers, both by the hundreds of thousands. No matter that the Share Our Wealth program was demonstrably impracticable as presented. It *was* believable: A limitation of fortunes to $5 million. An annual income minimum of $2000. An annual income maximum of $1,800,000. A homestead grant of $6000 for every family. Free education from kindergarten through college. Bonuses for veterans. Old age pensions, radios, automobiles, an abundance of cheap food through governmental purchase and storage of surpluses. The Share Our Wealth members had their own catchy song, "Every Man a King," their own newspaper, the mud-slinging *Louisiana Progress,* expanded now to the *American Progress.*

The movement was nothing less than a new political party, heir to the yearnings and frustrations of the Populists, the Whisky Rebels, the Know-Nothings, the Free Silverites, of all the have-nots of capitalism. The New Deal became worried, and began to use its Louisiana patronage accordingly.

By legislative action, Long made sure that no Federal relief money could be obtained by any Louisiana municipality or county except with the approval and supervision of an agency of his own. The Federal administration retaliated by withholding PWA project funds. Revenue agents roved through Louisiana from 1932 until well after Long's death and eventually with decisive results. A Senatorial committee timorously held hearings in New Orleans relative to the corruption which accompanied the election to the Senate of a Long ally, John Overton; and, after being defied, browbeaten and ridiculed by Huey and his gibing lieutenants, exonerated Overton.

As the Share Our Wealth chorus swelled, Huey, like a wise military tactician, took care to protect his rear. In a spectacular, degenerative series of special sessions in 1934 and 1935, his legislature reduced Louisianians almost literally to the status of Indian wards. Together with this final elimination of the actualities of democratic self-government—to the unconcern of a majority of the unconsulted electorate—came new benefits: homestead tax exemption, theoretically up to $2000; abolition of the one-dollar poll tax; a debt moratorium act—and

new taxes: an income tax; a public utilities receipt tax; an attempted
"two cents a lie" tax on the advertising receipts of the larger newspapers, which the United States Supreme Court pronounced unconstitutional.

Huey's figurehead governor, O.K. Allen, was given the power to
call out[442] the militia whenever he—or Huey—wished. The governor
could—and did—expand the state police force into a swarm of private
agents, some uniformed and some not, their number and the identity
of the un-uniformed alike a secret. The State Attorney-General was
empowered to supersede any district attorney in any trial. The State
Tax Commission was given the right to change any city or county tax
assessment, so that a misbehaving corporation or individual might
know just who held the economic stranglehold. An ironically-desig-
nated civil service board was created, without appointive control over
all fire and police chiefs; and a school budget committee with the right
to review the appointments of every school teacher and school employee.

v

It is perhaps a corollary that in the last year of his life, Long
became obsessed with a fear of assassination. He increased his armed
bodyguard, and took other unusual precautions to insure his personal
safety. In July 1935 he charged on the floor of the Senate that enemies
had planned his death with "one man, one gun and one bullet" as the
medium, and with the promise of a Presidential pardon as the slayer's
reward. This plot, he said, was hatched in a New Orleans hotel at a
gathering of his enemies. A dictograph, concealed in the meeting room,
had recorded the "murderous conversation." I was at that meeting. It
was a caucus of die-hard oppositionists, dolefully trying to decide what
to do for the next state campaign. And the "plotting" was limited to
such hopefully expressed comments as "Good God, I wish somebody
would kill the son of a bitch."

And somebody did. That July, the white horse of death, foreseen
by Mason Spencer earlier in the year, was but two months distant.
On the night of September 8, a slender, bespectacled man in a white
suit stepped from behind a marble pillar in the capitol as Long,
accompanied by his closest aides and bodyguard, hurried to the governor's office. Dr. Carl Austin Weiss, the man in the white suit, drew a
small pistol and fired once. Seconds later, the assassin lay dead, his
body and head riddled by 61 shots. Huey Long staggered away with one
bullet wound, perhaps a second, in his stomach. Thirty hours later he
died.

The principal legatees of the kingdom effected an uneasy peace
among themselves, settling upon one Richard Leche, a fat, easy-going
minor henchman who held a judgeship, as a compromise candidate for

governor. They had a limitless war chest and the election machinery. The Share Our Wealth Clubs were out to avenge their martyr. The repeal of the poll tax had almost doubled the voting lists, and the overwhelming majority of the new voters were remembering the man who had given them this free privilege and their roads and school books and a circus besides.

We took up the fight against[443] Long's heirs. On our side we had only the Federal patronage. In a vote-getting sense, this consisted mainly of WPA work orders which were distributed by the thousands to the anti-Long organizations. They didn't help much. The poor jobless devils took the work orders readily enough, but they didn't vote WPA.

Few among us could have won even in an honestly conducted election. In the eyes of too many old and new voters, the hands of the opposition were stained with Huey's blood. And we had nothing to offer except the promise that self-government would be returned to a people apparently content without it. The campaign was macabre. The heirs of Long did almost everything in his memory except display his body on the platform. And by the thousands upon thousands the Louisiana electorate voted vengeance for their martyr against the mythical "bloody murderers" whose indictments and convictions were a Leche campaign pledge. We would have been defeated even in an honest election; yet it was a bitter thing to stand by helplessly while the pre-marking of ballots through the endless chain device insured machine majorities in most of the boxes where the issue might otherwise have been in doubt.

No wealth-sharing ideologist or political rough-and-tumbler, Leche ushered in an era of comparably good feeling and incomparably good pickings. His morals as flaccid as his body, he took things easy, and his fellow-freebooters took almost everything easily. "When I took the Governor's oath I didn't take the vows of poverty," quipped fat Dick.

With an eye on Louisiana's electoral votes in the 1936 Democratic National convention, the more practical politicians of the New Deal made a special kind of deal with Louisiana. Income tax prosecutions were dropped. Dick visited Washington, called upon and was photographed with President Roosevelt and some of the lesser figures of the administration. He was visited in turn in Louisiana by the President and Attorney General Murphy.

And then in 1939 the haunted, graft-debased house of Long began to fall apart. President James Monroe Smith of Louisiana State University went to the penitentiary for stealing state bonds. Dick Leche went to Federal prison. So did Seymour Weiss, the treasurer, Abe Shushan, one of the earliest Louisianians to support Long and to profit from that support, and several others. One grafter killed himself.

Earl Long, the flamboyant, politically unsuccessful brother of the

Kingfish, tried to carry the flickering torch. Running for a full term, he was opposed by James Noe, a wealthy oilman and ally of Huey, whom the gang had shunted aside and who made it pay for the snub; Sam Jones, a young, incorruptible attorney who had spent most of his mature years fighting Longism; and James H. Morrison, a brass-voiced newcomer[444] who in platform technique was another Long. Earl Long led in the first primary, with Sam Jones second, Noe third, and Morrison a poor fourth. Noe's support in the second primary would determine the winner. He got even with Earl Long by supporting Sam Jones.

But even in 1944 the ghost of Huey Long was not laid. A Long man was almost elected governor. He was defeated, not by a forthright crusader against machine politics, but by a mild and pleasant composer and singer of hillbilly ballads, a former professor and public service commissioner, who campaigned with his band and said nothing against any opponent. Perhaps because they were tired of invective and hate, Louisianians elected Jimmie Davis governor. His administration was uneventful, untroubled by corruption and perhaps too colorless for a state accustomed to bread, thieves, and circuses.

Then, forgetting the past, a majority of Louisianians delivered themselves willingly, early in 1948, to the Long dynasty again. In January, vengeful Earl Long, lacking his brother's distorted vision and ability but as dictator-minded, drove to the governorship over Sam Jones, who in 1940 had undertaken the thankless housecleaning. And in July, 29-year-old Russell Long, Huey's spit-and-image son, triumphed in a much closer race for the Senate seat left vacant by the death of his father's old henchman, John Overton.

Beside them in their campaigns stalked the ghost of Huey Long, giving credence to their promises of help for the poor, identifying brother and son with the little people whose material needs he had filled, reminding the insecure, the class-conscious, the conscienceless and the ignorant of the continuing cleavage between the powerful and the small. Almost overnight, Louisiana became the most heavily taxed state, per capita, in the nation as Earl Long rammed through revenue measures to make good his promises of largesse. But that didn't bother the little people. Huey, too, had soaked the rich. Let his brother and his boy have a go at it. Long live the Longs and to hell with the high hats and the reformers!

No, the ghost is not yet laid, although Huey Long is dead these many long years. Nor will it be for many years to come. For this hideous thing that we remember as the rough-shod reign of the Kingfish was not hideous in its beginnings. Whether or not Huey Long himself was ever sincere in his protestations for the poor and downtrodden is, basically, beside the point. For he led a social-economic revolution in Louisiana; and after his death the entire South was debated ground.

V I

It was not his political genius and ruthlessness alone that made him possible. There were two other facts equally as important.

The first fact was that, after two hundred years, the people of Louisiana[445] were ready and waiting for a Messiah who would translate their needs into accomplishments. Theirs was the ground-swell of the little people, a people undisturbed by his tactics as long as they got the roads, the free bridges, the hospitals, the free schoolbooks, the public works; as long as the men whom he pilloried and broke and banished were identified with the leaders of the past, bumbling representatives of an indifferent, negative ruling class. The little people shrugged at graft because of their certainty that there always had been graft of a kind. This time, whatever the politicians skimmed off the top, they were getting theirs too. And they were getting something else. Revenge. A fantastic vengeance upon the Sodom and Gomorrah that was called New Orleans. A squaring of accounts with the big shots, Standard Oil and the bankers, the big planters, the entrenched interests everywhere.

The second fact was the weird make-up of the forces actively opposed to Long. His disunited enemies had difficulty from beginning to end in maintaining an alliance that had its base in military necessity alone. We were strange bed-fellows. Cynical spoils politicians of the Old Regular ring in New Orleans. Ardent, idealistic New Dealers. Inept leaders of the country parishes, turned out in short grass. Nonpolitical gentility awakened from their slumbers by rude knocking. The hitherto secure representatives of Big Business. Honestly disturbed, solid bourgeoisie. Our combined cries for good government made a dissonant chorus. Huey bowled us over like tenpins.

Even had Huey Long relied only upon his mesmeric appeal to Louisiana's masses and his ability to make promised delivery of the material things those masses wanted, it is probable that he could have dominated his state as completely and for at least as long as he did. But his compelling lust for power as such—a primary animating force in his political life—and the intense vindictiveness which from the start characterized his public career lured him to a morally indefensible position.

When impeachment seemed a certainty in those early months as governor, he simply bought and paid for enough legislators "like sacks of potatoes" to prevent the majority vote necessary for conviction. From then on, Long bought those whom he needed and could buy, and crushed those who had no purchase price or whose price was too high.

Nor was the control of a governor, a majority of legislators, a court majority enough. Even private citizens made their living by his sufferance. Long could have taxed to extinction any business, large or small, and business knew it. Men could be—and were—arrested by unidentified men, the members of his secret police, held incommunicado, tried and found guilty on trumped-up charges. A majority of the State Supreme Court became unabashedly his. Through his state printing board he popped an[446] economic whip over the rural and small town press, lashing all but a few into sullen silence. A thug, making a premeditated skull-crushing attack upon a Long opponent, could draw from his pocket in court a pre-signed pardon from the figurehead governor.

In the end, these things indirectly destroyed Huey Long himself. There are many conflicting tales as to why and how he was killed. This much is a certainty. His assassination was not plotted. It is not probable that Dr. Weiss went to the capitol the night of September 8, 1935 deliberately to kill Long. But he must have intended to protest a grave injury, the double-barrelled kind of injury Long delighted in inflicting. Dr. Weiss' father-in-law, an implacable enemy of Long, had been gerrymandered out of his judgeship. Two of the judge's daughters had been dismissed from their teaching positions in further retaliation. And worse, Long had circulated noisome rumors about the family's ancestry.

Political punishment compounded with savage slander. An old, tested formula for reducing enemies to impotence. But this time the formula distilled a deadly reaction. Those who knew young Dr. Weiss best say that he could have sought Long only to protest verbally or with his fists this grave slander. They say that he could have drawn his gun only because the bodyguards threatened him. Few in Louisiana believe the full, true story has been told, for Long's henchmen were the only spectators. Perhaps the single bullet, fired from Weiss' small pistol, fatally wounded Long. Perhaps there was a second wound, as many Louisianians believe, caused by a ricocheting bullet from a bodyguard's gun. One bullet, two bullets. It is unimportant now, unimportant even then. Out of the terror he created, out of the driving passion to destroy other men, out of the futility that warped the minds of the Louisianians who opposed him, Huey Long himself forged the weapon which felled him.

And it need not have been so. He might have served Louisiana and the South as had no other political leader. Before the numbed thousands of his followers, the worn and credulous who milled across the grounds of the capitol, Gerald L. K. Smith, the grasping opportunist who directed the Share Our Wealth clubs, spoke an epitaph deserving to have been said of a better man by a better man:

His body shall never rest as long as hungry bodies cry for food, as long as lean human frames stand naked, as long as homeless wretches haunt this land of plenty.

Close beside the bier crowded the thieves and sycophants of the inner circle. Beyond wept the poor.

Huey Long was no true revolutionary. Power for power's sake was his mastering god. No revolutionary but—the word is used not loosely but gingerly—a dictator. A dictator, *sui generis,* the first truly such out of the soil of America.[447]

✠

THE ACHIEVEMENTS OF HUEY LONG

T. Harry Williams

Huey P. Long was born in 1893 in Winn parish (county), the seventh in a family of nine children. There is a myth about his background that colors everything that has been written about him. It is that the Longs were abjectly poor, were without education or culture, were, in Southern terminology,[x] "hillbillies" or "trash." Long himself helped to father the myth—he operated in an age when politicians found it profitable to boast of a log cabin origin—but it has little foundation. Winn parish, with its thin soil and cutover timber patches, was undeniably poor in comparison with the more favored cotton and sugar parishes. It could not show an array of planter magnates, but it did have a substantial number of small farmers who worked hard and enjoyed a fairly comfortable living. The Longs were as well off as most people in Winn and, indeed, something above the average. Rather than scorning culture, they were highly respectful of it and eager to acquire it. Every member of the large family secured at least a touch of a college education. Huey Long, as he relates in the autobiography, had relatively little formal schooling at the higher levels—he exaggerates somewhat the work he took at Tulane University—but from boyhood he educated himself with a program of voracious reading. It is unlikely that many college graduates of the period had, for example, as wide a knowledge of history, or as much of a sense of history, as this product of the north Louisiana hills.

The members of the Long family, it needs to be noted for an understanding of the autobiography, were all intelligent and extremely individualistic in their relations with one another. Huey Long hints at this characteristic in referring to two of his brothers, whom,

From T. Harry Williams, "Introduction," *Every Man a King: The Auto-biography of Huey P. Long.* Chicago: Quadrangle Books, 1964. Pp. vii–xxvi. Reprinted by permission of the author and Quadrangle Books, Inc.

curiously, he does not name. The older brother mentioned in the early pages is Julius, who helped finance Huey's education and with whom he formed a law partnership. Yet Julius and Huey eventually broke[xi] and became bitter personal and political enemies. The younger brother described later who wanted to run for office is Earl Long, who was destined to be a political figure in his own right and three times governor. He and Huey broke too, although before Huey's death they were reconciled. All the brothers and sisters were in some degree interested in politics and active in it throughout their lives.

Perhaps there was something in the stark environment of Winn parish that was conducive to political interest. Winn had a tradition of dissent and protest that was rare in the rural South. In 1861 the parish had opposed secession and had shown but a scant enthusiasm for the Confederate cause. In the 1890's it had been the center of Populist strength in the state. In the early 1900's it had nurtured a Socialist party—more agrarian than Marxian, perhaps, but still daring to wear the collectivist label—that garnered a respectable vote in presidential elections and even won a number of local offices. Huey Long and his brothers and sisters grew up in an atmosphere of hot political debate, and many of the debaters challenged the basic assumptions held by many Americans. None of the Longs was a Populist or a Socialist. But the doctrines of these two factions, which Huey Long heard constantly in his youth, could not help but enter into his thinking. His own political philosophy was a kind of neo- or modified Populism. Drawn from his observation of local issues and conditions and his wide reading in past and current history, it was a down-with-the-big-man and up-with-the-little-man creed. He expressed it in definite terms when in 1918,[xii] at the age of twenty-four, he ran for his first office, and he never deviated significantly from it thereafter.

In the autobiography Long states that he decided to run for a place on the Railroad Commission because he was not old enough to try for any other office. The explanation is disingenuous. Although the age element may have had some influence, Long was moving with calculated shrewdness. For a politician who wanted to go to the top, the commission was the best possible starting point. Shortly to be renamed the Public Service Commission and given enlarged super-vision over all utilities, it was potentially one of the most powerful agencies in the state. It had been a moribund body. But after Long, who won an easy victory, took his seat, things changed fast. The commissioner launched a series of spectacular actions that he had undoubtedly planned from the moment he set eyes on the office. He instituted and prosecuted complaints and lawsuits against the biggest corporations in the state, with the gigantic Standard Oil Company heading the list of victims. Not all the decisions had the effect that Long claimed. But for the first time the commission had become an active, meaningful agency—and in the process Huey P. Long had become a figure with a state reputation, a man to be reckoned with as candidate for governor.

There can be no doubt that Long had planned from the first to run for governor. In fact, some of those closest to him think that he had mapped out a whole sequence of offices to be secured on a regular schedule—governor, United States Senator, and, finally, President. But he failed in his first try for the[xiii] governorship in 1924, although he ran a strong third. A variety of factors combined to undo him. He got in the middle of a fight over the Ku Klux Klan. Of the two other candidates, one was pro-Klan, the other, anti-Klan; Long, seeking to avoid the issue, lost votes in both camps. He lacked adequate finances and did not have an effective state-wide organization. The story in the autobiography, that rain on election day held back his full country vote, which has received wide credence, is without basis. What defeated him was an inability to roll up much of a vote in populous south Louisiana and the city of New Orleans. He tried to remedy this situation before running for the governorship again in 1928. To strengthen himself in the southern parishes he indorsed Senator Edwin S. Broussard's bid for re-election in 1926, in return for a pledge of Broussard's support. He also sought to create a more efficient organization in New Orleans. The Broussard deal worked. But Long was unable then and later to set up a combination in New Orleans that could cope with the ruling Old Regular machine. He finally, toward the end of his career, broke the Old Regulars, but he never won an election against them in the city proper.

Still, with more abundant finances and better organizational support, Long was able to win in 1928. He did not have the required majority of the popular vote in the first primary. But he was razor close, and when the third ranking candidate pulled out, with most of his leaders declaring for Long, the second runner also withdrew. Huey Long was governor, and a momentous change in the power structure of Louisiana[xiv] was about to take place. The new governor was determined to do many things, but first and foremost he meant to strike a deathblow at the hierarchy that had long controlled the state.

After Reconstruction, in all the Southern states the places of power were taken over by the upper income groups, the old planter class and the new and rising business interests. For generations these hierarchies ruled Southern politics, exercising their power through the medium of the one-party system, manipulating and combining factions in the Democratic organization. Occasionally rebels rose to challenge the existing order. They were men who claimed to speak for the masses and who demanded for the masses some voice in the councils of government and some share in the material rewards that government could bestow. In Southern historical writing they are called the demagogues. The demagogues made much noise and won some elections, but they did not alter in any fundamental way the nature of power relationships. Despite their violent denunciations of the ruling classes, they did little to raise up the masses. Some of them had no real interest in reform and were easily deflected into race baiting or into collaboration with the hierarchy. Those that had a program were unable to put it through; and for a fundamental reason—they lacked the ability, or more probably the will, to destroy the organization of the oligarchy and were eventually overthrown by it.

No demagogue had dared to defy the Louisiana hierarchy. Composed of the usual upper income groups and others peculiar to the local scene—the[xv] Standard Oil Company and gas and shipping interests—and allied with the New Orleans Old Regulars, the machine seemed especially strong and secure, and it was unusually conservative and complacent. It was capable of meeting demands for social change and absorbing and blunting them. It had, for example, to deal with the threat posed by the Progressive movement, which affected Louisiana and the South somewhat later than other sections. John M. Parker, who won the governorship in 1920 and who had Long's support, advocated some Progressive ideals, and as governor he steered some Progressive measures to enactment. But Parker, a man of ability, was himself a representative of the planter class, inhibited by his own standards and those of his group, and though he pushed harder than some associates thought he should, he did not push too hard. The Louisiana of the 1920's could hardly be said to be a modern state. It had less than 300 miles of cement roads, only 35 miles of roads with other surfacing, only three major bridges in the state highway system, an inadequate educational arrangement from the state university down to the elementary level, and archaic hospital and other public services. Both the place and the time were ripe, overly so, for a leader who would demand change. But few could have guessed what kind of change would come after 1928.

Long had promised change in both his campaigns. That he would succeed in getting much seemed doubtful to supporters and opponents and disinterested observers. He took with him into office only a minority of pledged followers in the legislature, and[xvi] everybody knew the vast power of the opposition to contain its enemies. Besides, Long was one of those demagogues. He would make a token effort for reform and then go to denouncing Negroes or Yankees and recalling Confederate glories in the Civil War and Southern suffering during Reconstruction. That was the way it always had been.

It was not going to be anything like that way. Long was the one Southern popular leader who promised something and then delivered. He was governor from 1928 to 1932. In 1930 he ran for the United States Senate, defeating the incumbent with ease. He could not take his seat, however, because of a conflict with his lieutenant governor, Paul Cyr. Long and Cyr had broken, and Huey would not go to Washington until he had made certain that one of his own men would succeed to the governorship. Not until January, 1932, could he safely leave the state. He was in the Senate after that date, but he was, in effect, still governor. His friend, O.K. Allen, was governor in name only. Long ran the administration and the state, ran both, his enemies charged, like a dictator.

The Long program of legislation was put into force over the period between 1928 and 1935. Although it took some time to enact, it was an impressive accomplishment. By 1935 Louisiana had 2,446 miles of cement roads, 1,308 miles of asphalt roads, twice as many miles of gravel roads as when Long took office, and over forty bridges in the state highway system. Appropriations for education, especially at the higher level, were increased, and the providing of free textbooks caused a 20 per cent jump in public school[xvii] enrollment. In a notable attack on ignorance, free night schools were set up that aided over 100,000 adult illiterates of both races. State hospitals and other public institutions were expanded and enlarged and their services were humanized. Repeal of the poll tax opened the political doors to a host of new voters, and the new, significant issues that Long introduced aroused popular interest in politics to a degree unmatched in any other Southern state. The huge costs of the Long program were met in a manner that anticipated the New Deal—by heavier taxes, especially on corporations, and by the issuance of bonds that increased the state debt to what was by the standards of that time an astronomical figure.

It took Long years to pass his program because he had to proceed against the implacable opposition of the ruling classes. The governor's announcement of his principal demands in 1928 led to an attempt in the following year to impeach him. He narrowly defeated the move by resorting to the device that became famous in Louisiana political history as the "round robin"—a sufficient number of state senators to block impeachment were persuaded to sign a document that they would not vote to convict. Long thus saved himself and continued to press toward his objectives. That this episode had a profound influence on him cannot be doubted. There is some question, however, as to its exact impact, and even his closest associates differ on this point. According to one version, Long was a fairly typical Progressive or liberal governor. Like similar executives in all sections, he entered office full of ideals and fired with a desire to pass legislation to[xviii] help the masses. He met unreasoning and even unscrupulous resistance from the conservatives, and this development changed him, making him more rancorous and ruthless, ready to use extreme methods to reach his goals. There is some merit in the analysis. The impeachment unmistakably hardened Long, and the stratagems of the opposition and his own stratagems to overcome theirs induced in him a measure of cynicism about the democratic process. But another explanation probably is closer to the mark. It is that from the very first Long knew pretty much what he was going to do and moved to do it, at his own schedule and on his own terms. He was an artist in power, like Abraham Lincoln or Franklin D. Roosevelt, and as he manipulated power he became increasingly fascinated with its uses.

Long's first objective after going into office was to perfect the organization that had elected him. He shortly welded together an extraordinarily effective machine. It covered the whole state and was one of the instruments that eventually enabled him to control the legislature almost completely. Before Long appeared on the scene, parish politicians, the "leaders" in local parlance, had exercised an inordinate influence in their own areas and on the state generally. The leader was usually, although not always, the sheriff, and if enough sheriffs could agree on a candidate and make a deal with the New Orleans Old Regulars, they could dictate the election of a governor. Long abruptly abolished this pattern. In his arrangement the sheriff might have a place, but he was only one of several leaders. Deliberately Long would set up[xix] in a parish a plural or committee type of organization. There were several leaders who divided power among themselves and watched one another and reported on the others to Long, and no one of them was strong enough to defy the big boss at Baton Rouge. Moreover, Long was accustomed to dealing directly with the voters. He was capable, as his local leaders uneasily knew, of invading their parishes and turning their own people against them.

But no machine, no matter how artfully constructed, can endure on symmetry alone. It has to be able, as Long was fully aware, to pass out material or prestige awards to its followers. The Long organization was deliberately geared to be abundantly appreciative. Its ability rested on a firm and frank basis of patronage and price. Immediately the regime reached out to grasp control of existing boards and bureaus, and then by constantly creating new agencies to perform new functions it kept enlarging the jobs at its disposal. Thus the number of state employees was steadily increased, some of them being added unnecessarily but with a candid admittance that depression conditions obligated the state to hire people. More jobs were made available through the huge road building program, which in part was a state public works project. Finally, the Long organization was self-sustaining in a financial sense. The road contractors, the contractors on other works, the distributors of highway machinery and supplies, and the companies that wrote the state's insurance were required to render regular contributions to the machine's campaign treasury, and for obvious reasons these interests met[xx] the assessments. The state employees had to pay a percentage of their salaries before an election, the so-called "deducts." Surviving Long leaders will argue that these dealings were moral because they were open and known to the public.

The organization was not beholden to any secret donors, they contend, and was hence independent and free to act in the public interest.

If Long had simply created an efficient machine, his achievement, while noteworthy, would not have been unusual, nor would it have won him the attention he secured in his own time or entitle him to the unique place he has in the annals of American politics. He went far beyond the pattern of previous leaders in the South or any section. He was the first mass or popular leader to set himself, not just to establish a machine of his own or to bring his enemies to terms, but to over-whelm utterly the existing organization and force it to enter his own apparatus. He systematically deprived the opposition of political sustenance, until finally he brought even the Old Regulars to their knees. At the time of his death by assassination in 1935, he had compelled most political elements in the state to affiliate with his organization. Each had a place and received certain rewards—but he defined the terms. A Long henchman was governor, and Long appointees filled all the executive offices. Long followers dominated the legislature, and a Long majority sat on the state supreme court. More, a series of far-reaching laws passed by an obedient legislature gave the governor, that is, Long, a controlling influence over local governments. There was still opposition,[xxi] bitter and organized, but it seemed that the old power structure had been destroyed, that, in fact, one man had become the power structure of an American common-wealth. Nothing quite like it had ever been witnessed in the nation's history.

It was, without exaggeration, an imaginative and imposing edifice of authority, and the man who had envisioned and put it together was very possibly the most daring of all American politicians. Most observers of the political scene would add that Long was also the most dangerous of our leaders. In his own time he was called a dictator and likened to Adolph Hitler or Benito Mussolini. The comparison was natural in the 1930's and has won wide credence. But later students will wonder about this easy application of the dictator label. Long, a remarkably introspective politician, wondered about it himself. Not surprisingly, he denied the charge. What is surprising was that some of his reasons were perceptively sound. He was well aware, for exam-ple, that his machine was largely a personal creation and dependent on the magnetism of his name. (The Long machine of later years was similarly dependent on Earl Long's name.) He realized too that he had concentrated too many powers in his own hands, powers that he but no successor could wield. On numerous occasions he warned his associates not to attempt to emulate him. He knew, finally, that his so-called dictatorship would not survive him. (The Long machine was, in fact, *voted* out of office five years after his death.) Long was not an American Hitler. Rather, he was an American boss, typical in many ways of the type, atypical[xxii] in that he came to grasp for too much power, to look on power as something to be gained for the sheer pleasure of its use. It is fashionable to denounce Long as a power grabber. But no politician should be judged by just one aspect of his character or career. This is especially applicable to the great politician, the "shaker," the leader who picks things up and changes them, who leaves behind him a different, if not always a better, world. Such a man has to be evaluated in the round, to be rated by what he did to and for society and to and for himself.

Thus it is proper for detached commentators on the art of politics to point out that Huey Long had more power than any democratic leader should have. But they should also emphasize that unless he had been willing and able to take power he could not have done the things that he did—that he could not have lifted Louisiana from a condition of near feudalism into the modern world almost overnight or inspired thousands of poor white people all over the South to a vision of a better life or introduced into all of Southern politics, which had been pervasively romantic, a saving element of economic realism. The commentators might want to add, as a footnote, that in the Long story there is a great tragic query about politics and life itself. Robert Penn Warren poses the question in *All the King's Men*. How much evil may a good man have to do to do good—and how will he himself be changed by what he does? . . . [xxiii]

THE LEGACY OF HUEY LONG

Carl P. Leubsdorf

WASHINGTON (AP) Sept. 8, 1965—Thirty years after an assassin's bullet struck down Kingfish Huey Long, "we've not only done most of what he advocated but we've even gone beyond it," says his son, Sen. Russell B. Long, D.-La.

The flamboyant Kingfish, whose controversial "share the wealth" politics carried him from the backwoods of northern Louisiana to the U.S. Senate, was shot Sept. 8, 1935, in Louisiana's 32-story State Capitol Building at Baton Rouge. He died two days later.

"No one should be too rich and no one too poor" was the way he felt, the senator said in an interview. Sixteen at the time his father

An untitled Associated Press release, which appeared in many newspapers. Reprinted by permission of AP Newsfeatures.

was assassinated, he is now assistant Democratic leader of the Senate.

Welfare programs, government construction of highways and hospitals, abolition of poll taxes, and free education are just some of Huey Long's programs that have long since become law, the senator said, adding that the Social Security and welfare benefits go beyond what he envisioned.

"President Johnson has said he used to come over to the Senate and listen to Huey Long speak," the senator added, noting that a large part of the President's education and anti-poverty programs bear marked similarity to the Kingfish's ideas.

There have been differences too. "We've tried to help people own their own homes," he said. "He tried to give it to them debt free."

Much of what Long did was extremely controversial. He was impeached by the state Assembly within a year of taking office as governor. But he lined up enough state senators behind him—the charges were due to be tried by the Senate—so the trial never took place.

When Huey Long refused to resign as governor upon election as senator, opponents accused him of being a dictator. He finally left the governorship a year later after his close friend, O. K. Allen, had been elected governor.

After Long's death, many of his associates, including Richard Leche, who had been elected governor on the Long ticket in 1936, were sent to jail on various charges including fraud and income tax evasion in what became known as the "Louisiana scandals."

The Kingfish made no secret of his many relatives on the state pay roll, contending they deserved it because "they were among my political supporters of longest and most arduous service."

"By any objective standards," the senator contends, "he was the best governor Louisiana ever had. He was a doer, and he was enormously popular with the people."

"Many people have told me," Long said, "that they consider Huey Long responsible for Social Security."

"They think President Franklin D. Roosevelt became interested in it because he needed something to build a backfire against some of the headway Huey Long was making.

"He never told me he was planning to run for president but as a politician I could see all the signs," Sen. Long said.

"I think he figured as a third-party candidate he'd run well to the left of Roosevelt and pull enough votes away from Roosevelt that the Republicans could win. Then, in four years, he'd be the Democratic candidate and would be elected.

"A lot of wealthy Republicans would have helped him. They wanted to beat Roosevelt so badly they would have helped Huey Long even though they might have created a Frankenstein. They certainly didn't agree with everything Huey Long was for.

"I just don't know if he ever would have been elected," the senator said.

At the time of his assassination, Huey Long was only 42. Like his life, Long's death stirred controversy. The alleged assassin, Dr. Carl Weiss, was shot to death by Long's bodyguards within seconds of the Kingfish's assassination and some have accused them of shooting the senator.

"There's no doubt in the world" that Weiss did it, the senator said.

In the two days that he lay dying, Long said, his father asked his doctors: "I don't know why that boy did that. Who is he? Why did he do it?"

The senator says the main reason he knows is that the judicial district which Weiss' father-in-law represented on the state Supreme Court had been redistricted, forcing the judge to retire rather than face almost certain defeat. Of the idea that Weiss feared Long might accuse the family of having Negro blood, the senator said: "My father had no such idea and never cared about that."

Twenty years after Long died, his son said, a poll showed half the persons questioned regarded him as the greatest governor in the state's history. His political heirs, meanwhile, have continued to dominate the state's politics, which have generally matched the Longs against the anti-Longs.

LOUISIANA POLITICS AND *ALL THE KING'S MEN*
Robert Penn Warren

When I am asked how much *All the King's Men* owes to the actual politics of Louisiana in the '30's, I can only be sure that if I had never gone to live in Louisiana and if Huey Long had not existed, the novel would never have been written. But this is far from saying that my "state" in *All the King's Men* is Louisiana (or any of the other forty-nine stars in our flag), or that my Willie Stark is the late Senator. What Louisiana and Senator Long gave me was a line of thinking and feeling that did eventuate in the novel.

Robert Penn Warren, *"All the King's Men:* The Matrix of Experience," *Yale Review*, LIII (December 1963), 161–167. This essay appears also as the Introduction to the Time Reading Program edition of *All the King's Men* and is reprinted with the express permission of Time-Life Books, New York, New York.

In the summer of 1934 I was offered a job—a much-needed job—as Assistant Professor at the Louisiana State University, in Baton Rouge. It was "Huey Long's University," and definitely on the make—with a sensational football team and with money to spend even for assistant professors at a time when assistant professors were being fired, not hired—as I knew all too well. It was Huey's University, but he, I was assured, would never mess with my classroom. That was to prove true; he was far too adept in the arts of power to care what an assistant professor might have to say. The only time that his presence was ever felt in my classroom was when, in my Shakespeare course, I gave my little annual lecture on the political background of *Julius Caesar;* and then, for the two weeks we spent on the play, backs grew straighter, eyes grew brighter, notes were taken, and the girls stopped knitting in class, or repairing their faces.

In September 1934 I left Tennessee, where I had been living[161] on a farm near Nashville, drove down across Mississippi, crossed the river by ferry (where I can't be sure—was it at Greenville?) and was in North Louisiana. Along the way I picked up a hitchhiker—a country man, the kind you call a red-neck or a wool-hat, aging, aimless, nondescript, beat up by life and hard times and bad luck, clearly tooth-broke and probably gut-shot, standing beside the road in an attitude that spoke of infinite patience and considerable fortitude, holding a parcel in his hand, wrapped in old newspaper and tied with binder twine, waiting for some car to come along. He was, though at the moment I did not sense it, a mythological figure.

He was the god on the battlement, dimly perceived above the darkling tumult and the steaming carnage of the political struggle. He was a voice, a portent, and a natural force like the Mississippi River getting set to bust a levee. Long before the Fascist March on Rome, Norman Douglas, meditating on Naples, had predicted that the fetid slums of Europe would make possible the "inspired idiot." His predictive diagnosis of the origins of fascism—and of communism—may be incomplete, but it is certain that the rutted back roads and slab-side shacks that had spawned my nameless old hitchhiker, with the twine-tied paper parcel in his hand, had, by that fall of 1934, made possible the rise of "Huey." My nameless hitchhiker was, mythologically speaking, Long's *sine qua non.*

So it was appropriate that he should tell me the first episode of the many I had to hear of the myth that was "Huey." The roads, he said, was shore better now. A man could git to market he said. A man could jist up and git, if'n a notion come on him. Did'n have to pay no toll at no toll bridge neither. Fer Huey was a free-bridge man. So he went on and told me how, standing on the river bank by a toll bridge (by what river and what bridge was never clear), Huey had made the president of the company that owned the bridge a good, fair cash offer, and the man laughed at him. But, the old hitchhiker said, Huey did'n do nothing but lean over and pick him up a chunk of rock and throwed it off a-ways, and asked did that president-feller see whar the rock hit. The feller said yeah, he seen. Wal, Huey[162] said, the next thing you see is gonna be a big new free bridge right whar that rock hit, and you, you son-of-a-bitch, are goen bankrupt a-ready and doan even know it.

There were a thousand tales, over the years, and some of them were, no doubt, literally and factually true. But they were all true in the world of "Huey"—that world of myth, folklore, poetry, deprivation, rancor, and dimly envisaged hopes. That world had a strange, shifting, often ironical and sometimes irrelevant relation to the factual world of Senator Huey P. Long and his cold manipulation of the calculus of power. The two worlds, we may hazard, merged only at the moment when in September 1935, in the corridor of the Capitol, the little .32 slug bit meanly into the senatorial vitals.

There was another world—this a factual world—made possible by the factual Long, though not inhabited by him. It was a world that I, as an assistant professor, was to catch fleeting glimpses of, and ponder. It was the world of the parasites of power, a world that Long was, apparently, contemptuous of, but knew how to use, as he knew how to use other things of which he was, perhaps, contemptuous. This was a world of a sick yearning for elegance and the sight of one's name on the society page of a New Orleans paper; it was the world of the electric moon devised, it was alleged, to cast a romantic glow over the garden when the President of the University and his wife entertained their politicos and pseudo-socialites; it was a world of pretentiousness, of bloodcurdling struggles for academic preferment, of drool-jawed grab and arrogant criminality. It was a world all too suggestive, in its small-bore, provincial way, of the airs and aspirations that the newspapers attributed to that ex-champagne salesman Von Ribbentrop and to the inner circle of Edda Ciano's friends.

For in Louisiana, in the 1930's, you felt somehow that you were living in the great world, or at least in a microcosm with all the forces and fatalities faithfully, if sometimes comically, drawn to scale. And the little Baton Rouge world of campus and Governor's Mansion and Capitol and the gold bathroom fixtures reported to be in the house of the University contractor was,[163] once the weight of Long's contempt and political savvy had been removed by the bullet of the young Brutus in the Capitol, to plunge idiotically rampant to an end almost as dramatic as the scenes in the last bunkers of Berlin or at the filling station on the outskirts of Milan. The headlines advertised the suicides, and the population of penitentiaries, both Federal and state, received some distinguished additions.

But this is getting ahead of the story. Meanwhile, there was, besides the lurid worlds, the world of ordinary life to look at. There were the people who ran stores or sold insurance or had a farm and tried to survive and pay their debts. There were—visible even from the new concrete speedway that Huey had slashed through the cypress swamps toward New Orleans—the palmetto-leaf and sheet-iron hovels of the moss pickers, rising like some fungoid growth from a hummock under the great cypress knees, surrounded by scum-green water that never felt sunlight, back in that Freudianly contorted cypress gloom of cottonmouth moccasins big as the biceps of a prize-fighter, and owl calls, and the murderous metallic grind of insect life, and the smudge fire at the hovel door, that door being nothing but a hole in a hovel wall, with a piece of croker sack hung over it. There were, a few miles off at the University, your colleagues, some as torpid as a gorged alligator in the cold mud of January and some avid to lick the spit of an indifferent or corrupt administration, but many able and gifted and fired by a will to create, out of the seething stew and heaving magma, a distinguished university.

And there were, of course, the students, like students anywhere in the country in the big state universities, except for the extraordinary number of pretty girls and the preternatural blankness of the gladiators who were housed beneath the stadium to have their reflexes honed, their diet supervised, and—through the efforts of tutors—their heads crammed with just enough of whatever mash was required (I never found out) to get them past their minimal examinations. Among the students there sometimes appeared, too, that awkward boy from the depth of the 'Cajun country or from some scrabble-farm in[164] North Louisiana, with burning ambition and frightening energy and a thirst for learning; and his presence there, you reminded yourself, with whatever complication of irony seemed necessary at the moment, was due to Huey, and to Huey alone. For the "better element" had done next to nothing in fifty years to get that boy out of the grim despair of his ignorance.

Yes, there was the world of the "good families," most of whom hated Huey Long—except, of course, for that percentage who, for one reason or another, had reached an accommodation. They hated him sometimes for good reasons and sometimes for bad, and sometimes for no reason at all, as a mere revulsion of taste; but they never seemed to reflect on what I took to be the obvious fact that if the government of the state had not previously been marked by various combinations of sloth, complacency, incompetence, corruption, and a profound lack of political imagination, there would never have been a Senator Huey P. Long, and my old hitchhiker by the roadside would, in September 1934, have had no tale to tell me.

Conversation in Louisiana always came back to the tales, to the myth, to politics; and to talk politics is to talk about power. So conversation turned, by implication at least, on the question of power and ethics, of power and justification, of means and ends, of "historical costs." The big words were not often used, certainly not by the tellers of tales, but the concepts lurked even behind the most ungrammatical folktale. The tales were shot through with philosophy.

The tales were shot through, too, with folk humor, and the ethical ambiguity of folk humor. And the tales, like the political conversations, were shot through, too, with violence—or rather, with hints of the possibility of violence. There was a hint of revolutionary desperation—often synthetically induced. In Louisiana, in '34 and '35, it took nothing to start a rumor of violence. There had been, you might hear, a "battle" at the airport of Baton Rouge. A young filling station operator would proudly display his sawed-off automatic shotgun—I forget which "side" he was on, but I remember his fingers caressing the polished walnut of·the stock. Or you might hear that there was [165] going to be a "march" on the Capitol—but not hear by whom or for what.

Melodrama was the breath of life. There had been melodrama in the life I had known in Tennessee, but with a difference: in Tennessee the melodrama seemed to be different from the stuff of life, something superimposed upon life, but in Louisiana people lived melodrama, seemed to live, in fact, for it, for this strange combination of philosophy, humor, and violence. Life was a tale that you happened to be living—and that "Huey" happened to be living before your eyes. And all the while I was reading Elizabethan tragedy, Machiavelli, William James, and American history—and all that I was reading seemed to come alive, in shadowy distortions and sudden clarities, in what I saw around me.

How directly did I try to transpose into fiction Huey P. Long and the tone of that world? The question answers itself in a single fact. The first version of my story was a verse drama; and the actual writing began, in 1938, in the shade of an olive tree by a wheat field near Perugia. In other words, if you are sitting under an olive tree in Umbria and are writing a verse drama, the chances are that you are concerned more with the myth than with the fact, more with the symbolic than with the actual. And so it was. It could not, after all, have been otherwise, for in the strict, literal sense, I had no idea what the now deceased Huey P. Long had been. What I knew was the "Huey" of the myth, and that was what I had taken with me to Mussolini's Italy, where the bully boys wore black shirts and gave a funny salute.

I had no way of knowing what went on in the privacy of the heart of Senator Long. Now I could only hope, ambitiously, to know something of the heart of the Governor Talos of my play Proud Flesh. For Talos was the first avatar of my Willie Stark, and the fact that I drew that name from the "iron groom" who, in murderous blankness, serves Justice in Spenser's Faerie Queen should indicate something of the line of thought and feeling that led up to that version and persisted, with modulations, into the novel.

Talos was to become Stark, and *Proud Flesh* was to become[166] *All the King's Men.* Many things, some merely technical, led to this transformation, but one may have some bearing on the question of the ratio of fact and fiction. In 1942 I left Louisiana for good, and when in 1943 I began the version that is more realistic, discursive, and documentary in method (though not in spirit) than the play, I was doing so after I had definitely left Louisiana and the world in which the story had its roots. By now the literal, factual world was only a memory, and therefore was ready to be absorbed freely into the act of imagination. Even the old man by the roadside—the hitchhiker I had picked up on the way down to take my job—was ready to enter the story: he became, it would seem, the old hitchhiker whom Jack Burden picks up returning from Long Beach, California, the old man with the twitch in the face that gives Jack the idea for the Great Twitch. But my old hitchhiker had had no twitch in his face. Nor had I been Jack Burden.

I had not been Jack Burden except in so far as you have to try to "be" whatever you are trying to create. And in that sense I was also Adam Stanton, and Willie Stark, and Sadie Burke, and Sugar Boy, and all the rest. And this brings me to my last notion. However important for my novel was the protracted dialectic between "Huey" on the one side, and me on the other, it was far less important, in the end, than that deeper and darker dialectic for which the images and actions of a novel are the only language. And however important was my acquaintance with Louisiana, that was far less important than my acquaintance with another country: for any novel, good or bad, must report, willy-nilly, the history, sociology, and politics of a country even more fantastic than was Louisiana under the consulship of Huey.[167]

HUEY LONG IN FICTION

Louis D. Rubin, Jr.

The late Huey Pierce Long, governor of and United States Senator from Louisiana until his assassination in 1935, has been credited with inspiring four novels since his death. Two of them, Robert Penn Warren's *All the King's Men* and Adria Locke Langley's *A Lion Is in*

Louis D. Rubin, Jr., "All the King's Meanings," *Georgia Review*, VIII (Winter 1954), 422–434. Reprinted by permission of the author and the publisher.

the Streets, have been best sellers. The other two, John Dos Passos' *Number One* and Hamilton Basso's *Sun in Capricorn,* have not done so well financially.

Of the four, *All the King's Men* seems to be the one that has the best chance for an extended literary life; it is one of those rare books that make their appeal both to the intellectual and to the popular reader. Now it has gone into the Modern Library reprint series, the proprietors of which select their titles with a view toward the long haul. In his preface to the new edition, Mr. Warren ascribes the book's general popularity to its journalistic relevance, and he declares emphatically that *All the King's Men* is not about Huey Long at all. "Certainly it was the career of Long and the atmosphere of Louisiana ✓ that suggested the play that was to become the novel," he admits. "But suggestion does not mean identity, and even if I had wanted to make Stark a projection of Long, I should not have known how to go about it." Mr. Warren goes on to say that Long was but one of the figures implicit in the character of Willie Stark, and that another was "the scholarly and benign figure of William James."

Mr. Warren ought to know what the tie-in is between Huey Long and Willie Stark if anyone knows; and yet an annoying paradox exists here: because the fact is that of the four novels "about" Huey Long, it is most certainly *All the King's Men* that best captures the picture of the historical King Fish, and of Louisiana during the 1920's and 1930's when the King Fish governed. No one, I believe, who can read these four novels with reasonable dispassion will dispute that. To be sure, Hamilton Basso did, in a rather long essay on the Huey Long Legend in *Life* magazine several years ago. But Mr. Basso was prominently identified with the anti-Long faction in Louisiana during the [422] 1930's, and I suspect that his complaint that Mr. Warren has eulogized the King Fish is at least partly explained by that quite understandable partisanship. Mr. Basso even objected to *A Lion Is in the Streets* on the same score, and I doubt that any halfway objective reader would conclude after perusing Mrs. Langley's novel that Long came out very well. Whatever the artistic faults of *A Lion Is in the Streets,* no one could reasonably claim that Mrs. Langley advocates or is even willing to tolerate men like Long in politics.

Mr. Basso's objections to the contrary, I think that most readers familiar with the South of the 1930's will testify that *All the King's Men* is a remarkably accurate reporting on those times. And this is not only in the more intangible "atmosphere" of those times, but even in the events themselves; Mr. Warren's account of the death of Willie Stark, and the causes, is factually closer to the death of Long, for instance, than are the death scenes in any of the other three novels.

Yet Mr. Warren denies the identification, which certainly seems paradoxical; and so that I may attempt to resolve the apparent paradox, I am going to propose what may be another paradox. This is, that

Mr. Warren was able to write the best book "about" Huey Long *because* he was furthest from his subject. His very lack of motivation and dedication to "tell the truth" about Huey was what made it possible for him to do just that. What is meant by this can best be seen through a look at the four "Long" novels.

Mr. Basso's *Sun in Capricorn* is rather easily disposed of; it is a slight affair, with no great pretension about it. The central character of the book becomes the victim of a slander plot engineered by one of the lieutenants of "Gilgo Slade," the Long-like governor of the state. The attack is directed against the central character because his uncle is Gilgo Slade's opponent in the gubernatorial race, and it takes the form of an accusation that the central character's girl friend has violated the state moral code by going to bed with him. The last several chapters are built around a race to get the young lady on a train for New York before the police come. A political rally for Gilgo Slade causes the highways to be blocked off and almost results in the girl's being caught, but finally she gets away, and Gilgo Slade is shot to death by the central character's brother—though for political reasons only.

The novel is neither high drama nor a commentary on the state of man on Louisiana earth during the 1930's. It is simply a thriller. It attempts no development of the character of Gilgo Slade, who remains[423] a sinister but shadowy background presence. The novel fulfills Mr. Basso's own criterion for novels "about" Huey Long: there is no doubt that Gilgo Slade is a fascist, a menace, a scoundrel, and a despot. But he is not much of a fictional character; and since Mr. Basso was attempting a novel and not a treatise on unconstitutional government, he failed to achieve his purpose entirely. No matter what one might think of its political attitude, *Sun in Capricorn* is indifferent art.

A Lion Is in the Streets, by Adria Locke Langley, is a book of considerably more pretension than *Sun in Capricorn*. It is about four times as long, and of all the "Long" novels it has had the best sale, topping even Mr. Warren's book and far outdistancing both Mr. Basso and Mr. Dos Passos.

Mr. Basso singled out *A Lion Is in the Streets,* along with *All the King's Men,* for castigation because it presented Huey Long in partially favorable terms. How he arrived at this evaluation is somewhat puzzling. On the political plane, Mrs. Langley's novel is faithfully anti-Long. Using flashbacks to review the career of "Hank Martin," the Lion, Mrs. Langley tells a tale about a poor boy burning with zeal to improve his lot and the lot of those around him. He rises to political power, but immediately he is corrupted by it. In the end he is assassinated by one of the "little people," who thus preserves democracy and popular government. The whole point of the book is that power corrupts and absolute power corrupts absolutely, and Mrs. Langley eschews both subtlety and symbolism to make it crystal clear that that is what she means. Thus Hank Martin's wife Verity, the "conscience" of the novel, is actually glad that her husband has been done to death:

> The glow of the western sky pinked the leaves of oak and magnolia, and in the distance was the sheen of the silvered river. A great love of this country swelled and pushed within her. Spreading her arms toward the world she pleaded silently, Don't—oh, don't turn on your bed as a door on its hinges. You're my kinsmen—you're the people! Only the people can blow the trumpet —the incorruptible trumpet of faith and justice, of equality and truth. And blow certain, she pleaded. Oh, trumpet, blow certain!

The only possible objection that Mr. Basso could have to Mrs. Langley's politics would be that she made her Huey Long-like protagonist honest and public-spirited at first, and then let him grow corrupt[424] as he gained power, instead of making him thoroughly hypocritical and corrupt from the very outset. Surely, even granted Mr. Basso's objectives, that seems rather too partisan and unfair. A much more legitimate complaint is that *A Lion Is in the Streets* is a badly written book. The characterization, from Hank Martin on down, is stereotyped; the transformation in Hank Martin's character is simply not credible in terms of the novel's structure. We are told that Hank is becoming corrupt and is losing his principles; the author leaves it up to us to make it believable. Hank is overdrawn all the way through, too; the dialogue that Mrs. Langley invents for him approaches the burlesque.

> "... There's a clear, bright somethin' liken to a fast-runnin' brook in you, 'n I come to that brook 'n I spill the blackness in me, 'n I feel all clean agin." Taking her hand he placed it over his heart and sealed it there with one of his own. " 'N I get all filled up 'n go as plain as if it was the handwritin' for me on the wall. My beginnin's is allus with you. Liken to that brook y' got in y'. Its beginnin's is in some high place."

Mrs. Langley is laying it on rather thickly there, and it is a fairly representative passage. The whole of *A Lion Is in the Streets* is flashy and gaudy; in particular there is one outlandish scene in which a big city underworld king is eaten alive by thousands of brightly plumaged birds, with Hank Martin and a vixen named Flamingo officiating. It might really have happened, for all I know; but in the novel it is comically bizarre. The vixen Flamingo is not one of Mrs. Langley's happier creations. We first meet her when she attempts to feed Hank Martin's wife Verity to an alligator, and thereafter she keeps turning up time after time, jarring our tolerance of fictional coincidence on each occasion. A chapter on the art of fiction could be written by comparing Mrs. Langley's use of coincidence with that of Mr. Warren in *All the King's Men*. The apparent coincidences become the structure of Mr. Warren's novel, and are not really chance meetings at all. They are brought off by the inevitability of fate and the plot, and are no more haphazard, at the last, than the events of the Oedipus plays that they so resemble. Whereas Mrs. Langley's coincidences occur because of the apparent luck of the draw, to make the plot work out smoothly.

A more exciting comparison for *All the King's Men* is with Mr.[425] Dos Passos' *Number One,* the second volume of his Spotswood trilogy and since published along with the other two novels under the general title of *District of Columbia.* For in John Dos Passos we have a worthy adversary for Mr. Warren, and the measure of Mr. Warren's achievement in *All the King's Men* is more fully understood when the book is considered alongside of *Number One.*

Both novels have several technical and structural similarities. Both Mr. Warren and Mr. Dos Passos chose to focus their attention not on the Huey Long-like politician, but on one of his aides. In neither novel does the aide serve simply as a chorus; neither *All the King's Men* nor *Number One* achieves its final meaning in the rise and fall of the Boss, but rather in the effect of the Boss's fortunes upon the aide. Indeed, in *Number One* the Boss doesn't suffer either assassination or disaster; when threatened, he merely offers up the aide, Tyler Spotswood, as a convenient scapegoat.

The figure of Homer Crawford is less easily likened to Huey Long than is Mr. Warren's Willie Stark. Crawford is the backwoods messiah type, with some of the mannerisms and traits we recognize as Long's, but there is not the strong similarity in setting and historical events that we find between Willie Stark and Long in *All the King's Men.* And the main reason for this is that Mr. Dos Passos never goes in much either for setting or for historical events. His Chuck Crawford is simply a demagogue, obviously inspired by Long, and Crawford's role in *Number One* is to show by example that strong men endanger democratic government. The lesson is meant for Tyler Spotswood, and us. Much of Homer Crawford's success is due to Tyler Spotswood's help, and when Homer then ditches Tyler as soon as it becomes expedient, we have the final irony to make Tyler—and us—aware of Crawford's ruthlessness and lack of principle. Tyler Spotswood finally learns what it means to play with fire, and is at last able to realize that as an American citizen it is his responsibility to fight power, not abet it. Through Tyler's misfortunes we are taught a lesson in political attitude.

Robert B. Heilman has said of *All the King's Men* that "the author begins with history and politics, but the real subject is the nature of man; Warren is no more discussing American politics than *Hamlet* is discussing Danish politics." This I think is just about as valid for *Number One* as it is for Mr. Warren's novel; the vast difference between the two novels lies in their authors' tremendously disparate[426] conceptions of what is involved in "the nature of man." I think this difference is apparent in almost every phase of the two novels, and we can get at it from the very beginning.

All the King's Men opens as Jack Burden and his companions are driving along a white concrete highway in Louisiana:

MASON CITY.

To get there you follow Highway 58, going northeast out of the city, and it is a good highway and new. Or was new, that day we went up it. You look up the highway and it is straight for miles, coming at you, with the black line down the center coming at and at you, black and slick and tarry-shining against the white of the slab, and the heat dazzles up from the white slab so that only the black line is clear, coming at you with the whine of the tires, and if you don't quit staring at that line and don't take a few deep breaths and slap yourself hard on the back of the neck you'll hypnotize yourself and you'll come to just at the moment when the right front wheel hooks over into the black dirt shoulder off the slab, and you'll try to jerk her back on but you can't because the slab is high like a curb, and maybe you'll try to reach to turn off the ignition just as she starts the dive. . . .

From the highway Mr. Warren proceeds to the countryside, the rednecks who inhabit it, and then begins on the people who share the car with Jack Burden, showing how they are reacting to the trip. We see Sugar Boy, the bodyguard-driver; then Tom Stark, son of the Boss; then Lucy Stark, Tom's mother and the Boss's wife; until finally the car pulls up to a stop at a drug store. Before that car has stopped and Willie Stark has gone into action, Mr. Warren has given us perhaps two thousand words to get us into the situation. In the long third sentence of the opening passage he evokes several varieties of sensory experience, and in the sentences that will follow he continues this process. Even the rhythm of the prose contributes to the mood, constructed as it is with a multitude of short coordinate clauses coming one after the other, and joined by the same conjunction each time, with none of the variety possible through subordinate construction. The whole passage is designed to get across the sense of a drive through Louisiana on a hot day, with one image after another looming up and then receding behind the speeding car, to touch off the casual and rather monotonous thought patterns. There is a quietly desperate feeling about the whole thing, and Mr. Warren shows us how this[427] feeling is in various degrees shared by the participants of the scene that is to follow. Were this not done, then the electric effect of Willie Stark orating at the drug store would not be properly grasped. The riders in the automobile are not content to sit back and enjoy the trip; they are bored and nervous, and they are anxious to get where they are going even though they have no particular desire to go there. What they are waiting for is the emotional stimulus of Willie Stark's personality, which they know will necessarily be available when they arrive and he goes to work.

By contrast, Mr. Dos Passos gets *Number One* under way with a prelude, in italics:

When you try to find the people, always in the end it
comes down to somebody,
somebody working, maybe:
a man alone on an old disk harrow yelling his lungs
out at a team of mean mules (it's the off mule that gives
the trouble, breaking and skittish, pulling black lips back
off yellow teeth to nip at the near mule's dusty neck); it's
March and the wind sears the chapped knuckles of the hand that
clamps the reins; levers rattle; there's a bolt loose under
the seat somewhere . . .

and so on for about six hundred words. The passage is filled with details, and yet paradoxically it is a completely abstract piece of writing.
It is not a particular place or individual being described, but merely
a farmer—any farmer: "the people." Something of the same effect might
have been achieved had Mr. Dos Passos chosen to include a painting
as a prelude, instead of the prose passage. Its link with the story that
follows is completely on an ideological plane, by intention of the
author; and this is true as well of several other such italicized passages
inserted between chapters of *Number One*. In them the author shows
us "the people," in specimen form—a mechanic, a radio ham, a busi-
nessman, and finally a catalogue of occupations, which ends with the
injunction that

> *weak as the weakest, strong as the strongest,*
> *the people are the republic,*
> *the people are you.*

To repeat, these passages have no structural or textural relationship to the story proper; when the plot opens, the scene is a hotel
room,[428] and we get Tyler Spotswood thinking for perhaps a hundred
and fifty words before the dialogue between him and a cohort begins
and the plot proceeds to advance. The italicized preludes serve by their
very contrast to remind us of what the "real people" are. But the only
real people in *Number One* are the politicians. The "real people" remain out of it entirely, so that when Tyler Spotswood is reminded at
the finish to keep his faith with them, the credibility of that final resolution depends entirely upon the reader's willingness to accept that
evaluation of their democratic worthiness. And while I am quite able
to do this, I do not like being told to do so by a novelist. I prefer him
to prove his case on its own artistic merits.

Tyler Spotswood "discovers" democracy in the process of political
betrayal. Mr. Dos Passos' novel makes its appeal to the reader as
political animal, and this is true from the first pages onward. On any
other plane save the political, there would be no need and no reason
for the reminder about the "real people."

By contrast, the opening pages of *All the King's Men* begin unfolding for us no merely political animals. Right away we sense that it

is not simply a political reason that has those people driving toward Mason City with Willie Stark. What we get is several people going somewhere in Louisiana on a hot day; immediately Mr. Warren gets about his appointed task of giving us these people in their time and place *on many planes of activity*. The devotion to the sensory texture of the scene, rather than to the political affiliations alone, begins the job. Whereas Chuck Crawford of *Number One* possesses life and importance only insofar as he symbolizes a political strong man, Willie Stark of *All the King's Men* becomes a compelling person in his own right, and the political implications are only part of the total story. This is apparent from the first chapter on. Nor is the figure of Willie Stark made the ultimate object of the novel's meaning; instead it becomes the cause of the action, upon which all the various planes of the characters' individual existences are focused, thus giving a unity and a progression to the multitudinous scene about it.

Like *Number One*, Mr. Warren's book is a political novel, in that the question of civic attitude toward government is prominently aired. But unlike *Number One*, it is also a social novel, a moral novel, a philosophical novel—a novel of the meaning of history and society and of man in a time and place. At the end of it Jack Burden, the central character, has come through to a knowledge possible only through [429] tragic experience, and I think it possible to say that *All the King's Men* possesses the proportions of tragedy.

Jack Burden's tragic experience lies in the knowledge of time. It is symbolized by the Cass Mastern journal. Jack has not been able to make sense of it. He cannot understand why Cass Mastern acted as he did. Not until the events transpire that cause Anne Stanton to become Willie Stark's mistress, kill Willie, Adam Stanton, and Judge Irwin, and paralyze Tom Stark, does Jack comprehend the meaning of the journal. And the meaning is that man must take care to move and act in the convulsion of the world, accepting full responsibility for his acts both as they draw on the past and create the future. Because Jack was a divided man, he could not fathom the motives that impelled Cass Mastern to act as he did. Cass Mastern had accepted the full implications of his responsibility; and Jack could not understand why.

Therefore, Jack Burden put aside the journal of his ancestor, which he had proposed to edit as his doctoral dissertation, and he went to work for Willie Stark. He believed in Willie's good faith, and he found in Willie's realism and strength a kind of absolute. Yet it was not satisfactory, and when Jack did reprehensible things because he thought Willie Stark's ends justified them, he was attempting to live a role as a divided man. He tried to ignore his responsibility to both himself and society, to separate artificially his personal loyalties and beliefs from his work with Willie Stark—and the world tumbled down on him.

It is the split sensibility of Jack Burden that causes him to kill

Judge Irwin, his true father—and in so doing to discover that the Judge is his father. The Judge has brought Jack up as a child and has been his friend, but Jack works for Willie Stark, and he turns up evidence for Willie to show that the Judge once accepted a bribe. It is "true," and so Jack will use it without regard for personal loyalty, old friendships, or the knowledge that the Judge has done full atonement and has lived an upright life ever since. For Jack Burden can compartmentalize his life into separate experiences, or thinks he can, and thus refuse to consider one action as having any bearing on another. But unfortunately for his peace of mind, that was not so. As Jack says, "It was the 'Case of the Upright Judge' and I had every reason to congratulate myself on a job well done. It was a perfect research job, marred in its technical perfection by only one thing: it meant something" (203/*191*).[430]

Split sensibility, evasions of responsibility: these things bring death to Willie Stark, cause Jack Burden to kill his father, and make the whole world of *All the King's Men* possible—and impossible.

Yet Mr. Warren's counsel in his novel is not for one moment that of the subjective idealist. He is not declaring that Jack Burden's actions, or Willie Stark's, either, violated some sort of abstract ethical principle and that therefore the disasters came. Indeed, one of Jack Burden's sins is a bit of subjective idealism in his make-up, Mr. Warren intimates: he rationalizes away personal responsibility for his own misdeeds by considering only what he believed was the ideal end of his action. Jack refuses to consider "the truth" in the light of the whole situational context, and of his knowledge of human fallibility, and instead he separates his "research" into the Judge's past from all other considerations. And his father dies. Similarly—Adam Stanton's downfall comes about because, as Robert B. Heilman says, he "takes insufficient account of the facts" when they fail to conform to abstract ideals.

The lesson of the Cass Mastern story is that wholeness embodies the acceptance of evil and guilt, and it is wholeness that Jack Burden finally learns to seek. As Norton Girault has written, Burden learns at last "that it is only through an acceptance of the evil in his nature that man can achieve good." He learns, too, that the knowledge given to men is never quite certain. And finally, Jack Burden realizes that men must strive "for that state *least* wasteful of human good."

And here is the answer to those who, like Hamilton Basso, contend that *All the King's Men* is a deification of men like Huey Long. If Mr. Warren has any political message in his novel, it is that in any realm, including the political, a supposedly desirable end does not justify vicious means. Willie Stark dipped too deeply in evil to achieve his purposes. In Girault's words, "the Boss's integration has been doomed to fall because it has rested on an unsound base." We recall Willie's advice to Jack Burden: "Man is conceived in sin and born in corruption and he passeth from the stink of the didie to the stench of the shroud. There is always something" (54/*49*).

Jack Burden finds "something." He finds out that Judge Irwin, whom Willie Stark wants to ruin, had in his youth accepted a bribe. When he confronts the Judge with this knowledge, the Judge commits suicide. And then Jack's mother tells him that the Judge was his father.

Judge Irwin could have made Jack Burden withhold the evidence[431] of the long-ago dishonesty had he wished, merely by telling Jack that he was his father. But the Judge didn't. He preferred to go to his death rather than make that claim.

It is Judge Irwin's example, more than anything else, that makes Jack Burden realize that honor has its place, along with the stink and stench, in the life of man. And the full realization of this comes later, after Willie Stark and Adam Stanton are dead, and Jack knows, now, that his mother, whom he had thought selfish and cold and loveless, has been in love herself. She questions him about the night of the interview with Judge Irwin which resulted in the Judge's death:

> "—did he—was there—" she was looking away from me.
> "You mean," I said, "had he got into a jam and had to shoot himself? Is that it?"
> She nodded, then looked straight at me and waited for what was coming.
> I looked into her face and studied it. The light wasn't any too kind to it. Light would never be kind to it again. But she held it up and looked straight at me and waited.
> "No," I said, "he wasn't in any jam. We had a little argument about politics. Nothing serious. But he talked about his health. About feeling bad. That was it. He said good-bye to me. I can see now he meant it as the real thing. That was all."
> She sagged a little. She didn't have to brace up so stiff any longer.
> "Is that the truth?" she demanded.
> "Yes," I said. "I swear to God it is."
> "Oh," she said softly and let her breath escape in an almost soundless sigh. (456–457/*431*)

The interview has taken place at the railroad station, and afterward Jack's mother boards the train and it pulls away for the West:

> I looked after the dwindling train that was carrying my mother away until it was nothing but the smudge of smoke to the west, and thought how I had lied to her. Well, I had given that lie to her as a going-away present. Or a kind of wedding present, I thought.
> Then I thought how maybe I had lied just to cover up myself.
> "Damn it," I said out loud, savagely, "it wasn't for me, it wasn't."
> And it was true. It was really true. (458/*432*)

If Burden were Warren, or merely speaking for Warren much as a Greek chorus represented the commentary on the action, the import of this scene would only be that Warren wished to inform his readers that Burden had done an act of selflessness rather than selfishness[432] when he lied to his mother. But that is not the impact of that last line at all. What it means to the reader, and must mean in the context of the novel, is that Jack Burden as protagonist has faced up to his responsibility at last, and realizes that he has done so.

Nor is it any vacant, burned-out finish that Jack Burden and Anne Stanton have achieved. The conclusion of *All the King's Men* does not leave them in a Snug Harbor such as the characters of *Strange Interlude* find, in which they will "pick flowers together in the ageing afternoons of spring and summer." Jack Burden disavows any such idea as that when he remarks that "it looks as though Hugh [Miller] will get back into politics, and when he does I'll be along to hold his coat. I've had some valuable experience in that line." Burden has by no means abandoned the world to seek his salvation in the hermitic fashion that the scholarly attorney did. This is not at all the solution of *All the King's Men*. On the contrary, Mr. Warren has Burden declare at the last that he and Anne must "go into the convulsion of the world, out of history into history and the awful responsibility of time."

So that now we may return to the question of whether *All the King's Men* is "*about*" Huey Pierce Long of Louisiana. I think the answer is, yes, it is "about" Long, but not "about" him in the way that *A Lion Is in the Streets* is "about" him. Rather, it is the very detachment with which Robert Penn Warren as artist could observe the Louisiana scene that makes the novel both an independent work of art which does not require a predetermined set of political attitudes for its effect, and at the same time a breathtaking depiction of the time and place of Long in Louisiana. Where other, lesser novelists were constricted and hampered in their art by their engagement in the political milieu from which they were attempting to draw the raw material for their art, Mr. Warren was able to see Huey Long in relation to the world in which he existed, and through his superior insight and artistry present the total picture—not just the political side of it, not just one man's role in it, but something of the total length and depth.

It is the failure to recognize what Mr. Warren was doing that resulted in all the complaints about *All the King's Men* being a glorification of Huey Long, and Mr. Warren as apologist for fascism, and so forth. The usually astute Mr. Robert G. Davis, for example, interpreted, in the New York *Times*, Mr. Warren's novel as the author's guilty rationalization for having edited the *Southern Review* with Long money,[433] and he concluded his review with the complaint that "Warren does not ask—the question apparently has no imaginative appeal for him—whether American tradition does not demand that we fight men like Long with all the democratic means at our disposal in order to preserve in this country and in the world free, open, pluralistic societies in which individual rights are protected by law and in which ultimate control is vested below in the people and not above in Willie Stark." Had Mr. Warren set himself to work along the lines of the problem as seen by Mr. Davis, *All the King's Men* would have been not a novel, but a political tract. Mr. Davis asks, purely and simply, that when Mr. Warren writes a novel involving a political figure, he drop everything else and dedicate all his efforts to attacking the political figure. Unless *All the King's Men* presents a political sermon designed to produce results on election day, it ·has failed; that in effect is what Mr. Davis's approach would maintain.

Even on ideological grounds, Mr. Davis's contention, and the way he phrased it, are invalid. American tradition does not "demand" that a novelist fight anybody or anything; rather it is the land of novelists like Ilya Ehrenburg that makes that particular demand. Mr. Davis would surely not maintain that because Hamilton Basso's *Sun in Capricorn* fulfilled the ideological requirement he set up, it is a better work of art than *All the King's Men;* and yet that is what his theory would imply.

There is a philosophical moral implicit in all this, but it is in the literary moral that I am interested. Mr. Warren achieved both the tragedy and the social commentary, and transcended the regional and political limitations, by heeding that counsel of wholeness—sound and shape, smell and feel, ethics and politics, sociology and dramatics—in the telling of his tale. If one may borrow Mr. Warren's own summation of William Faulkner's achievements and apply it to *All the King's Men,* "he has taken our [Southern] world, with its powerful sense of history, its tangled loyalties, its pains and tensions of transition, its pieties and violence, and elevated it ·to the level of a great moral drama on the tragic scale." In the last analysis it was the story that mattered to Robert Penn Warren: all the magnificent social, political, and philosophical portraiture was incidental to his artistic purposes. Mr. Warren's story gave the counsel of wholeness, but it was because *All the King's Men* itself embodied the wholeness that it succeeded where other novels fell short. [434]

Three Literary Sources

PURGATORIO: CANTO THREE

Dante Alighieri

Inasmuch as the instantaneous flight
    Had scattered them asunder o'er the plain,
    Turned to the mountain whither reason spurs us,
I pressed me close unto my faithful comrade,
    And how without him had I kept my course?
    Who would have led me up along the mountain?
He seemed to me within himself remorseful;
    O noble conscience, and without a stain,
    How sharp a sting is trivial fault to thee!
After his feet had laid aside the haste
    Which mars the dignity of every act,
    My mind, that hitherto had been restrained,
Let loose its faculties as if delighted,
    And I my sight directed to the hill
    That highest tow'rds the heaven uplifts itself.
The sun, that in our rear was flaming red,
    Was broken in front of me into the figure
    Which had in me the stoppage of its rays;
Unto one side I turned me, with the fear
    Of being left alone, when I beheld
    Only in front of me the ground obscured.[255]
"Why dost thou still mistrust?" my Comforter
    Began to say to me turned wholly round;
    "Dost thou not think me with thee, and that I guide thee?
'Tis evening there already where is buried
    The body within which I cast a shadow;
    'Tis from Brundusium ta'en, and Naples has it.
Now if in front of me no shadow fall,
    Marvel not at it more than at the heavens,
    Because one ray impedeth not another

From *The Divine Comedy of Dante Alighieri*, translated by Henry Wadsworth Longfellow. Boston: Houghton, Osgood, and Company, 1879.

To suffer torments, both of cold and heat,
    Bodies like this that Power provides, which wills
    That how it works be not unveiled to us.
Insane is he who hopeth that our reason
    Can traverse the illimitable way,
    Which the one Substance in three Persons follows!
Mortals, remain contented at the *Quia;*
    For if ye had been able to see all,
    No need there were for Mary to give birth;
And ye have seen desiring without fruit,
    Those whose desire would have been quieted,
    Which evermore is given them for a grief.
I speak of Aristotle and of Plato,
    And many others";—and here bowed his head,
    And more he said not, and remained disturbed.
We came meanwhile unto the mountain's foot;
    There so precipitate we found the rock,
    That nimble legs would there have been in vain.
'Twixt Lerici and Turbìa, the most desert,
    The most secluded pathway is a stair
    Easy and open, if compared with that.
"Who knoweth now upon which hand the hill
    Slopes down," my Master said, his footsteps staying,
    "So that who goeth without wings may mount?"
And while he held his eyes upon the ground
    Examining the nature of the path,
    And I was looking up around the rock,
On the left hand appeared to me a throng
    Of souls, that moved their feet in our direction,
    And did not seem to move, they came so slowly.
"Lift up thine eyes," I to the Master said;
    "Behold, on this side, who will give us counsel,
    If thou of thine own self can have it not."
Then he looked at me, and with frank expression
    Replied: "Let us go there, for they come slowly,
    And thou be steadfast in thy hope, sweet son." [256]
Still was that people as far off from us,
    After a thousand steps of ours I say,
    As a good thrower with his hand would reach,
When they all crowded unto the hard masses
    Of the high bank, and motionless stood and close,
    As he stands still to look who goes in doubt.
"O happy dead! O spirits elect already!"
    Virgilius made beginning, "by that peace
    Which I believe is waiting for you all,

Tell us upon what side the mountain slopes,
    So that the going up be possible,
    For to lose time irks him most who most knows."
As sheep come issuing forth from out the fold
    By ones and twos and threes, and the others stand
    Timidly, holding down their eyes and nostrils,
And what the foremost does the others do,
    Huddling themselves against her, if she stop,
    Simple and quiet and the wherefore know not;
So moving to approach us thereupon
    I saw the leader of that fortunate flock,
    Modest in face and dignified in gait.
As soon as those in the advance saw broken
    The light upon the ground at my right side,
    So that from me the shadow reached the rock,
They stopped, and backward drew themselves somewhat;
    And all the others, who came after them,
    Not knowing why nor wherefore, did the same.
"Without your asking, I confess to you
    This is a human body which you see,
    Whereby the sunshine on the ground is cleft.
Marvel ye not thereat, but be persuaded
    That not without a power which comes from Heaven
    Doth he endeavour to surmount this wall."
The Master thus; and said those worthy people:
    "Return ye then, and enter in before us,"
    Making a signal with the back o' the hand
And one of them began: "Whoe'er thou art,
    Thus going turn thine eyes, consider well
    If e'er thou saw me in the other world."
I turned me tow'rds him, and looked at him closely;
    Blond was he, beautiful, and of noble aspect,
    But one of his eyebrows had a blow divided.
When with humility I had disclaimed
    E'er having seen him, "Now behold!" he said,
    And showed me high upon his breast a wound.[257]
Then said he with a smile: "I am Manfredi,
    The grandson of the Empress Costanza;
    Therefore, when thou returnest, I beseech thee
Go to my daughter beautiful, the mother
    Of Sicily's honour and of Aragon's,
    And the truth tell her, if aught else be told.
After I had my body lacerated
    By these two mortal stabs, I gave myself
    Weeping to Him, who willingly doth pardon.

Horrible my iniquities had been;
>
>> But Infinite Goodness hath such ample arms,
>> That it receives whatever turns to it.

Had but Cosenza's pastor, who in chase
>
>> Of me was sent by Clement at that time,
>> In God read understandingly this page,

The bones of my dead body still would be
>
>> At the bridge-head, near unto Benevento,
>> Under the safeguard of the heavy cairn.

Now the rain bathes and moveth them the wind,
>
>> Beyond the realm, almost beside the Verde,
>> Where he transported them with tapers quenched.

By malison of theirs is not so lost
>
>> Eternal Love, that it cannot return,
>> So long as hope has anything of green.

True is it, who in contumacy dies
>
>> Of Holy Church, though penitent at last,
>> Must wait upon the outside this bank

Thirty times told the time that he has been
>
>> In his presumption, unless such decree
>> Shorter by means of righteous prayers become.

See now if thou hast power to make me happy,
>
>> By making known unto my good Costanza
>> How thou hast seen me, and this ban beside,

For those on earth can much advance us here."[258]

ON POLITICAL EXPEDIENCY

Niccolò Machiavelli

Agathocles the Sicilian rose not only from private life but from the lowest and most abject position to be King of Syracuse. The son of a potter, he led a life of the utmost wickedness through all the stages of his fortune. Nevertheless, his wickedness was accompanied by such vigour of mind and body that, having joined the militia, he rose through its ranks to be prætor of Syracuse. Having been appointed to this position, and having decided to become prince, and to hold with violence and without the support of others that which had been constitutionally granted him; and having imparted his design to

From *The Prince and The Discourses*, translated by Luigi Ricci, revised by R. P. Vincent. New York: Modern Library, 1950.

Hamilcar the Carthaginian, who was fighting with his armies in Sicily, he called together one morning the people and senate of Syracuse, as if he had to deliberate on matters of importance to the republic, and at a given signal had all the senators and the[31] richest men of the people killed by his soldiers. After their death he occupied and held rule over the city without any civil strife. And although he was twice beaten by the Carthaginians and ultimately besieged, he was able not only to defend the city, but leaving a portion of his forces for its defence, with the remainder he invaded Africa, and in a short time liberated Syracuse from the siege and brought the Carthaginians to great extremities, so that they were obliged to come to terms with him, and remain contented with the possession of Africa, leaving Sicily to Agathocles. Whoever considers, therefore, the actions and qualities of this man, will see few if any things which can be attributed to fortune; for, as above stated, it was not by the favour of any person, but through the grades of the militia, in which he had advanced with a thousand hardships and perils, that he arrived at the position of prince, which he afterwards maintained by so many courageous and perilous expedients. It cannot be called virtue to kill one's fellow-citizens, betray one's friends, be without faith, without pity, and without religion; by these methods one may indeed gain power, but not glory. For if the virtues of Agathocles in braving and overcoming perils, and his greatness of soul in supporting and surmounting obstacles be considered, one sees no reason for holding him inferior to any of the most renowned captains. Nevertheless his barbarous cruelty and inhumanity, together with his countless atrocities, do not permit of his being named among the most famous men. We cannot attribute to fortune or virtue that which he achieved without either. . . .[32]

We must assume, as a general rule, that it never or rarely happens that a republic or monarchy is well constituted, or its old institutions entirely reformed, unless it is done by only one individual; it is even necessary that he whose mind has conceived such a constitution should be alone in carrying it into effect. A sagacious legislator of a republic, therefore, whose object is to promote the public good, and not his private interests, and who prefers his country to his own successors, should concentrate all authority in himself; and a wise mind[138] will never censure any one for having employed any extraordinary means for the purpose of establishing a kingdom or constituting a republic. It is well that, when the act accuses him, the result should excuse him; and when the result is good, as in the case of Romulus, it will always absolve him from blame. . . .[139]

Whoever becomes prince of a city or state, especially if the foundation of his power is feeble, and does not wish to establish there either a monarchy or a republic, will find the[183] best means for holding that principality to organize the government entirely anew (he being himself a new prince there); that is, he should appoint new governors with new titles, new powers, and new men, and he should make the poor rich, as David did when he became king, "who heaped riches upon the needy, and dismissed the wealthy empty handed." Besides this, he should destroy the old cities and build new ones, and transfer the inhabitants from one place to another; in short, he should leave nothing unchanged in that province, so that there should be neither rank, nor grade, nor honor, nor wealth, that should not be recognized as coming from him. He should take Philip of Macedon, father of Alexander, for his model, who by proceeding in that manner became, from a petty king, master of all Greece. And his historian tells us that he transferred the inhabitants from one province to another, as shepherds move their flocks from place to place. Doubtless these means are cruel and destructive of all civilized life, and neither Christian nor even human, and should be avoided by every one. In fact, the life of a private citizen would be preferable to that of a king at the expense of the ruin of so many human beings. Nevertheless, whoever is unwilling to adopt the first and humane course must, if he wishes to maintain his power, follow the latter evil course. But men generally decide upon a middle course, which is most hazardous; for they know neither how to be entirely good or entirely bad. . . .[184]

I believe it to be most true that it seldom happens that men rise from low condition to high rank without employing either force or fraud, unless that rank should be attained either by gift or inheritance. Nor do I believe that force alone will ever be found to suffice, whilst it will often be the case that cunning alone serves the purpose; as is clearly seen by whoever reads the life of Philip of Macedon, or that of Agathocles the Sicilian, and many others, who from the[318] lowest or most moderate condition have achieved thrones and great empires. Xenophon shows in his Life of Cyrus the necessity of deception to success: the first expedition of Cyrus against the king of Armenia is replete with fraud, and it was deceit alone, and not force, that enabled him to seize that kingdom. And Xenophon draws no other conclusion from it than that a prince who wishes to achieve great things must learn to deceive. . . .[319]

☙

ON PRAGMATISM

William James

Some years ago, being with a camping party in the mountains, I returned from a solitary ramble to find every one engaged in a ferocious metaphysical dispute. The *corpus* of the dispute was a squirrel— a live squirrel supposed to be clinging to one side of a tree-trunk; while over against the tree's opposite side a human being was imagined to stand. This human witness tries to get sight of the squirrel by moving rapidly round the tree, but no matter how fast he goes, the squirrel moves as fast in the opposite direction, and always keeps the tree between himself and the man, so that never a glimpse of him is caught. The resultant metaphysical problem now is this: *Does the man go round the squirrel or not?* He goes round the tree, sure enough, and the squirrel is on the tree; but does he go round the squirrel? In the unlimited leisure of the wilderness, discussion had been worn threadbare. Every one had taken sides, and was obstinate; and the numbers on[43] both sides were even. Each side, when I appeared therefore appealed to me to make it a majority. Mindful of the scholastic adage that whenever you meet a contradiction you must make a distinction, I immediately sought and found one, as follows: "Which party is right," I said, "depends on what you *practically mean* by 'going round' the squirrel. If you mean passing from the north of him to the east, then to the south, then to the west, and then to the north of him again, obviously the man does go round him, for he occupies these successive positions. But if on the contrary you mean being first in front of him, then on the right of him, then behind him, then on his left, and finally in front again, it is quite as obvious that the man fails to go round him, for by the compensating movements the squirrel makes, he keeps his belly turned towards the man all the time, and his back turned away. Make the distinction, and there is no occasion for any farther dispute. You are both right and both wrong according as you conceive the verb 'to go round' in one practical fashion or the other." [44]

Although one or two of the hotter disputants called my speech a

From William James, *Pragmatism: A New Name for Some Old Ways of Thinking*. New York: Longmans, Green and Company, 1908.

shuffling evasion, saying they wanted no quibbling or scholastic hair-splitting, but meant just plain honest English 'round,' the majority seemed to think that the distinction had assuaged the dispute.

I tell this trivial anecdote because it is a peculiarly simple example of what I wish now to speak of as *the pragmatic method*. The pragmatic method is primarily a method of settling metaphysical disputes that otherwise might be interminable. Is the world one or many?—fated or free?—material or spiritual?—here are notions either of which may or may not hold good of the world; and disputes over such notions are unending. The pragmatic method in such cases is to try to interpret each notion by tracing its respective practical consequences. What difference would it practically make to any one if this notion rather than that notion were true? If no practical difference whatever can be traced, then the alternatives mean practically the same thing, and all dispute is idle. Whenever a dispute is serious, we ought to be[45] able to show some practical difference that must follow from one side or the other's being right. . . .[46]

Pragmatism represents a perfectly familiar attitude in philosophy, the empiricist attitude, but it represents it, as it seems to me, both in a more radical and in a less objectionable form than it has ever yet assumed. A pragmatist turns his back resolutely and once for all upon a lot of inveterate habits dear to professional philosophers. He turns away from abstraction and insufficiency, from verbal solutions, from bad *a priori* reasons, from fixed principles, closed systems, and pretended absolutes and origins. He turns towards concreteness and adequacy, towards facts, towards action and towards power. That means the empiricist temper regnant and the rationalist temper sincerely given up. It means the open air and possibilities of nature, as against dogma, artificiality, and the pretence of finality in truth.

At the same time it does not stand for any special results. It is a method only. . . .[51]

No particular results then, so far, but only an attitude of orientation, is what the pragmatic method means. *The attitude of looking away*[54] *from first things, principles, 'categories,' supposed necessities; and of looking towards last things, fruits, consequences, facts.* . . .[55]

. . . Pragmatism [is] a mediator and reconciler and . . . she 'unstiffens' our theories. She has in fact no prejudices whatever, no obstructive dogmas, no rigid canons of what shall count as proof. She is completely genial. She will entertain any hypothesis, she will consider any evidence. . . .[79]

Her only test of probable truth is what works best in the way of leading us, what fits every part of life best and combines with the collectivity of experience's demands, nothing being omitted. If theological ideas should do this, if the notion of God, in particular, should prove to do it, how could pragmatism possibly deny God's existence? She could see no meaning in treating as 'not true' a notion that was pragmatically so successful. What other kind of truth could there be, for her, than all this agreement with concrete reality?[80]

Touchstones

SELECTED LITERARY CRITICISM
Robert Penn Warren

Critics are rarely faithful to their labels and their special strategies. Usually the critic will confess that no one strategy—the psychological, the moralistic, the formalistic, the historical—or combination of strategies, will quite work the defeat of the poem. For the poem is like the monstrous Orillo in Boiardo's *Orlando Innamorato*. When the sword lops off any member of the monster, that member is immediately rejoined to the body, and the monster is as formidable as ever. But the poem is even more formidable than the monster, for Orillo's adversary finally gained a victory by an astonishing feat of dexterity: he slashed off both the monster's arms and quick as a wink seized them and flung them into the river. The critic who vaingloriously trusts his method to account for the poem, to exhaust the poem, is trying to emulate this dexterity: he thinks that he, too, can win by throwing the lopped-off arms into the river. But he is doomed to failure. Neither fire nor water will suffice to prevent the rejoining of the mutilated members to the monstrous torso. There is only one way to conquer the monster: you must eat it, bones, blood, skin, pelt, and gristle. And even then the monster is not dead, for it lives in you, is assimilated into you, and you are different, and somewhat monstrous yourself, for having eaten it.

So the monster will always win, and the critic knows this. He does not want to win. He knows that he must always play stooge to the monster. All he wants to do is to give the monster—the poem—a chance to exhibit again its miraculous power, which is poetry.[3]

From "Pure and Impure Poetry" (1943)

From Robert Penn Warren, *Selected Essays*. New York: Random House, 1958. Reprinted by permission of the author and the publisher.

. . . Is the kind of instruction expected of fiction in direct competi-
tion, at the same level, with the kind of instruction offered in Political
Science I or Economics II? If that is the case, then out with Shakespeare and Keats and in with Upton Sinclair.

Perhaps *instruction* is not a relevant word, after all, for this case.
This is a very thorny and debatable question, but it can be ven-
tured that what good fiction gives us is the stimulation of a powerful
image of human nature trying to fulfill itself, and not instruction in
an abstract sense. The economic man and political man are important
aspects of human nature and may well constitute part of the *materials*
of fiction. Neither the economic nor the political man is the complete
man; other concerns may still be important enough to engage the
attention of a writer—such concerns as love, death, courage, the point of
honor, and the moral scruple. A man has to live with other men in
terms not only of economic and political arrangements but also of
moral arrangements; and he has to live with himself, he has to define
himself. . . .[116]

From "Ernest Hemingway" (1947)

If *The Ancient Mariner* has a meaning, what is that meaning?

It is true that a poem may mean a number of different things. By
this I do not intend to say that a poem means different things to different readers. This is, of course, true in one sense, but true, first, only in
so far as the poet fails, as fail he must in some degree, in the exercise
of his creative control, and second, in so far as each reader must, as a
result of his own history and nature, bring to the poem a different mass
of experience, strength of intellect, and intensity of feeling. In this
second sense we may say that the reader does not interpret the poem
but the poem interprets the reader. We may say that the poem is the
light and not the thing seen by the light. The poem is the light by
which the reader may view and review all the areas of experience with
which he is acquainted.

I do not intend to say merely that a poem has different meanings
for different readers, but that it may have different meanings for the
same reader. For present purposes we may discriminate two senses
in which this is true.

First, it is clear that a poem has different meanings when placed
in different perspectives of interest. We may look at it as a document
in the history of a language, in the history of literary forms, in the history of political ideas, or in a thousand other different perspectives,
and in each of them discover a different kind of meaning. The significant factor in determining the difference among meanings in this sense
is that the reader, from outside the poem, prescribes the particular
perspective in which the poem is to be placed.

Second, a poem may have different meanings according[212] to the
different perspectives which are inherent in the poem itself and are not

proposed from outside. But it may be objected that the difference be-tween the *extrinsic* and *intrinsic* perspectives may not, in practice, really subsist. An illustration may clarify the distinction proposed. In the play *Julius Caesar* the topic of the transition from the Republic to the Empire appears. The same topic may be regarded in either the extrinsic or the intrinsic perspective. The decisive factor is this: If we regard it in the extrinsic perspective, we relate it to a body of facts and ideas many of which have not the slightest relation to the play. For instance, many of the facts pertinent to this perspective have been discovered and many of the ideas have been formulated since the date of composition of the play. If we regard the topic, however, in the intrinsic perspective, we relate the pattern which the topic receives in the play to other patterns in the play. For instance, the political theme (as we may call the topic as patterned in the play, as viewed in the intrinsic perspective) is related to the other themes, for instance, to the philosophical theme, which is here, I take it, primarily concerned with the question of free will and determinism. In other words, the various extrinsic perspectives disintegrate the play for their own special pur-poses; the various intrinsic perspectives merely define the themes which, it is assumed, the play unifies and makes mutually interpretive. Any substantial work will operate at more than one thematic level, and this is what makes it so difficult to define *the* theme of a profound creation; the root-idea will have many possible formulations and many of them will appear, or be suggested, in the work.

In *The Ancient Mariner* I wish to distinguish two basic themes, both of them very rich and provocative, and I shall, in the course of my discussion, attempt to establish their interrelation.

One theme I shall call *primary*, the other *secondary*. I do not mean to imply that one is more important than the other. But the one which I shall[213] call primary is more obviously presented to us, is, as it were, at the threshold of the poem. The primary theme may be defined as the issue of the fable (or of the situation or discourse if we are applying this kind of analysis to a poem which does not present a fable). The primary theme does not necessarily receive a full statement. In fact, in *The Ancient Mariner* it receives only a kind of coy and dra-matically naïve understatement which serves merely as a clue—"He prayeth best, etc." But the theme thus hinted at is the outcome of the fable taken at its face value as a story of crime and punishment and reconciliation. I shall label the primary theme in this poem as the theme of sacramental vision, or the theme of the "One Life." The operation of this theme in the poem I shall presently explore.

As the primary theme may be taken as the issue of the fable, so the secondary theme may be taken as concerned with the context of values in which the fable is presented and which the fable may be found ultimately to embody, just as more obviously it embodies the primary theme. I shall label the secondary theme in this poem as the theme of the imagination. . . .[214] We may look at the matter in this way: The theme of the "One Life," of the sacramental vision, is essentially re-ligious—it presents us with the world, as the crew of the ship are pre-sented with the Albatross, in "God's name." As we have seen, the poem is shot through with religious associations. On the other hand, the theme of imagination is essentially aesthetic—it presents us with the "great forms" of nature, but those forms as actively seized upon by the human mind and loved *not merely as vehicles for transcendental meaning but in themselves as participating in the reality which they "render intelligible."*. . .[249]

The type of critical analysis which I have just attempted always raises certain questions. I shall state them bluntly and in the terms in which they usually appear:

1. Assuming that certain interpretations can be "drawn out of" or "put into" the poem by an "exercise of ingenuity," how do we know that the poet "intended" them?

2. If the present interpretations are "right," (a) is the poem not obscure, since good and experienced readers of the past have "missed" them, or (b) how is it that such good and experienced readers, having missed the interpretations, have still been deeply affected by the poem?

These questions, it will be readily seen, have to do, in order, with the theory of poetic creation and the theory of poetic appreciation. To answer these questions properly would require a space not here at my disposal and a competence not at my command. But it is not to be expected that a reader will accept my interpretation if I am not willing to abide his questions. And so I shall indicate, at least, the lines along which I should try to frame answers.

I should begin by saying that the questions, *as stated,* are false questions. There are real problems concealed behind these questions, but these are false because they are loaded—they will not permit an answer which does not falsify the nature of the process under discus-sion.

Let us take the first one.

The falsity of the first question inheres in the word *intended* as the word is intended in the context. The implication here is that the process of poetic creation is, shall we say, analogous to the process of building a house from a blueprint: the poet has an idea, the blueprint, and according to it, plank[267] by plank and nail by nail, he makes a poem, the house. Actually, the creation of a poem is as much a process of discovery as a process of making. A poem may, in fact, start from an idea—and may involve any number of ideas—but the process for the poet is the process of discovering what the idea "means" to him in the light of his total being and his total experience (in so far as that total experience is available to him for the purpose of poetry—the degree here varies enormously from poet to poet). Or a poem may start from a phrase, a scene, an image, or an incident which has, for the poet, a suggestive quality—what, for him in the light of his total being and total available experience, we may call the symbolic potential. Then the process for the poet is the process of discovering why the item has caught his attention in the first place—which is simply another way of saying that he is trying to develop the symbolic potential. Or the original item may lead by some more or less obscure train of association to another item which will become the true germ of the poem, and whose symbolic potential may supplant that of the first item.

However the process starts, it is, of course, enormously complicated. The degree of effort may vary from instance to instance (the poet may dream up his poem in a flash or it may be laboriously accreted like coral), and the degree of self-consciousness may vary from instance to instance (the poet may or may not in the process of creation interlard his symbolical thinking with discursive and critical thinking). As Coleridge said, and as many other poets and even scientists have said, the unconscious may be the genius in the man of genius. But this is not to define the process as an irrational process. What comes unbidden from the depths at the moment of creation may be the result of the most conscious and narrowly rational effort in the past. In any case, the poet always retains the right of rejecting whatever seems to violate his nature and his developing conception of the poem. And the[268] process of rejection and self-criticism may be working continually during the composition of a poem. In the case of *The Ancient Mariner* we have good evidence that the poet was working in terms of a preconceived theme, and we know that the original composition required some months and that the process of revision required years.

Whatever the amount of possible variation from case to case in various respects, we can say that the process is a process of discovery which objectifies itself as a making. What the poet is trying to discover, then, is what kind of poem he can make. And the only thing he, in the ordinary sense, may "intend" is to make a poem. In so far as his process of discovery has been more than a rhetorical exercise, he cannot do otherwise than "intend" what his poem says, any more than he can change his own past as past, but he does not fully know what he "intends" until the poem is fully composed. A purpose "formally conceived" is not, as Wordsworth said, necessary, first to initiate the process of creation, or second, to give the finished poem a meaning ultimately expressive not only of the man but of his "ideas" in a restricted sense. But, Wordsworth went on to say, "habits of meditation have, I trust, so prompted and regulated my feelings, that my descriptions of such objects as strongly excite those feelings, will be found to carry along with them a *purpose.*"

If the poet does not have a blueprint of intention (and if he does happen to have it, we ordinarily have no access to it), on what basis may a poem be interpreted? What kind of evidence is to be admitted? The first piece of evidence is the poem itself. And here, as I have suggested earlier, the criterion is that of internal consistency. If the elements of a poem operate together toward one end, we are entitled to interpret the poem according to that end. Even if the poet himself should rise to contradict us, we could reply that the words of the poem speak louder than his actions.

But the application of the criterion of internal[269] consistency cannot be made in a vacuum. All sorts of considerations impinge upon the process. And these considerations force on the critic the criterion of external consistency. But consistency in regard to what? First, in regard to the intellectual, the spiritual climate of the age in which the poem was composed. Second, in regard to the over-all pattern of other artistic work by the author in question. Third, in regard to the thought of the author as available from non-artistic sources. Fourth, in regard to the facts of the author's life. These considerations cannot be applied in a mechanical fashion, that is, so as to confuse the material of the poem with the poem itself. If treated mechanically, the first, for example, will give us crude historicism, or the fourth will give us crude psychologism—both of which confound the material with the thing created, both of which deny the creative function of mind, both of which fail to provide any basis for distinguishing the excellent product from the conventional or inept. But treated as conditioning factors, as factors of control in interpretation, the considerations named above provide invaluable criteria.

I have said that both of the questions usually raised by the kind of interpretation I have attempted are false questions. They are false in themselves, without regard to the goodness or badness, the truth or falsity, of a particular interpretation. Just as the first question is false, as stated, because it is based on a misconception of the creative process, so the second is false because based on a misconception of the appreciative process. I shall repeat the second question: If the present interpretations are "right" (a) is the poem not obscure since good and experienced readers of the past have "missed" them, or (b) how is it that they, having missed the interpretations, have still been deeply affected by the poem?

The trouble is that the word *missed* here falsifies the relationship between the reader and the poem.[270] It implies a matter of yes-and-no. Actually, the relationship is not one of yes-and-no, but of degree, of gradual exploration of deeper and deeper levels of meaning within the poem itself. And this process of exploration of deeper and deeper levels of the poem may be immediate and intuitive. The reader may be profoundly affected—his sense of the world may be greatly altered—even though he has not tried to frame in words the nature of the change wrought upon him, or having tried to do so, has failed (as all critics must fail in some degree, for the simple reason that the analysis cannot render the poem, the discursive activity cannot render the symbolical). As for *The Ancient Mariner* itself, the great central fact of the poem, the fact which no reader could miss—the broken tabu, the torments of guilt and punishment, the joy of reconciliation—is enough to account for the first impact of the poem upon a reader. But beyond that, the vividness of the presentation and the symbolic coherence may do their work—as blessing sprang to the Mariner's lips—unawares. For the good poem may work something of its spell even upon readers who are critically inarticulate.

If this is true—if ideally appreciation is immediate and intuitive—why should critical analysis ever be interposed between the reader and the poem? The answer is simple: in order that the intuition may be fuller, that detail may be more richly and the central images more deeply realized. But in this case what becomes of immediacy of appreciation? Nothing becomes of it, if "immediacy" is read properly—if it is read as signifying "without mediation" of critical analysis and not as signifying "upon the first instant of contact." Let me put it in this way: A poem works immediately upon us when we are ready for it. And it may require the mediation of a great deal of critical activity by ourselves and by others before we are ready. And for the greater works we are never fully ready. That is why criticism is a never-ending process.

One last word: In this essay I have not attempted[272] to "explain" how poetry appeals, or why. I have been primarily concerned to give a discursive reading of the symbol which is the poem, in so far as I can project the import of the symbol in such a fashion. I humbly trust that I am not more insensitive than most to the "magical lines," but at the same time I cannot admit that our experience, even our aesthetic experience, is ineluctably and vindictively divided into the "magical" and the rational, with an abyss between. If poetry does anything for us, it reconciles, by its symbolical reading of experience (for by its very nature it is in itself a myth of the unity of being), the self-devisive internecine malices which arise at the superficial level on which we conduct most of our living.

And *The Ancient Mariner* is a poem on this subject.[273]

From "A Poem of Pure Imagination: An
Experiment in Reading" (1946, revised 1958)

KNOWLEDGE AND THE IMAGE OF MAN

Robert Penn Warren

Our general topic is Man's Right to Knowledge. To put my cart before the horse, the conclusion before the discussion, and let the cat out of the bag, I'll assert that to say man's right to knowledge is simply a way of saying man's right to exist, to be himself, to be a man.

That, of course, is the premise of our society—man's right to exist as a man, as a uniquely defined individual. Our society, we know well, violates this premise every day, but it remains fundamental to our democratic Western world.

We must distinguish this idea from the idea of the sanctity of life as such. More frequently in other societies than ours has the saint or sage turned from the caterpillar in the path or shrunk to pluck the lettuce for fear of the unhearable scream. No, we have limited and revised the idea of the sanctity of life. Human life we mean in our world, and human life not as existence but as the individual's right to exist as himself, the right to the hazards and glories of trying to develop most fully as himself.

I suppose that this notion of personality—the right to define one-self—despite all the distortions it has suffered from forces like Machiavellianism, Manchester economics, the Winning of the West, and progressive education, is a heritage of Christianity. Every soul is valuable in God's sight, and the story of every soul is the story of its self-defini-tion for good or evil, salvation or damnation. Every soul is valuable in God's sight. Or, with the secularization of things, we may say: every soul is valuable in man's sight.[182]

If we accept this notion, then we are committed to recognize the right of every soul to that knowledge necessary for its best fulfilment.

At this point, however, someone may object to the statement that man's right to knowledge, in our society at least, derives from, or is related to, our Christian history. The objector may recollect that every Christian church has, at one time or another, opposed the extension of

Robert Penn Warren, "Knowledge and the Image of Man," *Sewanee Review*, LXIII (Spring 1955), 182–192. Reprinted by permission of the author and the pub-lisher. This essay was originally an address given at the conference on the Unity of Knowledge at the Bicentennial celebration of Columbia University in 1954.

knowledge. To this objection one may say that the various churches are of this world and have made their worldly errors, and that opposition to the extension of knowledge, in any given instance, was accidental and not essential to Christianity; and one could paraphrase Jacques Maritain in another context: the glory of God does not demand that man go on all fours.

To be a man, to keep from going on all fours, implies the right to knowledge. But it is a sad fact that, though the glory of God does not demand that man go on all fours the glory of our democracy, by a last perversion, sometimes seems to make that demand. Since I am about to refer to the Age of the Common Man, I shall hasten to say that I was a New Dealer, with as few reservations and heart burnings as one can reasonably expect about a political process, and I don't take it back now. But one of the heart burnings I did have was precisely about Common Man-ism of the sort the New Deal *sometimes* promoted.

The prophets of the Common Man might have spoken gloriously —if they had really believed that that fellow-citizen whom they called the Common Man was really as good as they, the prophets, too often took themselves to be. But no, they often spoke with a nauseous condescension, and it was not glorious. They might have said something like this: As men we have in common certain capacities that make us men, the capacity to envisage ourselves in relation to nature and other men, the capacity for self-criticism, the capacity for a disinterested love of excellence. Let us try, therefore, to create a society in which each[183] man may develop as far as possible those capacities that distinguish his manhood, and in which each man will accept his responsibility for trying to realize his common humanity at its highest.

Perhaps some of the prophets did speak gloriously, but their voices were generally drowned out by voices that in declaring the Age of the Common Man uttered a doctrine of complacency. These voices, by implication at least, denied that democracy should mean the opportunity—and the responsibility—for the development of excellence, and uttered a doctrine carrying at its core the appalling convictions that the undeveloped, the unaspiring, the frustrated, the un-responsible, is somehow mystically superior to the excellent, and that a refusal of effort toward excellence is a gesture of moral worth.

In reading the history of our country we have met all too often this same old notion, the glorification of the un-excellent, this conviction that a mystic worth attaches to ignorance. Sometimes this was, we know, a way of pitting the honest coon-skin cap against crowns and coronets, an honest faith in democracy against Norman blood. But looking back on our forefathers, we know, too, that they were not above the human frailty of an awkward and strident defensiveness in the face of the learning, grace, and achievement of the Old World, and that, to keep their courage up, they whistled a little in the dark of their own heads.

Looking back, we can applaud the sturdy independence, the faith in democracy and destiny, and the lethal efficiency of the long-rifle levelled at a Redcoat. We can relish the juicy rambunctiousness and wild poetry and courage of the frontier, and see the pathos of its loneliness, malaria, and degradation. But this does not mean that, in the end, we have to take Davy Crockett as a philosopher superior to Immanuel Kant.

This isn't quite what happened in 1933, but it is uncomfortably close. And part of the sad comedy was that one of the places where the process flourished most rankly was in some classrooms[184] of literature, especially of American literature, and in learned books on that subject. To study our culture sometimes meant to seek out documentations of Common Man-ism. I am not referring merely to those students of our culture who made a Holy Alliance with Stalin and interpreted our history as a blundering and uninstructed provincial attempt to be Russian. No, I am referring to that far greater number who were devoted to the American Dream and the American Mission, but whose devotion manifested itself as an easy and sometimes false documentation of Common Man-ism, a process that took the place of the investigation of all other values, and I do not mean what it was sometimes fashionable to refer to as "merely literary values." I mean all values, including those of common sense and simple honesty.

Whitman was split down the middle and the part of his work that is humanly full was rejected for what was politically viable. Flaubert had nothing to tell us in an age of crisis. Down with Hardy and up with Ruth Suckow and Rölvaag or Grace Lumpkin. "Snowbound" is a great poem, and Henry James betrayed America. Conrad is not socially relevant, for he merely treats of man against geography. Faulkner is a Gothic fascist, and hates Negroes.

Most of the people who adopted these views were simply innocent, with decent human sympathies, but their very virtues made it possible in that context to accept the fashionable thing, and the fashionable thing simply amounted to the notion that only the easy and immediate is valuable. The spirit of God may not be in you, but the spirit of Democracy sure is, and if you are a Common Man, all things shall be added unto you, without your turning a hand, and anyway you've probably already got everything worth having. So the Right to Knowledge, which should have meant the glorification of our common human capacity to move toward excellence, to define ourselves in a communal aspiration, was betrayed by the prophets of Common Man-ism.[185]

Not only was the Right to Knowledge betrayed. There was an even more gross betrayal. The complacency fostered by the doctrine of Common Man-ism belied and betrayed that aspiration to excellence that is really in our midst, that has always marked much of our history, an aspiration that is sometimes blundering and confused but is indomitable and indestructible. It must be indestructible, more in-destructible even than the cat in the adage, for it has survived even the attempt of the New Deal to choke it with butter.

All this has been, in a way, an aside, the self-indulgent venting of old spleen, but too, I trust, a description of one extreme threat to the Right to Knowledge—the threat from well-meaning friends. We have less to fear sometimes from the Powers of Darkness than from would-be Angels of Light, and the would-be Angels of Light change their plumage from time to time. Right now the fashionable cut in wings and haloes is not that of the New Deal.

Let us come back to our beginning, the statement that the right to exist as a man assumes the Right to Knowledge.

It assumes the right because only by knowledge does man achieve his identity. I do not mean that the mere implements of knowledge—books, libraries, laboratories, seminars—distinguish man from the brute. No, knowledge gives him his identity because it gives him the image of himself. And the image of himself necessarily has a fore-ground and a background, for man is in the world not as a billiard ball placed on a table, not even as a ship on the ocean with location determinable by latitude and longitude. He is, rather, in the world with continual and intimate interpenetration, an inevitable osmosis of being, which in the end does not deny, but affirms, his identity. It affirms it, for out of a progressive understanding of this interpenetra-tion, this texture of relations, man creates new perspectives, discovers new values—that is, a new self—and so the identity is a continually[186] emerging, an unfolding, a self-affirming and, we hope, a self-corrective creation.

Despite this osmosis of being to which I have referred, man's process of self-definition means that he distinguishes himself from the world and from other men. He disintegrates his primal instinctive sense of unity, he discovers separateness. In this process he discovers the pain of self-criticism and the pain of isolation. But the pain may, if he is fortunate, develop its own worth, work its own homeopathic cure. In the pain of self-criticism he may develop an ideal of excellence, and an ideal of excellence, once established, implies a de-personalized communion in that ideal. In the pain of isolation he may achieve the courage and clarity of mind to envisage the tragic pathos of life, and once he realizes that the tragic experience is universal and a corollary of man's place in nature, he may return to a communion with man and nature.

Man can return to his lost unity, and if that return is fitful and precarious, if the foliage and flower of the innocent garden are now somewhat browned by a late season, all is the more precious for the fact, for what is now achieved has been achieved by a growth of moral awareness. The return to nature and man is the discovery of love, and law. But love through separateness, and law through rebellion. Man eats of the fruit of the Tree of Knowledge, and falls. But if he takes another bite, he may get at least a sort of redemption. And a precious redemp'ion. His unity with nature will not now be that of a drop of water iɴ the ocean; it is, rather, the unity of the lover with the beloved, a unity presupposing separateness. His unity with mankind will not now be the unity of a member of the tribal horde with that pullulating mass; his unity will be that of a member of sweet society.

I suppose that the ultimate unity of knowledge is in the image of himself that man creates through knowledge, the image of his destiny, the mask he stares at. This would mean that manipulative[187] knowledge, as well as knowledge of vision, calculation as well as conception—to take Shelley's distinction—works toward the creation of that image. Or to take another set of distinctions, the knowledge of *make,* that of *do,* that of *see,* that of *be,* however sharply we may distinguish them for various purposes, ultimately interfuse in our life process. Any change of environment—including any making—creates a new relation between man and his world, and other men. Any doing changes the doer. Any seeing changes the see-er. And any knowledge one has of his own being modifies that being, re-creates it, and thus changes the quality of making, doing, seeing.

Here let us remind ourselves most emphatically that a change in man's image of himself is not necessarily for the better. We do not ride a gravy train. We have seen, and see, in our own time, certain self-images of Frankensteinian horror that have captured the imagination of whole peoples. So new knowledge may give us new images absurd or dangerous, or may inadequately revise an old image so that it becomes absurd or dangerous, an anachronism. An intimate knowledge of fruit flies may lead us to think of human needs and values at the level of the fruit fly. A knowledge of the domestic arrangements of ancient royal houses of Egypt, or of Shelley's idea that incest is the most poetic of subjects, may lead us to a new admiration for the goings-on of the Jukeses and Kallikaks. And a knowledge of the structure of the atom may lead us to destroy ourselves. I say that knowledge *may* lead us to such unfortunate conclusions. But need it? And if it does, must we blame knowledge? No, we should blame incompleteness of knowledge—the fact that knowledge of human nature, human needs, human values, has not kept pace with knowledge of fruit flies and atoms, the fact that we have not achieved balance and responsibility in the ever-unfolding process of self-definition.

When we ourselves must combat the force of some absurd or dangerous image of man—the image of man, say, that stood behind[188] Nazism—we run the risk of assimilating the horror in the very act of wrestling with it. We run that risk because such an image, horrible though it may be, could not exist at all, or compel the imagination of millions, if it did not spring from, and satisfy, certain human needs, and give scope for certain human virtues. By our own similar needs and similar virtues we are vulnerable to the temptation of that image. As Coleridge says, all beliefs are true; at least, the fact of their existence proves that there is a kind of truth in them. To say this is not to condone a horror, but to realize its fullness in the fact that its energies of evil are a perversion of energies potential for good, that the will for destruction is but the will for creation swayed from its proper end.

And I am reminded here of the profound passage in Conrad's *Lord Jim,* when Marlow comments on the apparently aimless massacre by the brigand Brown:

> Thus Brown balanced his account with the evil fortune. Notice that even in this awful outbreak there is a superiority as of a man who carries right —the abstract thing—within the envelope of his common desires. It was not a vulgar and treacherous massacre; it was a lesson, a retribution—a demonstration of some obscure and awful attribute of our nature which, I am afraid, is not so very far under the surface as we like to think.

Even in the act seemingly most brutal and gratuitous, Brown has, somehow, in a last distortion, affirmed himself as human, not brute, has affirmed, paradoxically, the human need for moral vindication. And let us not forget that Jim, the redeemed, had confronted Brown, the damned, in a dark duologue of communion and complicity delivered back and forth across a jungle creek.

Each of us longs for full balance and responsibility in self-knowledge, in a recognition and harmonious acceptance of our destiny. Saints and sages may achieve that harmonious sense of[189] destiny, or the hero at the cannon-mouth, or the famous sergeant of Belleau Wood. But we lesser and more fumbling mortals may find at least some intimation of it in the unfolding pattern, however modest, of our own effort toward knowledge.

I know that this has been a congress of philosophers, and I have a becoming diffidence about offering my amateur and homemade product after the three-day exhibit of glittering articles. If I am invited here at all, it is with the credentials of one who tries to write novels and poems and not of one who tries to philosophize. And that would suggest that the thing I was supposed to do in the first place was to remark on what relation I find between my own profession and the topic of this meeting. So I'll say my say, though I find myself saying it in the last, not the first, place. But last place may be best, for what has gone before, if it has accomplished anything, will explain what now I try to say.

I'll start by making one of the most debatable statements one can make: Poetry—that is, literature as a dimension of the creative imagination—is knowledge.

In accidental or incidental ways, poetry may, of course, give knowledge, even very important knowledge, but I do not mean such accidental or incidental knowledge. I do not mean, for instance, the absurdity I now shall tell you about, an absurdity we have all encountered in many places but which I have most recently encountered in a philosophical journal. The author of this absurdity, who no doubt embarrasses his friends, announces himself as a logical positivist, then argues that the novel is the most valuable form of art, for some novels give valid historical, sociological, and psychological knowledge. True, all novels report human motives and actions, and the settings, spatial, temporal, and social, in which those actions take place. But such reports occur much more systematically in works of history, geography, psychology, etc., and most certainly cannot be taken as the thing that characterizes and differentiates the novel as an art form.[190] No, the novel, as novel, as art-form, is not reporting anything—how to drive chariots or govern cities. It is using certain materials, which may include valid knowledge of chariot-driving or city-government, for its characteristic purposes, etc. There is no use to pursue the argument. Let us blush, avert our eyes, and pass on from this scene of logical naiveté and terminological carnage and Hobbesian nonsense. In other words, knowledge by report is not the kind of knowledge I mean in this discussion.

Nor do I mean what, for lack of a better term, we may call knowledge by symptom, the knowledge we may get from a work by regarding it as a cultural or linguistic symptom, or the symptom of its age or author. True, we may learn much by regarding poetry as symptom—for example, about an age or author, if we know how to take the deep ambivalences, the condensations, the subtle distortions and essential purgations of an age or personality. But again, such knowledge is not characteristic or differentiating.

If knowledge by report and knowledge by symptom, however valuable and interesting such knowledge may be, are not characteristic and differentiating, then what kind of knowledge am I talking about? I should say: knowledge by form. No, knowledge *of* form.

By this I mean the furthest thing possible from any doctrine that might go as sheer formalism. I mean the organic relation among all the elements of the work, including, *most emphatically,* those elements drawn from the actual world and charged with all the urgencies of actuality, urgencies not to be denied but transmuted—as we are told Tintoretto transmuted the gamin divers of the Venetian canals into the angels of his painting. The form is a vision of experience, but of experience fulfilled and redeemed in knowledge, the ugly with the beautiful, the slayer with the slain, what was known as shape now known as time, what was known in time now known as shape, a new knowledge. It is not a thing detached from the world but a thing[191] springing from the deep engagement of spirit with the world. This engagement may involve not only love for the world, but also fear and disgust, but the conquest, in form, of fear and disgust means such a sublimation that the world which once provoked the fear and disgust may now be totally loved in the fulness of contemplation. The form is the flowering of that deep engagement of spirit, the discovery of its rhythm. And the form is known, by creator or appreciator, only by experiencing it, by submitting to its characteristic rhythm.

With this word *rhythm*, I am reminded of the necessary question: how does the knowledge of form give man an image of himself?

It does so insofar as it gives the image of experience being brought to order and harmony, the image of a dance on the high wire over an abyss. The rhythm is, as it were, a myth of order, or fulfillment, an affirmation that our being may move in its totality toward meaning. The soul faces some potentiality of experience, drawn from actuality, and the form is the flowing vibration of the soul, the abstraction of experience by imagination. The form gives man an image of himself, for it gives him his mode of experiencing, a paradigm of his inner life, his rhythm of destiny, his tonality of fate. And this evocation, confrontation, and definition of our deepest life gives us, in new self-awareness, a yet deeper life to live.

But not merely the life of contemplation, for the soul does not sit in self-regarding trance, like Rachel before her mirror all the day, in Dante's *Purgatorio*. No, that gazing prepares for the moment of action, of creation, in our world of contingency. It is, as Yeats puts it,

> ... Our secret discipline
> Wherein the gazing soul doubles her might.

The might is there for the moment when the soul lifts her head.[192]

AN INTERVIEW WITH WARREN

Ralph Ellison and Eugene Walter

Interviewers: What is the relation of sociological research and other types of research to the forms of fiction?

Warren: I think it's purely accidental. For one writer a big dose of such stuff might be fine, for another it might be poison.... I've known a good many people, some of them writers, who think of literature as *material* that you "work up." You don't "work up" literature. They point at Zola. But Zola didn't do that. Nor did Dreiser. They may have thought they did, but they didn't. They weren't "working up" something—in one sense, something was working them up. You see the world as best you can—with or without the help of somebody's research, as the case may be. You see as much as you can, and the events and books that are interesting to you[126] should be interesting to you because you're a human being, not because you're trying to be a writer. Then those things may be of some use to you as a writer later on. I don't believe in a schematic approach to material. The business of researching for a book strikes me as a sort of obscenity. What I mean is, researching for a book in the sense of trying to find a book to write. Once you are engaged by a subject, are in your book, have your idea, you may or may not want to do some investigating. But you ought to do it in the same spirit in which you'd take a walk in the evening air to think things over. You can't research to get a book. You stumble on it. Or hope to. Maybe you will, if you live right.

Interviewers: Speaking of craft, how conscious are you of the dramatic structure of your novels when you begin? I ask because in it there is quite a variety of sub-forms, folklore, set pieces like the *Ballad of Billy Potts* or the Cass Mastern episode in *All the King's Men.* Are these planned as part of the dramatic structure, or do they arise while you are being carried by the flow of invention?

Warren: I try to think a lot about the craft of other people—that's part of my long years of teaching. You've been explaining things like

From Ralph Ellison and Eugene Walter, "The Art of Fiction XVIII: Robert Penn Warren," *Paris Review,* No. 16 (Spring–Summer 1957), pp. 113–140. Reprinted by permission of the publisher.

how the first scene of *Hamlet* gets off ... thinking of how things have been done ... I suppose some of this sinks down to your gizzard. When it comes to your own work you have made some objective decisions, such as which character is going to tell the story. That's a prime question, a question of control. You have to make a judgement. You find one character is more insistent, he's more sensitive and more pointed than the others. But as for other aspects of structure and craft, I guess, in the actual process of composition or in preliminary thinking, I try to immerse myself in the motive and *feel* toward meanings rather than plan a structure or plan effects. At some point, you know, you have to try to get one with God and *then,* take a hard cold look at what you're[127] doing and work on it once more, trusting in your viscera and nervous system and your previous efforts as far as they've gone. The hard thing, the objective thing has to be done before the book is written. And if anybody dreams up *Kubla Khan,* it's going to be Coleridge. If the work is done the dream will come to the man who's ready for that particular dream; it's not going to come just from dreaming in general. After a thing is done, then I try to get tough and critical with myself. But damn it, it may sometimes be too late then. But that is the fate of man. What I am trying to say is that I try to forget the abstractions when I'm actually composing a thing. I don't understand other approaches that come up when I talk to other writers. For instance, some say their sole interest is experimentation: Well, I think that you learn all you can and try to use it. I don't know what is meant by the word *"experiment";* you ought to be playing for keeps. ... [128]

Interviewers: Speaking of critics reminds me that you've written criticism as well as poetry, drama, and fiction. It is sometimes said that the practice of criticism is harmful to the rest, have you found it so?

Warren: On this matter of criticism, something that appalls me is the idea going around now that the practice of criticism is opposed to the literary impulse. Is *necessarily* opposed to it. Sure, it *may* be a trap, it may destroy the creative impulse, but so may drink or money or respectability. But criticism is a perfectly natural human activity and somehow the dullest, most technical criticism may be associated with full creativity. Elizabethan criticism is all, or nearly all, technical—meter, how to hang a line together—kitchen criticism, how to make the cake. People deeply interested in an art are interested in the "how." Now I don't mean to say that that is the only kind of valuable criticism. Any kind is good that gives a deeper insight into the nature of the thing—a Marxist analysis, a Freudian study, the relation to a literary or social tradition, the history of a theme. But we have to remember that there is no *one, single, correct* kind of criticism, no *complete* criticism. You only have different kinds of perspectives,

giving, when successful, different kinds of insights. And at one historical moment one kind of insight may be more needed than another....[130]

Interviewers: ... Jack Burden in *All the King's Men* is a conscious
center and he is a highly conscious man. He's not there as an omniscient figure, but is urgently trying to discover something. He is involved.

Warren: Burden got there by accident. He was only a sentence or
two in the first version—the verse play from which the novel developed.

Interviewers: Why did you make the change?

Warren: I don't know. He was an unnamed newspaper man, a
childhood friend of the assassin, an excuse for the young[134] doctor,
the assassin of the politician, Willie Stark, to say something before he
performed the deed. When after two years I picked up the verse version, and began to fool with a novel, the unnamed newspaper man
became the narrator. It turned out, in a way, that what he thought
about the story was more important than the story itself. I suppose he
became the narrator because he gave me the kind of interest I needed
to write the novel. He made it possible for me to control it. He is an
observer, but he is involved....[135]

¥

THE DRAMATIC VERSIONS OF THE
WILLIE STARK STORY
William M. Schutte

Through literature the artist works his way toward the truths
underlying the world he knows. Some writers explore one facet of this
world and then pass on to another. Others cannot pass on in peace.
They keep returning to one facet, never quite satisfied with their
understanding of it, never sure that they have dug out the whole of
the truth in it. Such a writer is Robert Penn Warren.

Readers of Warren's preface to the Modern Library Edition of
All[75] *the King's Men* know that it began as *Proud Flesh,* an un-

William M. Schutte, "The Dramatic Versions of the Willie Stark Story." From
All the King's Men: A Symposium. Carnegie Series in English, Number Three.
Pittsburgh: Carnegie Institute of Technology, 1957. Pp. 75–90. Reprinted by per-
mission of the author and the publisher.

published poetic drama. From what he says there, one might perhaps assume that, having found the dramatic form too limited for the story he had to tell, he turned to the novel form, which alone could convey adequately his conception of the truth in the lives of Willie Stark and Jack Burden. In fact, however, the novel did not end his concern with Willie Stark's story.

After he completed the novel, he adapted it to the stage in a prose version, first produced late in 1947 by Erwin Piscator at the New School for Social Research in New York. . . . In recent years he has rewritten the prose drama for Broadway production and plans to put the poetic drama into a form that satisfies him.

Like Jack Burden, Robert Penn Warren is haunted by the figure of Willie Stark and the profound effect of this man of action on the spider web of American life. Each of the versions of Stark's story is a discrete entity. Each looks at the material of his life from a somewhat different angle. As a group they provide an examination in depth of a critical area of American democracy.

At the suggestion of Eric Bentley, *Proud Flesh* was first produced in April, 1946, at the University Theatre of the University of Minnesota under the direction of Frank Whiting. It is a verse drama in which poetry alternates with colloquial prose. Modeled loosely on the Greek tragedies, it concerns a modern *tyrannos* who falls because of a flaw in character which he himself cannot perceive. His tragedy, like that of Oedipus, is caused by arrogant insistence on following the truth as he sees it, ignoring the will of the powers that rule his world.

From Greek drama Warren borrows a chorus and chorus leader— in this play a chorus of surgeons. They are present throughout the action, seated in a raised, railed-in enclosure at the side of the stage. Apostles of the Fact, they present cool, dispassionate, "scientific" interpretation of the frequently violent and passionate actions of the characters. They deprecate the least tendency to act on the basis of emotion or sentiment. Their attitude is clearly indicated in the Chorus Leader's final speech.[76] Willie is in the hospital after the shooting. The Leader considers his chances:

His survival may, in fact, hinge on such an imponderable as the "will to live." Yes, even as men of science, we are forced, at times, to admit this factor into our calculations. But let us make no hasty generalization, certainly not one of a metaphysical nature, from this. The phrase, the will to live, we may take simply as a metaphor, the will to live—or will in any connection whatever—being as it were, a function of certain subtle biologic processes which have, thus far, eluded precise definition. But—I cannot refrain from making at this moment a comment of a more personal nature. Whatever we may have thought, as citizens, of the policies and methods of the patient during his incumbency as Governor of this State, we are bound in candor to confess that he did advance the cause of medicine and has provided more adequate facilities for the practice of humanitarian zeal.

The Chorus of Surgeons is severely limited in its ability to interpret Willie Stark's world because, unlike Adam, it is satisfied with the Big Twitch as the explanation for all events. In a sense, it plays a part of the role eventually assigned to Jack Burden, who for a time also interpreted Willie's world in the light of the Big Twitch.

In this play, Willie Stark, here known as Willie Talos,[1] is the only central character. Jack Burden appears as a very minor character in two scenes. The other Burden's Landing characters—except for Adam and Anne Stanton (Keith and Anne Amos)—do not exist. The story revolves around Willie's relations with Anne and Adam, with his political henchmen, and with his wife and son.

The play opens after Willie has decided, as a monument to himself, to erect an eight-million-dollar hospital and get Adam to run it. But convincing Adam that he should take the job is no easy task, for Adam feels a deep, fundamental revulsion from Willie and his methods. To him Willie is the "essential deformity," so loathsome that even the touch of his hand defiles. It is Anne who turns the trick. Her efforts to get state funds for an orphanage have brought her into contact with[77] Stark. Right after Adam is offered the job, she sees him at the Capitol. She admits that she knows—as everyone else, she says, knows—of the plan to offer Adam the Directorship. She insists that Adam must not live in the idyllic past and that only extreme vanity prevents him from seeing that

> If [a thing] is good, it's good, good in itself . . . ,
> No matter what [Stark] is, or the world is.

Adam is persuaded. Later when Hubert Coffee (Max Tully) tries to get Adam to use his influence about a contract for the hospital, Willie chokes off Adam's resignation by instantly firing Coffee from the payroll.

Anne's relationship to Willie at the opening of the play is apparently not confined to business. Her appearance just after the job has been offered to her brother suggests that she and Willie are working together. However, not until the night when she comes to his hotel room to tell him about Coffee's interference does she commit herself to him as his mistress. As in the novel, she enters this relationship with her eyes open:

> I lived in the clutter of time, and I found no reason.
> Therefore, I said: If, at all, there is reason,
> It lives in the affirmative instant out of time,
> For the past is dead and the future in it like maggots.
> I said, I will look steady at the heart of flame.

---

1 To reduce confusion I shall regularly use for each character the name he bears in the novel. The name he bears in the play under discussion—if it differs—will be indicated in parentheses.

> Therefore, I say that my conduct has been
> No accident, no casual remission of will.
> But for once—and after I had seen my time
> Untwist, gather like lint under a bureau—
> At last, at last, the attempt at unblinking acceptance.

Anne is not, as in the novel, propelled into her liaison with Willie by Jack Burden's destruction of her picture of the past; on the other hand, in this play there is no suggestion that the idyllic past has a strong hold on her. She commits herself because her life requires something positive. When it is over, she has no regrets. She is only disappointed at her inability to cope with the situation: "I had thought that it would be different, I had thought to be stronger."

Willie's political dealings are seen throughout *Proud Flesh* in a very different focus from that used in the novel. The hospital, we have seen, is to be a monument to himself. He is furious at Coffee not because he[78] has any particular desire to keep crooks out of the hospital deal, but simply because his orders have been disobeyed and his good faith jeopardized. The contract eventually goes to Gummy Larson (Gummy Satterfield) in a routine political deal. There is no special pressure on Willie. Gummy wants the contract; Willie needs the Fourth Congressional. Willie dislikes Gummy personally, but he is perfectly willing to do business with him. When Anne protests, he passes it off with a shrug and a "You know how things are." Only after he decides to make the hospital a memorial to his son, Tom, does he break off the deal with Gummy and begin to tear things apart in the Legislature. Even then there is no clear indication that he is doing more than lashing out at the stoic Gummy and at the pliant Tiny Duffy (Tiny Harper), who has arranged the deal, in order to compensate for the pain of losing Tom.

Because in *Proud Flesh* Willie has no reforming past to return to, Lucy's role and Lucy's character are stronger than in the novel. As her first speech reveals, she is a more understanding woman, one who has a somewhat more reflective and philosophical turn of mind:

> I shan't say anything for myself, for I am nothing.
> Or rather, I am all I need to be, for I need nothing,
> And since I need nothing, I can give all,
> Which is my love, for I love you.

For her, "love is its own fulfillment." But Willie has destroyed love. She knows that he has lived in darkness and that his will is "like death." When Willie insists on forgiveness, however, she finds herself unable to stand firmly against him:

> If it were not dark, or if it were just dark and the dark
> Were not vexed by ambiguities and if
> I could know the nature of dark, not feel its uneven
> Breath. . . .

Ultimately the memory of the past, of how things had been once, to which she has been constantly returning, will not let her reject him.

We find the Willie of the early play a far less complex character than the Willie of the novel. He is a *tyrannos* who has found the prescription for controlling men's votes, for leading men where he wants them to go. He is given no past—we only learn that he was a poor country boy, "a crummy little wide-eyed snot" according to Sadie (Sue Parsons).[79] So far as we know, he has never been a reformer, has never fought the bosses. And though he changes after Tom's death, there is no clear-cut effort to make everything different. He dies without uttering the important "last words" of the novel.

Willie sees Adam Stanton as a "romantic" who is abstracted from the real world where men must reach down for mud to make their bricks. Ironically, Willie's fall in this play is caused by his own inner need for self-definition in Adam's terms. His return to Lucy is the result of Tom's death, which forces him to re-examine the values on which he has based his life. He is terrified by what he sees:

> O, [Lucy]! I've heard in my mind
> Blunt horrors lurch and grind, like streetcars.

This cry comes at the end of the interview in which Lucy finally agrees tentatively to take him back. Following almost immediately is an evaluation of the situation by the Chorus of antiseptic surgeons, who understand the implications of Willie's decision:

> His period of usefulness has clearly come to an end—
> We regret to admit it, for he was, in a sense, our friend,
> And he took an almost scientific view
> Of the mechanism with which he had to do.
> But there was a defect, the flaw, the taint in the blood,
> The one little thing in himself which he never understood:
> The secret need at last to justify himself by the abstraction of Good.

The implications of this ironic reversal of the position of the Greek tragic hero are many, and they add a new dimension to the meaning of the play. From the Chorus' point of view, the man who has to justify his acts on the basis of abstract values has lost his status as a "scientist." His usefulness has come to an end: he can no longer view life "scientifically."

The remainder of the play makes it clear that the change in Willie also destroys his usefulness in the world which for so many years he controlled. He controlled it because he had no need to justify his actions on any but pragmatic grounds. His view of the world was consistent and ordered. It accounted for everything. His inner certainty gave him the power to dominate the fragmented lives around him. With the loss of inner certainty he has become a hollow shell, and he must fall.[80]

The significance of the change in Willie is most graphically illustrated in his relationship to Anne. She had gone to him because her
life was empty, and she counted on his strength to give it meaning. She
had looked, as she said, at the heart of the flame; but what she saw
was an optical illusion. She had gone to him "for strength," but
suddenly she found him asking her for

> Something I had thought that I would never need. . . .
> And it is a thing which I had never surmised
> In daylight, or heard like a word sudden in the half-light
> Of dawn, or defined in the sleepless and grit lidded hour
> Before dawn.

This was not the Willie whom she had known. There is despair in her
reply:

> If you are fragmentary, what of us others?
> What of me, for my need by your needlessness only
> Is answered.

Willie's fatal weakness is an underlying need for precisely the kind of
"romanticism" which had amused him when he found it in Adam
Stanton.

One element in *Proud Flesh* is likely to confuse its audience. As
in all of the versions of the story, Warren faces the problem of making
the change in Willie psychologically and dramatically convincing. In
the novel, the return to Lucy is clearly an attempt to return to the
early, idealistic Willie. In the play there is no such Willie to return
to, and there is no clear-cut commitment to make things "different."
The death of Tom does not really seem sufficient to cause Willie
suddenly to realize that he must justify his actions by the abstraction
of Good. There may be blunt horrors lurking and grinding in his
head, but the audience has not been adequately prepared for them.

It would be wrong to suggest, however, that this weakness destroys
the over-all effectiveness of the play. Because the plot is less complex
than that of later versions, there is a concentration on basic elements
and little diffusion of effect. If in most of the scenes there is too much
talk and too little action, there are some scenes which are charged by
violent and conflicting emotions and others which are given a new
dimension by the effective use of poetry. The verse is uneven in
quality[81] .and its level sometimes seems jarringly inappropriate to
the characters. The highway patrolman who at one moment says,
"Reckless drive-en, thar's reckless drive-en, all right. Seventy-five miles
an hour, and on them curves, and passing a car. Buddy, I'm doen you
a favor, hit's a favor," suddenly proceeds to describe his revolver:

> And name now this other, and praise it—
> The steel husk wherein sleeps amazement,

Steel pod where the dark drowses darkly
Like seed locked, like light locked in darkness.

But at its best the verse is highly effective, especially in the mouth of
the Chorus. Warren's brilliant use of images of light and darkness, of
birth and death, of gnawing teeth, of the garden of Eden, of foetal mass
and rotten pool help to underline the central meanings of the play.

Warren's second attempt to put the story of Willie Stark on the
stage came shortly after the publication of the novel, and bore its title.
This new version was first presented in 1947 by the Dramatic Work-
shop of the New School for Social Research under the direction of
Erwin Piscator and has since been given elsewhere with minor changes
in the script. It is essentially a dramatization of the novel, and one is
forced to agree in part with the stricture leveled against it by Wolcott
Gibbs (*The New Yorker*, January 24, 1948, p. 45) that "Mr. Warren
... [has] exercised almost no selection, and the unnecessary complex of
stories on the stage might easily be quite incomprehensible to anybody
who hadn't read the book." The second part of Gibbs' sentence is
perhaps too strong. True, the action is sometimes difficult to follow,
but there are enough powerful scenes to make this play exciting
theatre.

Toward the end of *Proud Flesh* Warren had made some use of the
flexible technique of moving rapidly from brief scene to brief scene
by alternately lighting and blacking out various areas of the stage. In
the play *All the King's Men* he makes extensive use of this technique
and achieves further flexibility by reducing the chorus to a single Professor of Science who remains on the forestage throughout the action
(though he is not always visible). The Professor introduces the play,
evaluates from a "scientific" point of view the events going on behind
him, occasionally fires a question at a character, and carries on a
running argument about the significance of the Stark story with Jack
Burden,[82] who sometimes joins him on the forestage. His role in the
proceedings is considerable during the early scenes but gradually
diminishes. In the final act he has very little to say; his role as commentator is to a large extent taken over by Jack Burden.

The action is divided into twenty-four scenes, a few of which
contain two or more related episodes taking place in different locations.
In one "scene," for example, Anne talks to Jack on the dock, trying to
persuade him to get Adam to take the job as Director; then as part of
the same scene there is a conversation about the Littlepaugh documents
between Anne and Adam. At the beginning of this scene Jack talks to
the audience; at the end the Professor talks with Adam. With so many
scenes and interludes, the play is a patchwork in which the pattern is
sometimes obscure. And because so much has to be included, the
"big" scenes of the novel are truncated and their effectiveness reduced.

The plot is the plot of the novel—somewhat condensed. The only important omissions are the events involving Byram B. White which lead up to the impeachment attempt (no specific event triggers it in the play) and the Cass Mastern story. Everything else of importance in the novel is either referred to in conversation (largely between Jack and the Professor) or presented on the stage. The result is a play whose full implications are likely to be understood only by those in the audience who have read the novel. Because the Burden's Landing background has to be hastily summarized, neither Jack nor Anne nor Adam is fully motivated. And because "Cousin Willie from the country" is only suggested, the portrait of Stark is harsher, less sympathetic than in the novel. The Professor is an irritating "Johnny One Note" with his supercilious assurance that nothing is of any significance except the "verifiable phenomenon," that man is important only as creator of end products, that all his actions are explainable in terms of basic drives.

If this retelling of the Willie Stark–Jack Burden story is memorable, it is memorable for a few individual scenes of inherent power and for the blood-tingling First Act conclusion, where Willie, his arms raised above his head, screams to an audience "Blood on the Moon!" The effectiveness of such scenes, however, is reduced by the awkward narrative method and the attempt to jam everything from the novel into a three-hour drama for the stage.[83]

Warren's most recent interpretation of the story is an as yet unproduced drama tentatively called *Willie Stark: His Rise and Fall.* It is more than a rearrangement of the earlier prose version. In many ways it is closer to *Proud Flesh,* from which its final scenes are taken with minor changes in emphasis. Perhaps as a result of the criticism that the play *All the King's Men* tried to do too much, Warren has recast the story so that it can be told forcefully in terms of the stage.

One major revision is the dropping of the Chorus. And with the Chorus goes the direct expression of the "scientific" point of view against which Warren has made a case in each of the earlier versions. Instead of using the Chorus or the Professor as commentator, he sets the new play in a frame—a speech by one Dr. Shipworth at the dedication of the Tom Stark Memorial Hospital. On the platform with the speaker are Governor Duffy, Senator MacMurfee, and William Larson, "builder, financier, philanthropist," all of whom, Dr. Shipworth notes, "have helped give a great dream [its] beautiful embodiment" in the hospital. Like the Professor of the preceding play, Shipworth insists, in the Prologue, that the only important "fact" is the present existence of the hospital. "It does not matter," he says, "how it came to exist." But to Jack Burden, observing from the forestage, it *does* matter. With his protest, unheard by the platform group, the play about Willie Stark begins.

This time the story is told in twelve scenes instead of twenty-four, and the few interludes serve as bridges between major scenes. Warren clearly has moved a long way now toward rethinking his story in terms of the stage. The result is no longer a staged novel. By eliminating large quantities of material, by moving incidents around so that more than one event may occur in a single scene, and by making one major character out of two, Warren has improved on the preceding version. What is left after the changes have been made is a more effective drama than either of the others on the same subject, and one which gives a somewhat different picture of events than either.

The rearrangement of materials is immediately apparent. The play opens with what in the novel was the Byram B. White scene. But Warren has made Tiny Duffy the cause of the trouble: it is Tiny who has stuck his nose in the trough, whom Stark bullies, who is forced to write out[84] his undated resignation. Standing in the corner observing the scene is not Hugh Miller, but Judge Irwin, the Attorney General. Because Willie refuses to throw Duffy to the wolves, Irwin offers his resignation. Most of the more philosophic parts of the conversation, which in the earlier versions occurs at Burden's Landing after Stark's midnight drive, are transferred to this scene and integrated with material from the Stark-Miller conversation in the novel. In this scene, too, after Irwin leaves, Willie conceives the plan for the hospital as a memorial to himself and asks Jack to get Adam to agree to be Director. He also tells Jack to dig on Irwin and prepares to resist a possible impeachment attempt. This first scene, then, is a full-length, integrated scene of considerable power, using materials which in the kaleidoscopic earlier prose version were scattered among several scenes. The remainder of the play continues to combine scenes from the older versions. This combining process is especially in evidence during the first two acts.

But, as already suggested, the recasting of the materials results in a considerable change in the characters. The portrait of Willie Stark, for example, has lost some of its subtlety. As in *Proud Flesh* we see him largely in his present aspect. Except for a reference or two to his rather commonplace early married life with Lucy, a speech in which he talks about his boyhood on a poverty-stricken farm, and Sadie's references to the "crummy little wide-eyed snot of a hick" she made over, all of his past is wiped out. There is no Willie from the country, no Willie the honest county official, not even Willie the crude but predestined savior of the red necks. Once again there is only the Boss.

And since in this play the Boss ultimately commits himself, as he did not in *Proud Flesh,* to the attempt to make things "different," Warren here faces a more difficult task than in either of the other versions. Within the limits of the present action he must make us believe in Willie's ultimate conversion to a "different" view of the world. At first glance Warren seems to make his job even more difficult by insisting at the start on the worst side of Stark's personality. In the novel and the earlier prose version, for example, Willie throws his drink in

Tiny's face at a point late in the story, right after he has been forced to deal with Larson, when he is both drunk and under intense emotional strain. In *Willie Stark: His Rise and Fall* he throws the drink at the very start of the play[85] when Tiny tries to explain his reasons for doing a little grafting on the side. So placed, it shocks the audience, which as yet is uncommitted about Willie, and establishes him as a vicious bully. Significantly, in both of the other versions, Tiny himself curbs the impulse to fling himself on Willie; in this one it is Sugar-Boy's "No - no - no - no, y - y - you don't" that stops him, and the audience's impression of Willie as a bullying gangster is further consolidated.

In the second scene, this impression is modified. We get a brief glimpse of his early poverty. We see his love for his son. We hear Lucy complain about what he is doing to Tom, but we also learn that he wants Tom not to have to drudge as he did. We are almost sorry for him when we are shown the monster whom he loves and in whom he vicariously lives the college life he was himself denied. Finally, we see him in action trying with a mixture of pure charm and disarming forthrightness to talk Adam into taking the hospital job. His attack is directed at Adam's deepest convictions. He tries to do what Jack succeeds in doing later: he tries to change Adam's picture of the world. He insists with Adam, as he has with Irwin, that the trouble with the "Silk Hat Gang" is that they want to do good but don't want to pay the price that has to be paid for it. He offers Adam the chance to do good, and he offers to pay the price himself. For, he says, he has no scruples about getting his hands dirty. Essentially he is doing for Adam what he did for the Judge (or in the novel for Hugh Miller), to whom he gave the chance to "make the fur fly." But Adam is suspicious and self-righteous, and only by challenging his "first principles" can Willie hope to persuade him to accept. Actually, Adam merely agrees to think over the offer; but that in itself is a victory. Jack and Anne finish the job by destroying Adam's image of Judge Irwin.

Stark's behavior at the Judge's home is far cruder than in earlier versions. He insists on accompanying Jack to Burden's Landing, accuses him of disloyalty, pushes him into Irwin's study, and then breaks rudely in himself before the Judge tells Jack whether or not he will continue to support MacMurfee. These bullying tactics are so crude that even the phlegmatic Jack is disgusted. He orders both Stark and Sugar-Boy out of the house. The pistol shot which follows Jack's departure and concludes the second act puts the seal on the viciousness of Willie Stark.[86]

In this play, too, we are given graphic proof of Lucy's twice-repeated assertion that Willie has ruined everything he has touched. Most importantly we find that each of the central characters—except Lucy—is here less sympathetic than in the earlier versions. The last scene of the second act begins with a symbolic tableau. The stage is dark at first. Then Jack comes out to announce: "So he has us all now." And as he names those whom Stark "has"—Anne, Sadie, Lucy, Tom, Adam, Sugar-Boy, Tiny, and himself—each appears in a spotlight. Willie has them all. His corruption taints each one. Tiny, as we have seen, is even more treacherous and more oily than he has been. Jack is again relegated to a minor and frequently less than sympathetic role. But Sadie and Anne suffer most. In one scene, the one in which she reveals to Jack that Anne is Willie's mistress, Sadie tells us what a hell her own life has been. But we are not, as we are in the novel, prepared to be sympathetic; for we have heard nothing from her but vicious comments about Anne and whining complaints about Willie's ingratitude. And the description of her early life is followed by her telling Jack in Anne's presence that Anne is Willie's mistress. The whole situation might have been used to create sympathy for Sadie, but her attack on Anne is so "venomous" (to take a word from Warren's stage direction) that most of our sympathy is for Anne and Jack, not for her. Through the remainder of the play she is essentially unchanged. There is nothing of the smart cookie who knows her way around; this Sadie has no control either of herself or of the world around her. As a result, one of the most sympathetic characters of the novel has become one of the least sympathetic in this play.

Anne's character suffers, too. Warren sketches in briefly the idyllic background of Jack and Anne as a framework around the first scene of Act II, in which Jack tells Willie that he has found something on Irwin and in which Tiny is blown up for suggesting a deal with Larson. The next scene is the one on the wharf in which Anne pleads—almost hysterically—with Jack to make Adam take the hospital job. The violence of her speech comes as a surprise to the audience. Without the background supplied by the novel she seems merely neurotic about her brother. Furthermore Warren injects into this scene for the first time an exchange which cannot but lead the audience to suspect her motives,[87] especially as the scene is followed almost immediately by the one in which she admits to being Willie's mistress. Here is the exchange. The subject is her effort to persuade Adam to accept:

ANNE. Don't you see why I'm doing it?
JACK. Well?
ANNE. I'm doing it for him. For him.
JACK. For who? For who did you say?
ANNE. For Adam—for Adam, of course—you knew we were talking about Adam.
JACK. Sure, but Governor Stark is the most interested party, and it just occurred to me that—
ANNE. What are you saying? (*Recoiling*) Are you saying that I'd put something before Adam—before Adam's good—that I'd put somebody's wishes first—Oh, Jack, how could you?

Thus Warren sows a seed of suspicion in the reader's mind. And if there is anything to the suspicion, the vehemence of Anne's insistence that her whole concern is for Adam convicts her of the worst kind of hypocrisy. The scene on the wharf is her big scene. Thereafter she has little to do. Her last significant appearance occurs after Willie has decided to return to Lucy and the "better" way of life. She is given a moment to tell the audience what her affair with him has meant to her. The speech provides an interesting contrast to her despair in *Proud Flesh* when she discovers Willie's need to lean on her. Here she says:

> Oh, I understand now. I understand now, and would not have it otherwise. And what I had loved in you was what, in the end, made you leave me. I had loved you because I knew there was a truth in you, and if, in the end, you found that truth, why should I complain that that truth had no place for me? But oh, it was hard, it was hard.

Anne says that Willie has found the essential truth in himself and must therefore become something other than what he has been. Once again Warren is faced with the problem of making the audience accept the essential change in his protagonist. And in this play he must work with a Willie who is more vicious than any we have seen before. To be sure, in the second scene he gains some stature as a human being whose view of the world is consistent, who is willing to look steadily at "first[88] principles," and who can be immensely persuasive and charming. And later we find him violently castigating Tiny for trying to deal Larson in on the hospital contract: he will have no crooks messing around *his* hospital. Nevertheless, we also find that Judge Irwin's suicide and the ugly rumors it breeds force Willie to make the deal with Larson in order to kill the impeachment. Drunk, as in the novel, he then threatens Larson and shouts at Jack, "I never wanted his dirty hands on it. But they made me. I tell you they made me. Do you understand? Do you understand?"

This scene is followed directly by one at the hospital in the middle of which Tom's death is reported to his mother and father. On this scene Warren depends for making the audience believe in Willie's "conversion." Before the fatal message comes, Willie is belligerent, tender, and optimistic by turns. Above all he is, as he says, confused. He has so far lost contact with Lucy that he expects her to be happy at his idea of naming the hospital after Tom. After Adam has made his report, Lucy gives vent to her bitterness. "And now you have your son," she tells him, "but you cannot have mine." She knows that Willie didn't mean to kill Tom, "But you ruin everything you touch." She believes, too, that she knows why their world originally collapsed. The basic reason is the one stressed in *Proud Flesh*. Willie had failed in love. "Love," she insists, "would have made a world that love could live in." Willie is crushed. He has no reply. He drops to his knees be-

won the pit, and this novel is a best-seller, which is to say that there is
a level of dramatic tension more widely accessible than one expects in
the philosophic novel. The plot involves public figures, but the record is
nally of the private agony (as with Macbeth and Oedipus). The author
begins with history and politics, but the real subject is the nature of
an: Warren is no more discussing American politics than *Hamlet* is
cussing Danish politics. Then there are the ironic intra-family con-
tradias and injuries, the repercussions of generation upon genera-
n, with Hamlet and Orestes—a type of situation which, it may be
erven passing, Aristotle praises. As with the older tragedy, all
calk like steaming melodrama if one wants to stop at the deed
ed simply forget about meanings. But as in the older poetic
ed is, beneath all the explicitnesses, a core of obscure con-
s, ves partly clouded, of calculations beset by the uncalcu-
d, impasses in which both action and inaction may damn,
Outy be Oresteian guilt.

ng's Men is the tragedy of incomplete personalities
onship is rooted, in part, in the impulse to complete-
y of will." Anne Stanton cannot find it in the un-
young Jack Burden, sardonic in a detachment closer
objectivity; by contrast the rude, better-directioned
rk acts compellingly upon her. Dr. Adam Stanton,
off, driving himself with ascetic, self-destructive
apparently acting unwillingly, a liberating[155]
ies him with Willie Stark, the man of fact—the
d himself, as symbolic modern characters, pro-
sophic groundwork of the story. Jack Burden,
rewd, speculative, but unintegrated, lacking,
gives his life an appearance of personal form
o Willie, who has cohesion and aim and a
organizes and excites—and that still calls up
hich Jack, in evidence of his never quite
ways keeps asking. Everybody's needs are
grotesque gunman, Sugar Boy, the stut-
e Willie "can talk so good." Willie com-
is a centering and a commitment; but
f. In a complex of polarities that are
ut the novel, Willie also seeks comple-
with idea and tradition, and with the
ses an entryway into a realm beyond
act, there is the paradox of action;
lete; action is necessary but is never
but imposes its conditions. Adam
ions of action, and Willie cannot
lie cannot save himself from his
understand himself; the man of

fore her as he says "I have come a long way, and I didn't see the way,
and—oh, Lucy, I have horrors in my head—they lurch and grind like
streetcars."

In the hands of sensitive, capable actors, this scene should convince
an audience that Willie's attempt to reform is genuine. The helplessness and inarticulateness of the normally articulate and dynamic Governor give to his final statement about the horrors in his head a conviction lacking in the comparable speech in *Proud Flesh*. His behavior
here suggests, too, that in the following scene he really means it when,
after ordering Tiny to break the news to Larson, he tells Sadie, "Whatever it was that I was [before becoming a successful politician] it was
better."

But whatever it was that he was, Willie cannot go back to it. In
the very process of turning the money-changers out of the temple, he
has to act like the Willie Stark of old. "You got to start somewhere," he
tells the uncomprehending Sadie. "Yeah—you start, and then you find
it[89] is just the same. You find you're just heaving yourself around like
you did. You find yourself saying the same things. You find yourself
heaving your weight around just like you did. You find yourself
just . . ." This comment throws an ironic light on Willie's final speech.
Jack may, as he says in the epilogue, believe that things might have
been different. But the truth is that they could only have been different
if Willie had made a world in which love could live. By the time
Willie learned his lesson, it was too late. And when he denied the self
he had lived by, he condemned himself to destruction.

In these three dramatic versions of the Willie Stark story, we find
Warren striving to set down what at three different periods the story of
Willie Stark has meant to him. In *Proud Flesh*, Stark is a strong man
who stays in the saddle until the shock of his son's death brings to the
surface a fatal flaw, a need to justify his acts by referring to abstract
values. In *All the King's Men*, the play, he is the reformer Willie of
the novel who became a demagogue as a result of the traumatic revela-
tions of Upton and is returned to the paths of righteousness by the
shock of his son's death. And in *Willie Stark: His Rise and Fall*, the
emphasis is on the inability of the dictator by an act of will to change
the world he has created with his power or change his ways of action
in it. Like other men he is caught in the maze he has contrived for
himself.

In each of the last two versions of the story, Willie returns to say
to those left behind, "Being a man, I did not know what I was, nor
what might be the fullness of man. But being a man, I yearned toward
that definition, even in the dark night of my ignorance." Through his
plays about Stark, Warren has sought to work his way toward a final
definition of a distinctive creation of American political life.[90]

First Analyses

ALL THE KING'S MEN AS TR

Robert B. Heilman

Everybody knows that the eighteenth
literature, the disappearance of tragedy a
neo-classicism set in, something happene
thing which included the growth of t
subtle adulteration of the Christian
stance, the pressure of prudential upo
a weakening of the grasp of man's i
ties upon which tragedy, and for t
pends. In its direction the novel
cern was less the troubled man t
to a consideration of troubles at
and easily catalogued: Joneses,
beth Bennets, Micawbers, Be
the[154] content of experienc
that level some men of lette
perience, however much E
imaginations: the novel, i
determination, has kept
ness of life which dram
lish fiction is the Ques
to now, begins to cu
further; James, Con
that do not match
tensities. Robert
the history of th

Recovery i
Greek, traged

Robert B
Sewanee Re
South. Reprin

action becomes the self-critic in action when,, in every phase of the hospital drama, he actually, if not overtly, repudiates his working half-truths.

A plurality of heroes is one symbol of a riven world. There are in Warren's novel other partial men; there is especially Jack, whose story, he says, is Willie's story: he is the riven world which produces Willie and serves him and yet always keeps a last thin aloofness from him, and which through him comes to a possibly saving understanding—the note of hope, of spiritual discovery, which completes tragedy. Jack is a scarred Ancient Mariner telling what happened and what he learned; he stubbornly tells it in a style which recreates things as they were to him, without benefit of the exceptions he might now make in his maturity.

I have stressed Mr. Warren's belonging to the tragic tradition because his book has brought into focus a very disturbing situation—our sheer incompetence to read tragedy. A large number of critics have beaten Mr. Warren around the ears and cried that he should[156] have written a political melodrama. He woos a long-neglected Melpomene, and is told he should be doing a carmagnole with an up-to-date Clio. He tries to give his readers the universal in the unique form which is the individual work of art, and they bawl at him for not sticking to social platitudes. He gives them metaphysics, and they call pettishly for sociology. Well, he does give them some social documentation, all right, but he gives it to them the hard way: he pictures for them the spiritual condition—the decline of tradition, the loss of an integrating force, the kind of split—which results in Willie-as-hero; he makes it still harder for them by pointing out the kind of greatness Willie had to have to be to a society what he was. Warren says, I take it, that a universal complement has to be a little more than a melodrama villain. But they do not want understanding—because it involves the pain of self-scrutiny. They know in advance that Willie, insofar as he is Humpty, is a bad egg who ought to have had a fall; we should simply and happily hoot him. And feel ever so warm a glow inside. But we can get a warm glow from liquor or likker, and some prefer chemical analysis.

Most of the daily and weekly reviewers who tell America what to read still have the simplified view of *belles lettres* deriving from the eighteenth century. Of some two score of them whose reviews of *All the King's Men* I have been able to see, precisely two have a complete grasp of the work as tragedy: Henry Rago in *Commonweal* and Brainard Cheney in the Nashville *Banner,* both of whom do brilliant analyses. Four others come close: Victor Hamm in the Milwaukee *Journal,* Paul Engle in the *Chicago Tribune,* Granville Hicks in the *American Mercury,* and Lee Casey in the *Rocky Mountain News.* Surely these publications would not come to mind as the first six most likely sources of critical light in America. But by their diversity and distribution they establish the public intelligibility of Mr. Warren's novel; it is clearly not a work for club members only. Besides these six, about fourteen—in all, a little less than half of those I have seen— recognize that the novel is of philosophic dimensions. George Mayberry of the *New Republic* and James Wood of the *Saturday Review* read the book very intelligently; but the philosophic insight of others is often neither large nor secure. Most reviews are laudatory, some of them grudgingly, and others clearly uncertain why. The *Daily Oklahoman* headlines its review, "Nothing To Do But Like This Gay Old Cuss." From such a journalistic cradle, presumably typical, it is, paradoxically, not too[157] far to the mature journeyman critics, a dozen or so of them, who provide the real problem for discussion. They are the ones who fear that Mr. Warren fails to show the dangers of dictatorship, or who outright accuse him of defending or aiding fascism. If these were all journalistic hillbillies, one could shed a tear for the darkness of the underbrush and forget it; but they furnish part of the candlepower of some of the stronger fluorescent lights in Megalopolis— the New York *Times, PM,* the *Nation,* and the papers that subscribe to John Cournos and Sterling North. Further, Fred Marsh of the *Herald-Tribune* fails so completely to understand the book that he finally hypothesizes that it may be "intended only as melodrama in modern prose."

It would be easy to compile a florilegium of critical quaintnesses. Only two reviewers, for instance, indicate awareness that the management of the religious theme at the end is more than a pious postlude. The *New Yorker* and the Chicago *Sun* both regard Jack Burden as an interloper; *PM* and Sterling North regard the Cass Mastern episode, which is of high structural importance, as an intrusion. Most of the commentators on style should go to Henry Rago of *Commonweal* for a lesson on the quality and functional role of the style. Of three reviewers who use the word *slick,* only Robert Gorham Davis of the *Times* adduces evidence—two sentences, both of which, he fails to realize, are indications of the attitude of Jack Burden; the second he particularly mistreats by lifting it, without explanation, from a bitterly ironic context. But what is one to think of reviewers' sense of style in general when he can find applied to Mr. Warren's writing two such beautifully irreconcilable judgments as those of Fred Marsh in the *Herald-Tribune* and Laban C. Smith in the Chicago *Sun?* The former's words: "elaborately stylized prose (since nobody ever either talks or writes like this)." Mr. Smith's comment on figures of speech: "most of them very familiar if not trite, and the full development of these figures and their repetition frequently corrupts . . . a strong and intelligent style."

But the heart of the matter is this: why can so few critics read tragedy, and what are the implications of this disability of theirs? In the muddling over *All the King's Men* we can see several main tendencies, overlapping and not always properly distinguishable; perhaps they are all facets of a central cultural phenomenon. As a group the reviewers exhibit certain habits of mind that have been familiar since the eighteenth century—habits which appeared as tragedy began to[158] disappear and which, as long as they are general and uncorrected, are, without necessarily intending to be so, hostile to tragedy and to the insights made possible by the tragic sense. Perhaps the presence of these habits means simply the absence of the tragic habit of mind. Then the novelist faces the hard task of creating it for himself. The habits against which he will have to contend are the Puritanical, the sentimental, the scientific, the social-topical, and the lotos-eating or slothful.

The Puritanism that one finds in the reviews of *All the King's Men* is of the pale, literal, unhand-me-sir kind that, when Troy is falling, complains of, or even rises to a certain vice-squad petulance against, naughty words on the wall. Eunice Ross Perkins grieves, in the Macon *Telegraph,* that there is "no really fine" woman in the book and that Mr. Warren has not caught sight of the really very nice things in the South. The same obtuseness appears in two ecclesiastical organs, with which *Commonweal* is in encouraging contrast: Harold C. Gardiner in *America* abuses the book as blasphemous and immoral, and Daniel Poling in the *Christian Herald* regrets that Mr. Warren "goes into the gutter." Mr. Warren is trying to tell them about Troy, and they call for The Story of the Good Little Boy. A man's search for truth is too tough substance for these sentimental hand-me-downs from a simpler day. A cousin of theirs, Ethel Dexter of the Springfield *Republican,* wonders how women can really fall in love with such a fellow as Willie. These are familiar cries for familiar pluckings of the heart-strings. Give the cries a political twist, and they become demands for praise of reigning dogmas, and caveats against inquiry into underlying truths.

The scientific mind turns from aesthetic problems to the provenience of the book, the man behind the book, the book's effect on society, etc.: a perverse factuality trespasses on the domain of the imagination. Certain reviewers cannot separate Willie Stark from Huey Long; some actually fear that Mr. Warren is not *biographically* accurate. Such minds cannot distinguish fact and fiction, the point of departure and the imaginative journey; they cannot realize that a few biographical facts are merely, and can be no more than, an alterable design for a mold into which the artist pours such dramatic body and such values as his insight permits. How can these people read Shakespeare? Some of them, self-consciously sharp, scream "special pleading"; Sterling North and Robert Davis consider the novel a personal apologia, an[159] apologia, Davis says outright, for having edited *The Southern Review* at Louisiana State University. It may be remarked parenthetically that Mr. Davis's criterion, if applied with any sort of consistency at all, will deprive most universities of their faculties and most moneymaking periodicals of their reviewers. What is of critical interest, however, is not Mr. Davis's squinting detectivism, but the pseudo-scientific, psychology-ridden cast of mind, with which he is obviously well satisfied, that makes it literally impossible for him to read and understand the literary evidence. He cannot tell what the story says; he simply cannot grasp the author's detachment and integrity.

This category of incompetence overlaps the next, where we find the science-and-society frame of mind. Historically, this kind of reader represents the main tradition of the English novel, which finds its tensions in social patterns, in problems of relationship in society rather than in the individual. But societies change, and with the evolutionary friction the social becomes the topical. To us, in our day, the social appears as the real, and atmospheric pressures tend to convince the writer that literature ought to be an adjunct of societal reordering. Now this concept, if taken as profoundly as possible, could accommodate high literature; Mr. Warren *is* concerned with society: his very subject is the split personality of an age. But the self-conscious practitioner of social consciousness does not want such radical investigations; he has already done the diagnosis, and all he wants is a literary pharmacist to make up the prescribed vitamin and sulfa pills.

The social-topical critics, bound by their inflexibly applied theory of literature, cannot read the individual work. But there are degrees of subtlety among them. Granville Hicks, as I have already said, gives so sensitive an account of *All the King's Men* that he does not belong with the table-pounders at all—except for one small point: he notes Shaw's and Steffens' insistence on changing a corrupt society, and adds that Mr. Warren says nothing of socialism. That is all; yet it suggests that Mr. Hicks wants the novel to do something which is hardly in its province. But he holds to his dogma with such tact that he is not blinded to the goodness of what has been done. It is quite a step down, therefore, to Saxe Commins, who in the Cleveland *News* pays formal tribute to Mr. Warren's various skills but goes on to express regret for Mr. Warren's indifference to Negroes and "the people who should be the concern of the state." Mr. Commins' social concern is familiar: he wants a conventional conflict developed by standardized[160] dramatic symbols; he wants the novelist to be a one-man pressure-group instead of a man of tragic vision. So, dogma-bound, he gravely warns that the novel serves to glamorize the man in the "bullet-proof limousine" and thus to "invite disaster." Diana Trilling of the *Nation* imagines that Mr. Warren is defaming Hegel's relativism and hence gets things so out of focus that she perpetrates an extraordinary series of misreadings. She calls Jack Burden's Twitch theory "embarrassingly maudlin"—and completely misses Jack's repudiation of the theory. She says that Jack's "moral awareness" is of "low quality" and that he has a fine eye but "no equivalent gift of inward vision." She utterly misses his long search for truth, his reflectiveness, his later understanding of Cass Mastern, his insight into the Adam-Willie cleavage. What must a man do to exhibit vision? Declaim the Bill of Rights? Mrs. Trilling thinks the hospital is meant to establish Willie as a benefactor and that Mr. Warren approves of Willie because Willie is Jack's "hero." Even a strong commitment to liberal dogma seems hardly sufficient to explain, in a justly distinguished professional critic of fiction, such gross oversimplification of what a book says.

Dawn Powell gives the readers of *PM* little more than flippancies; but she closes with the warning that increasing regard for the strong-man legend may be paving the way "for a really successful Willie Stark." Sterling North's purely literary comments are too genuinely stupid to warrant mention; what he lacks in insight he makes up in insolence and malevolence. But is he, in his political and moral judgments, really the honest barbarian he looks? Beats there a heart of gold below the red neck? Or is he the slicker in the backroom who knows what the customers want? Are there pleasant little pills in the innocent, downturned palm?

Diana Trilling, Dawn Powell, and Sterling North—a pretty bedful. And when we find the somewhat primly schoolmasterish Robert Davis's head on the same pillow—he assures us that Warren is playing Parson Weems to Huey's Washington—the picture has a wonderfully satisfying completeness. For what do they all do but pull the covers up over their heads and refuse to listen to the real warnings about the society they are so preciously and loudly concerned about? They have taken the symptom for the disease, and they want the symptom denounced; out, out, dark pimple. When an artist takes the symptom and traces it to radical causes—and when he even shows the kind of consciousness that nourishes the causes and with a severely disciplined[161] hopefulness shows a possibly saving alteration in that consciousness—they mistake him for a germ-carrier. The artist proceeds from the region to the civilization, and from the civilization to the dangers of disintegration implicit in human life; this is tragedy; but they cannot read it, and in their confusion they are as complacent as if they were protecting Humpty down there under the covers.

Before we turn out the light and tiptoe away from this dormitory and its fantasies, we need to note that, aside from missing what is in the book, Mr. Davis prescribes a formula for contemporary fiction: that "we fight men like Long with the utmost resolution . . . to preserve . . . free, open, pluralistic societies. . . ." One may doubt whether *Macbeth* would have been improved if it had been conceived as a recipe for the curtailment of royal abuses. Mr. Davis makes the old confusion of citizen and artist; but, what is far worse, he is apparently bent on imposing upon the artist a topicality, and a predetermined point of view, which must dull and destroy his insight. It is dangerous to read badly; but it is a terribly serious matter when an élite itself—I

refer to most of the critics I have quoted—when this élite, as if moved
by a devastating self-distrust, calls for easy propaganda in place of the
difficulties of tragedy. It is easy to hate a villain; and it is usually the
groundlings who want life reduced to a manageable melodrama. What
if all artists give in?

In many of these readers of *All the King's Men* there is plain sloth-
fulness—not as a personal vice but as a public habit which appears to
have grown since the eighteenth century, to have been nourished upon
and in turn to have insisted upon, a relatively simple, one-dimensional
literature. Not that there has not been difficult, complex, poetic
writing; but it has been exceptional, and, until lately, rather much
neglected. It is obviously not quite fair to pick Leo Kirschbaum of
Commentary as the sole exemplar of the well-intentioned, easy-going
readerhood, for he has tried not to be careless or casual, and has indeed
worked hard at his assignment. But in him the moral becomes beautifully clear: as a sharp reader of Elizabethan tragedy, and as one who
understands poetic values, he is precisely the person who ought to
read *All the King's Men* with especial discernment. Yet his trouble is
that, as a man of the long post-1700 age of prose, he somehow
approaches the novel with a totally different set of assumptions—an
approach which is tantamount to an abdication of his critical powers.
As a modern work, the novel is going to be explicit, straightforward,
resonantly in[162] favor of the accepted goods, adapted to intelligent
upper-middle-class sentiments, not too poetic, and with the philosophy,
if any, prompting pretty audibly from the wings; and if the work
draws its skeletal materials from modern history, it must stick faithfully to what we all know to be the truth about those materials. Now
Dr. Kirschbaum would never read Shakespeare or Sophocles like that.
He would unconsciously junk all these preconceptions and start with
the text. But in his modern *acedia*—and perhaps it is the literary *acedia*
of any age—he starts, alas without knowing it, with something else that
the text is supposed to fit into. So he misses entirely the central theme
—the split in modern consciousness; in Jack's unrelenting philosophical
inquiry he finds only callow, even pathological insufficiency; and the
complex attitude of Jack to Willie, which involves not only his being
hypnotized by the genius of action, but also his sense of guilt and his
paradoxical detachment and critical distance from Willie, Kirschbaum
takes to be an "amoral and mystical approval of the American fascist
Willie Stark."

It may be worth repeating, as we leave the reviewers, that enough
of them glimpse the novelist's intention to establish his power of communication. Those who miss it are, in the main, not at all dull; but
by some habit of thought, some cast of mind, which seems to come
from the mental sets of the civilization, they are blocked off from
seeing how the novel, as tragedy, works. Mr. Warren treats them as
independent minds, able to slip away from societal apron-strings. In

fact, he never condescends to his readers; those who would read him aright will have to work out careful patterns. It would have been easy to supply a chorus identifying Willie's half-truths as half-truths; but Warren does it indirectly by having Willie in effect repudiate—his attitude to the hospital denies his formal relativism—his own announced positions, and by having the implicit repudiation seen through the awareness of a Jack Burden who is himself experimenting with concepts. Jack could have underlined his reservations about Willie, but we only see those reservations nibbling at the edges of an apparently whole-souled commitment. In the midst of strenuous muckraking Jack tells Willie, "I'm not one of your scum, and I'm still grinning when I please," and thus we see both the split in Jack and the withheld area of self which differentiates him from the Duffys and Larsons. The split in Jack—that is, the split in an age—finds a symbol in half-truths, with which the difficulty is precisely that they are partly true.[163] While striving toward a whole, Jack veers from half to half. In early years he is inactive, his personality is diffuse and amorphous. There is no imperative in either tradition or work; as a lover he ends —this is one of the most delicately managed episodes—in a hesitation which is in origin an echo of an old honor, thinned out now into a wavering sentiment, and which is in effect a negation. What Anne does not find in Jack she finds in Willie; what Jack does not find in himself he finds in Willie—resolution. But, riding on another man's activeness, Jack the doer is never free of Jack the self-critic; he justifies by half-truths, but: he also accepts half-truths uttered in judgment. The photographer says, ". . . you work for Stark and you call somebody a son-of-a-bitch." He is half right, half wrong, Jack thinks, "and in the end that is what paralyzes you" (427/403). Now the sense of paralysis is ironically a symbol of reorientation: Jack is trying to make his action and his idea cohere—a private parallel to his outward act of bringing Adam and Willie together. But the still more embracing irony, the irony which is all the preachment for which anybody could wish, lies in Willie's relation to this half-truth world. For his dubiety of his official philosophy is activated too late. For him the half-truth of acting according to the facts has been a whole truth; of the paralysis of others he is born; from the start he is always shown acting; and in turn all the spirit, the essence of action has somehow formed young Tom Stark. What is the end of Tom Stark? In the hospital bed he lies *paralyzed* —a fine climax to the counterpoint of kinesis and paralysis and a symbol of Willie's real failure. Willie, as Jack says, "could not tell his greatness from' ungreatness and so mixed them together that what was adulterated was lost."

Who would read the book aright, we have said, must find the patterns. Jack, searching for a past, kills his father; Willie, searching for a future, may be said to kill his son. What Willie learns, there is not enough life left to define wholly; it is Lucy who seizes, in a quiet irony, the instrument of continuity into the future. Jack finds a truth, a basis for values, a faith. All this is part of a very complex theme of past-and-future, a theme which is really another way of presenting the split in the world. Here the split is defined chronologically; the separation of fact and idea is also man's separation from his roots, a separation which appeared extensively in *At Heaven's Gate* and which appears intensively here. Jack's separation from the past is so extreme that at first he cannot understand·Cass Mastern's acute sense of moral responsibility;[164] the essence of his inner development is his coming to terms with the past, knowing the reality of guilt, and learning, with Cass, that "the world is all of one piece." There is a skillfully managed irony in the ambivalence of the past: when it is no longer a nourishing tradition, it is a terrifying skeleton: *the* past is gone, and each man has only *a* past that he can be coerced with. The skeleton, the sterilizing past, is all that Willie professes to believe in (even while being drawn to the Burdens, who represent traditions, the fertilizing past); Jack digs up each man's past and discovers *the* past; from case histories he progresses to the meaning of history. He moves away from his old misvaluation of the past, of which the two faces are cynicism and sentimentality. ". . . we can keep the past only by having the future, for they are forever tied together" (329/*311*). ". . . only out of the past can you make the future" (461/*435*). Faith is proved by deed, and fruitful deed comes only out of the long wisdom. He is, at last, prepared to face history, to enter "the awful responsibility of Time" (464/*438*).

Shift a few pieces on the board, and the history-theme becomes the knowledge-theme, which can be traced from episode to episode and from reflection to reflection. "Life is Motion toward Knowledge," Jack argues. Willie's career is a progression in self-knowledge, and Jack's is a passion for knowledge that leads from factual to moral awareness. ". . . all knowledge that is worth anything is maybe paid for by blood" (455/*429*). Jack's self-criticism is important here—the innumerable passages in which he catches himself at lying, or self-deception, or histrionics; or understands his feeling that Duffy "had . . . like a brother winked at me." (422/*417*). Or shift a few pieces again, and the action-theme becomes a study of participation and withdrawal, with its echoes in Jack and Adam and Hugh Miller, and the conclusion to which it leads, that there are no perfect choices: ". . . there is always a price to make a choice" (364/*363*). In one sense the body of the work is the regeneration theme: the variations range from a prefrontal lobectomy to the Scholarly Attorney's efforts with "unfortunates" to the acquisition of new insights by Cass Mastern and Jack Burden.

As the consciousness of an age, Jack also embodies its philosophic searchings. Jack appears first as an Idealist, and there is a nice implied contrast between his version of Platonism, which rationalizes away responsibility, and Adam's, which takes insufficient account of the facts. Then Jack plunges into pragmatism, but it is a drug and never a very efficient one; under the pressure of pain he falls into Mechanism—the[165] Twitch theory. But eventually he rejects the world as Idea, the world as Act, and the world as Mechanism; these are the half-truths of a disintegrating order. What he envisages is a saving union of the idealist and pragmatist impulses of modern man; while the brilliance of Willie is his executive mastery of fact, his greatness, in which the others "must" believe—the margin between him and the ordinary political operator—in his emergent awareness of the inadequacy of fact. If they cannot believe in that, there is nothing left; but they can believe, for tragedy reaffirms the whole truth which measures the failure of the incomplete man. Humpty is Willie and he is also Jack—that is, the man who has broken into parts. Nor will men and horses, human intention and mere animal strength, reunify man. That is, reintegration transcends the secular; Jack moves, at the end, toward the deepest possible grounding of his world-view, a grounding in theological terms. He assents, "in his own way," quasi-committally, to a metaphysic which accommodates evil, not to despair, but to define salvation. The reader recalls the earlier words of the Scholarly Attorney, "God is Fullness of Being" (160/*150*). Humpty is partialness. The fall in the old rhyme becomes a version of The Fall.

Some such matters the critics may reasonably be expected to see. Let it be said, if it need be said, that no one expects them to see more than the evidence. They need not like the evidence—a situation which, as we all know, *non est disputandum;* they need not consider the evidence sufficient to prove what the author wants proved. For various reasons they may not like the author's looks. If they think him unhandsome, that's their privilege; but, it may be repeated, they are wholly obliged to take a good, long, direct look at him instead of using one of those hasty city-street snapshots at 25 cents a peep. What contests he will win will appear in time. But those who have looked close enough to realize the intellectual and imaginative richness will know that they have been at least in the neighborhood of greatness. There is room, perhaps, for further coalescence of the gifts that appear brilliantly in, for instance, the vitality of Willie, the ironic commentary of Jack, the Jack-Anne idyl and the weak spot where it is breached, the bursting fullness of image, the reflective probing. For the present reader there is room, still, for some reproportioning and for some filling-out, with the logic of feeling and motive and the immediate concretenesses of man in action, of the immensely moving symbolic paradigms whose rightness carries one into wholeness of admiration and into all but wholeness of assent.[166]

꧁

IRONY IN *ALL THE KING'S MEN*

Joseph E. Baker

In Robert Penn Warren's *All the King's Men* the narrator, Jack Burden, begins the fifth chapter with a reference to his research on Cass Mastern, which has occupied the preceding chapter:

> That was the end of my first journey into the enchantments of the past, my first job of historical research. It was, as I have indicated, not a success. But the second job was a sensational success. It was the "Case of the Upright Judge" and I had every reason to congratulate myself on a job well done. It was a perfect research job, marred in its technical perfection by only one thing: it meant something. (203/*191*)

When a poet and critic like Warren suggests concerning any art that it should not "mean" but "be," he surely thinks of creative literature and the whole question of technique for technique's sake. Certainly this is not the only passage which will recall such problems to any reader familiar with the "New Criticism" of John Crowe Ransom, Cleanth Brooks, Warren himself, *et al.* We may well ask: Does this technically excellent job, *All the King's Men*, "mean" something? Or is it just a "thing made"? Does it "say" something that should turn our attention primarily to things outside of art? Obviously it does, in the eyes of its reviewers. Most of those who wrote critiques of the novel evidently never thought of judging it merely "for art's sake." But this is not so simple as it sounds.

Life, in an article entitled "The Huey Long Legend" by Hamilton Basso (December 9, 1946), says that this is one of the novels that "idealize the Kingfish," and as "a fair sample of the sort of idealiza-tion[122] Mr. Warren goes in for" quotes an "Abe Lincoln" passage out of its context where it might convey precisely the opposite implications to any reader with a sense of humor. Conservative organs like the *New York Times* (August 18) attacked the novel for not being liberal enough. On the other hand, the liberal *New Republic* (September 2) and the *Nation* (August 24) either attacked it for not being morally conservative or actually praised this supposed romanticizing of an

Joseph E. Baker, "Irony in Fiction: *All the King's Men*," *College English*, IX (October 1947), 122–130. Reprinted with the permission of the National Council of Teachers of English and Professor Joseph E. Baker.

American Fascist! An author who can stir up such complex and con-
tradictory reactions has produced a fascinating work indeed, one worth
re-examining from different angles: Left, Right, the North, the South,
from high above the battle in an ivory tower, or from some still
superior vantage point like "the sun, or like God's eye" (200/*189*). For
the purpose of this essay I shall not ask what the essence of this work is
as an idea in the mind of God, or in the dialectic of history, though
concerning the latter enough is said in the novel to lead us astray. I
intend to approach it from a point of view voiced by the author not so
long ago.

Between us and his own mind the author has interposed a narrator, "something like Henry James's 'sensitive observer' "—"Jack Burden, Willie Stark's ambiguous 'secretary' and 'research' man—whose
primary task is to pin something on all the Boss's opponents. Jack
Burden himself is the book's major misfortune.... His regeneration
at the end of the book is as repulsive and unconvincing a 'happy
ending' as I have ever encountered." I have quoted this from Hiram
Haydn's review in the Phi Beta Kappa *Key Reporter* (Winter, 1946).
But I do not agree with all of it. True, Jack is "the renegade aristocrat
—the hollow man"; but therein lies the strength of some of the
strongest scenes ever written by an American novelist. Consider the
terrific power with which the first chapter ends. And by "terrific" I
mean that it inspires pity and terror. At first Jack has shown Willie
Stark to us as a demagogue who feels at home in the company of a
gunman, a cheap politician, and a couple of willing tools. We have
been given a lively picture of the dictator's fraudulent publicity, his
shamelessness, his willingness to act outside the law and without justice.
Beyond what is actually described, sinister suggestions have been added
to build up an atmosphere of hardboiled toughness. We would not be
surprised at any ruthless act. In contrast, up to that point we have had
sympathy for Jack Burden. His aristocratic sensibility, his noncom-
mittal sense of humor, his realism, his complex imagination—so far we
have seen these only in the best light; we have not yet felt how they can
all be used for evil. (In one sentence the author is to cure us of our
superficiality and enable us to see with a gasp of horror that evil cannot
attain its full growth except by the aid of complex imagination, aristocratic sensibility, a humorous detachment, and a cynical realism; but
that is the last sentence of the chapter.) Up to this point Jack has let
"the Upright Judge" charm us with his attractive personality and win
our admiration with the courage and firmness of his character. He was
"more of a father to me than those men who had married my mother,
and come to live in Ellis Burden's house. And the Judge was a man"
(44/*40*). Jack has made it clear that in his own mind he feels that he
owes the Judge everything (except his present disreputable job)—his
education, the chance to develop his imagination and his knowledge
of the human past in the Judge's library, his happiest hours, clear back

to[123] his boyhood when his old friend played with him, took him duck hunting, taught him how to shoot.

But the Judge has announced that he will oppose the candidacy of one of the Boss's political henchmen, so Jack is given the nasty assignment of digging up some dirt on this fine old gentleman who stands in the way of the vulgarian's greed for power. And this research job will not be technically satisfactory if it leaves the Judge any possible way out; whatever is discovered must be made to stick. The first chapter ends thus:

> Judge Irwin is dead, who leaned toward me among the stems of the tall gray marsh grass, in the gray damp wintry dawn, and said, "You ought to have led that duck more, Jack. You got to lead a duck, son." And the Boss is dead, who said to me, "And make it stick."
> Little Jackie made it stick, all right. (54/49–50)

The author has achieved here a great effect, one of the greatest in all American literature. We suddenly realize that the narrator is the collaborationist type of intellectual, a brilliant technician without those feelings of natural loyalty that make men decent. He has none of that quality the Romans—the ancient Romans—demanded and called *pietas*. Religions and civilizations may change, but we would still agree with Aeschylus and Dante that the ungrateful traitor is the worst of sinners. Here is an example of filial ingratitude fit to place Jack Burden alongside Goneril and Regan; yet the author has had the boldness to make him his own spokesman. For at times Burden is nothing but the author's loudspeaker, a device by which certain philosophical generalizations can be spoken to a wider audience than will hear a lyric poem or a piece of criticism. And Burden accounts for only some of the several types of ambiguity by which Warren has disturbed the political readers of his novel.

Then he turns about and begins to show the other side of Willie Stark's career. The reader becomes almost entirely sympathetic with this "kingfish" and "all the king's men"—or one of them, Jack—by the time the young politician delivers his first effective public speech. Burden's discovery that the Judge had once taken a bribe convinces our reason that such an aristocrat may have done great harm politically; but it does not lessen our distaste for Jack Burden. Then another reversal occurs, contrived, as Aristotle would say, in the best way, coincident with a "recognition"—that the Judge is Jack's father, whom he has killed by his technically perfect piece of dirty research.

I I

"Concerning the subject of irony," the well-known college textbook *Understanding Fiction*, by Cleanth Brooks and Robert Penn

Warren, has this to say—and we may take it as the authors' personal contribution to the subject since they admit that they "have, perhaps, been guilty of wrenching the word from its usual context":

> The unity which the fictional structure possesses is of a very special kind. It is not the result of a purely genial conspiracy among the constituent elements. There is conflict and tension present, and the structure involves almost as much of vindictive opposition as of genial conspiracy.

The wrenching of the word "irony" to cover more than might ordinarily be expected turns out to be no perversion of its meaning but the occasion for some brilliant insight. But first we should notice that, when this passage speaks of the conflict as between "constituent elements" of the "structure," the word "structure" is not being used to mean "form"—rather it means something more often assigned to "content," for[124] "the fact of conflict as an essential aspect of fiction is clearly stated in every handbook. In its most obvious form it concerns a collision of interests in the external world." Then in "somewhat more subtle and sophisticated form conflict concerns a division of interests or obligations in the self." I would take, as an example of this, Huckleberry Finn's humane desire to free the slave Jim and, in collision with this deep obligation "in the self," his sincere belief that, if he does so violate the code of his society, he will "go to Hell" as a thief. These are elements of "structure" by the terminology of this "New Criticism." But the usual sense of the word "structure" is more relevant to the third type of conflict mentioned:

> In an even more subtle and sophisticated form, it concerns the alignment of judgments and sympathies on the part of the author—the problem of his own self-division. The dogmatist who is author paints a world of black and white, a world in which right and wrong, truth and falsehood, are clear with statutory distinctness, a world of villain and hero. The artist who is author paints a world in which there is, in the beginning, neither black nor white, neither right nor wrong which can be defined with absolute certainty. The certainty can only come in terms of the process, and must be *earned,* as it were, through the process.

This is very close to words that Warren puts into the mouth of Willie Stark—a little incongruously, for Stark at other times talks like a Calvinist. He tells Stanton that you cannot inherit Goodness:

> "You got to make it, Doc. If you want it. And you got to make it out of badness. Badness. And you know why, Doc? . . . . Because there isn't anything else to make it out of. . . . What the hell else you think folks been doing for a million years, Doc? When your great-great-grandpappy climbed down out of the tree, he didn't have any more notion of good or bad, or right and wrong, than the hoot owl that stayed up in the tree. Well, he climbed down and he began to make Good up as he went along." (272–3/257)

And the critic's reference to the "statutory distinctness" of right and wrong in the mind of the dogmatist (as contrasted with the artist) becomes this in the mouth of Willie Stark:

> "Hell, the law is like the pants you bought last year for a growing boy, but it is always this year and the seams are popped and the shankbones to the breeze. The law is always too short and too tight for growing humankind. The best you can do is do something and then make up some law to fit and by the time that law gets on the books you would have done something different. Do you think half the things I've done were clear, distinct, and simple in the constitution of this state?" ... (145/*136*)

And this passage, in turn, is important in the artistic justification of the dictator in his violation of constitutional government, in his achievements, often technically admirable—outside the law. This example from the novel shows something of the range of what Warren meant when he signed the introductory chapter of *Understanding Fiction*—to which I now return, continuing the quotation:

> In other words, the artist is sporting enough to put the best case possible for the opposition. But this is not mere sportsmanship. The artist realizes that, if the opponent—"villain" or "idea"—is a straw man, the conflict will lack interest. In a simple example such as *Richard III*, we observe that Shakespeare makes the traditional and historical Tudor villain the vessel of certain virtues which the Tudor age seems to have admired inordinately. Without this ironical ambivalence, the play would be a tedious recital of butcheries to prove that you can't kill all of the people all of the time. ...

This might serve as Warren's defense of his novel about a "villain."

> Or, to glance at other simple cases, we may recall that in *Uncle Tom's Cabin* Simon Legree is a Yankee, and that in Hemingway's *For Whom the Bell Tolls* the scene of greatest brutality is that of the massacre of Fascists by[125] Loyalists. ... In all of these cases, the irony is intended, on the one hand, to intensify the implications of the conflict, and on the other, to raise the issue above the level of merely dogmatic and partisan vilification.

Those who accuse *All the King's Men* of "fascism" feel that some evils are so bad as to deserve partisan vilification.

Warren's admiration for Hemingway does not end here—as anyone can see by comparing their fiction or by consulting *Understanding Fiction* for Warren's "Interpretation" of Hemingway's "The Killers." The story, it may be observed, contains fewer words than the "Interpretation," which is astute indeed, technically. Not astute morally. The gangster, we are told by the critic, accepts "the terms by which he lives—terms which transcend the small-town world. He lives, as it were, by a code, which lifts him above questions of personal likes or personal animosities." That is, he is a double-crossing criminal, in a gang which does not hesitate to kill a man without asking for any human justification at all, even personal anger! Warren is wrong; the moral issue here has nothing to do with Small Town *vs.* City. Men in cities are still humanly motivated. And Warren's use of the word "code" here has always disturbed me greatly. It seems to glorify what is really an un-principled lack of any code. To call such dead-end wretchedness "the gallantry of defeat" is not astute.

To find an "ethic" here is to find a "message" where there is no message, not even a perverse one. At least that is what Brooks and Warren would say if they found another critic reading in this way. We can be sure of this because in their earlier anthology, *Understanding Poetry,* they have warmly condemned "message-hunters" for confusing "scientific and poetic communication." In 1940, in the autumn issue of *American Prefaces,* Cleanth Brooks went still further, asserting: "The poet is a maker, not a communicator. . . . Meanwhile practitioners of the craft who believe in the theory of communication exist and flourish. They accept the reader's challenge—'you must show me, you must put it across to me.' . . . perhaps the most extreme proponents of this view are to be found contributing to the publications of Mr. Ber-narr Macfadden." (Neither Brooks nor Warren would seem to draw any essential distinction, in this respect, between fiction or drama in verse and fiction or drama in imaginative prose.) And in the first volume of the *Southern Review,* which he edited with the assistance of Robert Penn Warren from 1935 to 1942, Cleanth Brooks quoted with approval I. A. Richards' statement that "it is never what a poem says that matters, but what it is."

But *All the King's Men* says a great deal, and puts it across, and makes it stick all right—in the craw of conservative liberals.

I I I

These two attitudes toward the use of literature *as a means of communication* are in such sharp contrast that it is worth pausing to re-consider them, this time with some attention to chronology. Following the lead of Oscar Wilde who said, "Art never expresses anything but itself," Warren (and Brooks) declared in 1937 (*American Review,* February), "A poem must communicate poetry." And I have quoted above Brooks's attack on communicators in 1940. Warren and Brooks did not seem to be aware of any notable difference between their literary theories when they collaborated to produce *Understanding Poetry* in 1938 or even *Understanding Fiction* in 1943. Yet[126] in the latter book one looks almost in vain for this characteristic doctrine of aestheticism.

Then in 1946 Warren emerged definitely on the other side, re-jecting what he refers to as the "notion that a poem should not 'mean' but 'be' "—in his edition of *The Rime of the Ancient Mariner,* where he is concerned entirely with the moral and religious meaning of the poem as an expression of Coleridge's philosophic ideas. In fact, he declares roundly that "we may say that the poem is the light and not the thing seen by the light." In freeing himself from the restrictive view that the reader's main business is to "interpret the poem" *as such,* Warren has still not completely realized the full value of his perception of irony. At times he has swung to false extremes. Looking back on *Understanding Fiction* from the vantage point that Warren has afforded us three years later, we can now see that the book went to romantic lengths to squeeze an "ethic" out of brutality. There "the tough man" is equated with "the disciplined man,"

apparently, insensitive. But only apparently, for the fidelity to a code, to a discipline, may be an index to a sensitivity which allows the characters to see, at moments, their true plight.... The individual toughness (which may be taken to be the private discipline demanded by the world), may find itself in conflict with some more natural and spontaneous human emotion; in contrast with this the discipline may even seem to be inhuman; but the Hemingway hero, though he is aware of the claims of this spontaneous human emotion, is afraid to yield to those claims because he has learned that the only way to hold on to "honor," to individuality, to, even, the human order as against the brute chaos of the world, is to live by his code.

That is, by the code of gangster discipline. So stated, this may be the Fascist's unprincipled "code" of inhuman disorder and dishonor, whether or not the critic is justified in reading it in Hemingway's "The Killers." As moralizer, Warren is still not sure of himself.

But in *All the King's Men* how much do we find of this conflict between "sterile intellectuality" and the "simple virtues" of a storm trooper? The reviewers mislead us when they make us expect the novel to be an application of such "moral" theories. They have ignored the "ironical ambivalence" of the work of art.

I V

In what they call a "discussion of their general views" Brooks and Warren tell us that one of the functions of irony

is to indicate an awareness of the multiplicity of options in conduct, idea, or attitude—an awareness of the full context. This suggests one of the objections which may be brought against the emphasis on irony; the objection that such an emphasis ends in the celebration of a smug and futile skepticism which is at variance with the actual effect which most successful literary compositions leave upon the reader. The editors... would not endorse an irony which precluded resolution but they would endorse an irony which forced the resolution to take stock of as full a context as possible.

In other words, irony is a device necessary to tell the whole truth about human life, in all its complexity. Without dramatic language, says Lloyd Morgan, "no adequate account of what happens in human life is possible."[1] According to *Understanding Poetry,* "all poetry, including even short lyrics or descriptive pieces, involves a dramatic organization . . . every poem implies a speaker . . . the poem represents the reaction of such a person to a situation. . . ." And when "ironical comment" is found (e.g., in "The Love Song of J. Alfred Prufrock"), the critics' analysis recognizes as a merit "the poem's sense of fidelity to the[127] whole situation—its willingness to take into account so many apparently discordant views and points of view."

Can we add: so many different things seen from these different points of view? In *Understanding Fiction* the authors speak of the relation of irony "both to the completed literary structure and to the process of exploration which led to the creation of the structure." But is it just the process and not what is found that makes the exploration valuable? If that was what *Understanding Fiction* meant, Warren has gone beyond that point now in understanding history and politics. In *All the King's Men* a passage moralizing on political graft speaks of "the moral neutrality of history . . . Process as process is neither morally good nor morally bad. We may judge results but not process. The morally bad agent may perform the deed which is good. The morally good agent may perform the deed which is bad. Maybe a man has to sell his soul to get the power to do good" (418/*393–394*). Such passages bothered the *Nation* reviewer, Diana Trilling. Writing in the August 24 (1946) issue, she found in this a dangerous, Hegelian, moral relativism. But it is not relativism at all. The morality here is absolute. It is not Hegelian. "We may judge results" according to whether they "do good." What we really have here is the irony of life, or perhaps merely the irony that can be built up by tensions between words—the literary technique of using the word "good" in two different senses, an ambiguity that is closer to the pun than to serious philosophical speculation or to observation of the historical process. Even mere ambiguity can give literary pleasure. Is that all Warren intends? *Understanding Fiction,* in spite of all we have quoted concerning irony, seems to imply that this is art for art's sake, or for pleasure's sake only, not for the communication of truth at all, when it goes on to add: "The reader wants the resolution, but he does not want it too easy or too soon. He wants to see the knockout, but he does not want to see it until the fifteenth round." In the postulates and practice of Robert Penn Warren there is no reason now why he should not go on and say that "poetic language," or, indeed, any means of literary expression, "is a form of description, and since there is no such thing as a description that describes 'nothing,' there always arises the question of the truth of the description. In other words poetry 'says something,' . . .

---

[1] Quoted in W. M. Urban, *Language and Reality* (London: Allen & Unwin, 1939), p. 465.

the question is as to what it says and whether it speaks truly." But actually this passage is not by Warren; it is from *Language and Reality* by W. M. Urban (p. 464). And in sharp contradiction to Urban's view is that of Warren's colleague Cleanth Brooks in the first volume of the *Southern Review* that "the question of belief or disbelief never arises when we are reading well." If it does, "we have for the moment ceased to be reading and have become astronomers, theologians, or moralists, persons engaged in a quite different type of activity." And he observed, in the *Kenyon Review* (August, 1940), that a professor "often does not know how to *read*." I suppose that those who have taken "Brooks and Warren" as twin pillars of the "New" aesthetic movement might still follow this line and dismiss political review as the attacks of irrelevant moralists who are unable to perform the act of reading *as such*. But *All the King's Men* was surely not written upon those principles. And, though Warren calls his introductory essay to *The Rime of the Ancient Mariner* "An Experiment in Reading," he is not now afraid that he will[128] have "ceased to be reading" if he pursues ideas of interest to "theologians or moralists." Indeed, he says, "The poem is the light by which the reader may view and review all the area of experience with which he is acquainted." Hence "the reader does not interpret the poem but the poem interprets the reader." Warren certainly knows that we gain from literature our deepest insights into the history of emotional attitudes and mores. And he has his narrative spokesman say:

What we students of history always learn is that the human being is a very complicated contraption and that they are not good or bad but are good and bad and the good comes out of bad and the bad out of good, and the devil take the hindmost. But Adam [Stanton, the surgeon who later murders the Boss], he is a scientist, and everything is tidy for him, and one molecule of oxygen always behaves the same way when it gets around two molecules of hydrogen, and a thing is always what it is, and so when Adam the romantic makes a picture of the world in his head, it is just like the picture of the world Adam the scientist works with. All tidy. All neat. The molecule of good always behaves the same way. The molecule of bad always behaves the same way. (263/*248*)

Something like that might be called the theme of the novel. Of course the meaning of an artistic communication about human life cannot be fully stated in an abstract generalization, or the art would be redundant. That is very different from saying that it has no meaning, does not communicate, is *about* nothing.

v

Until we are two-thirds of the way through this novel, we feel that we are reading one of the richest pieces of twentieth-century fiction. It takes rank with those great "first parts" in American literature—the first hundred pages of *Babbitt,* the first seventeen chapters of *Life on the Mississippi.* Then Warren begins to lose his deft objectivity and to use Jack Burden more and more as a mouthpiece for general theorizing. By the end of the novel the author is as omnipresent as in any Victorian novel; the mask is thinner than that supplied in *Pendennis.* It is as if he had taken flight into the interior of Jack Burden, abandoning the grand irony, the "awareness of the full context" and the subtle conflict "of judgments and sympathies on the part of the author"—except in certain splendid passages in which Jack sees himself on a level with Sugar Boy and Tiny, just another one of the king's henchmen.

Whose story is it? "This story of a Southern Governor who is a scoundrel and a saint," Sinclair Lewis calls it, casually. And he ought to know, for he wrote *It Can't Happen Here* with the same governor in mind. The reader has almost finished *All the King's Men* before he realizes that its author has decided that this is not the governor's story. And finally, with only three pages yet to go, as if to clinch the matter, Jack Burden actually argues with the reader, pettishly: "This has been the story of Willie Stark, but it is my story too."

Well—Jack is mistaken. And the author is mistaken. Or his conscious decision has unfortunately rebelled against his artistic intuition. The instinct of all readers and reviewers on this matter is sound: It is a story of dictatorship. But its "multiplicity of options in conduct, idea, or attitude" disturbs the forthright simplicity of minds accustomed to journalism and to anti-Nazi melodramas. We may object to an aestheticism which claims that creative literature in no way communicates any "message"; but it is not necessary to swing to the opposite extreme and give our highest admiration to fiction that tries to lead us too directly. Warren's novel is quite mistaken in saying:[129]

As we know, reality is not a function of the event as event, but of the relationship of that event to past, and future, events. We seem here to have a paradox: that the reality of an event, which is not real in itself, arises from other events which, likewise, in themselves are not real. But this only affirms what we must affirm: that direction is all. (407/*384*)

If so, the novel lacks all, for it lacks direction. It is certainly not pointed in the direction of dictatorship; nor is it pointed in the opposite direction. The individual events are what have reality in this novel: the "scholarly attorney" feeding chocolate to his "unfortunate" bum; "Miss Littlepaugh in her foul, fox-smelling" lair in Memphis; the Boss trying to get the old dog propped up as if it were glad to see him —for a photographer; Jack getting information from four old men sitting on a bench; his mother offering her face to men like "a precious present"; the story of Cass Mastern, which is structurally what we would call an "episode" in an eighteenth-century novel. The Cass Mastern episode, far from gaining its reality from its relation to the rest of the novel, only by its strong existential quality justifies itself and thus tempts us to find excuses for its lack of any explicit relation to Huey Long.

All this is the way supreme irony would have it—one chunk of reality that to a superficial observer might seem to point in one direction laid down alongside an utterly incongruous chunk of reality to shock us out of our easy sense of direction, our dogmatism, into a deeper understanding of the complex nature of the fuller truth about human life and character. Warren is deeply concerned to show complexity, not to show direction. He makes this abundantly clear. His novel has done more than one could believe possible if one still remains within the limit of his theories. There are more things in the world he has created than are dreamt of in his philosophy, or in his philosophy of history. Warren's writing is at its best not in abstract formulation but in metaphor. And his own criticism relates metaphor very closely to irony. We may ask ironically if he is now willing to recognize the full meaning of one of his metaphors: "Cass Mastern lived for a few years and in that time he learned that the world is all of one piece" (200/*188*). No isolation, then, of Science and Poetry; here a "communication" and there a "thing made"; contemplation tidily separated from morality; fiction unrelated to politics. No. It is "all of one piece." That is the irony of it. And so the metaphor:

He learned that the world is like an enormous spider web and if you touch it, however lightly, at any point, the vibration ripples to the remotest perimeter and the drowsy spider feels the tingle and is drowsy no more but springs out to fling the gossamer coils about you who have touched the web and then inject the black numbing poison under your hide. It does not matter whether or not you meant to brush the web of things. Your happy foot or your gay wing may have brushed it ever so lightly, but what happens always happens and there is the spider, bearded black and with his great faceted eyes glittering like mirrors in the sun, or like God's eye, and the fangs dripping. (200/*188–189*)[130]

W

THE NARRATOR'S MIND AS SYMBOL

Norton R. Girault

If we are to judge from many of the reviews, *All the King's Men* is a very difficult novel to "explain"—difficult, it appears, mainly because of the oblique first-person narrator point of view. There have been many comments about the irrelevance of Jack Burden, as if he were a sort of displaced person who had found his way into the novel through the servants' entrance, or an exhibit guide with an annoying habit of stopping in the middle of his discourse upon the exhibit to digress on his domestic problems. Actually the novel is a dramatic monologue on a grand scale, and Jack Burden is as much the protagonist as he is the commentator. But it is apparent that the story has not been read as a product of Jack's mind. Attempts to explain Willie Stark, for example, have often dodged the problem of taking Jack's statements in character; apparently it has been assumed that the reader sees Willie Stark at first hand and not through Jack's sensibility, and that Willie can be understood and interpreted whether Jack is or not. Such an assumption is enough to cause serious misreading, because out of the first-person narrator point of view grows an important aspect of the novel's theme—that an understanding of the world depends upon an understanding of the self: Jack Burden cannot understand Willie Stark until Jack understands himself. (There is a question, of course, as to whether Jack ever fully understands either himself or Willie Stark.) We can get at an understanding of Robert Penn Warren's interpretation of the Boss only through a perception of the way in which the Boss's story was experienced by Warren's first-person narrator.

1.

Jack's story is so intimately related to Willie's that, as the narrative develops, their stories are told simultaneously. But phrases along the way like "at least that was the way I argued the case back then" (373/351) remind the reader of the fact that Jack has lived through the

Norton R. Girault, "The Narrator's Mind as Symbol: An Analysis of *All the King's Men*," *Accent*, VII (Summer 1947), 220–234. Reprinted by permission of the author and the publisher.

actions he is describing and that he is trying to reorient himself in relation to them. It becomes more and more apparent as the story develops that Jack is telling it as a means of defining to himself what actually did happen to him: the manner in which he reconstructs the story gives the reader an insight into the nature of Jack's experience. For example, the fact that Jack withholds his father's identity until he learns that Judge Irwin has killed himself implies that he wants the discovery of the truth about his paternity to make the same shocking impact upon the reader that it made upon him; it is his way of dramatizing his reaction to the discovery. And when he attempts to describe subjective reactions to events that are past,[220] the metaphors he uses provide the reader with an insight into why Jack Burden is an appropriate first-person narrator. A study of those metaphors indicates that they support a basic symbolism of rebirth that runs through the novel and unifies it, and after our participation in the total experience of *All the King's Men*, we realize that it is because Jack has been reborn, though not of woman (in a sense defined by the symbolism), that he is qualified to tell us what happened to Willie Stark.

The symbolic event that brings the rebirth symbolism into focus is Jack's being awakened in the middle of the night by his mother's screams. It is a "bright, beautiful, silvery soprano scream" (370/*348*) that awakens him, and his mother, hysterical, accuses him of having killed his father. The accusation comes as the sudden revelation of the truth about his paternity: Judge Irwin, not the Scholarly Attorney, suddenly becomes his father. Jack has, as his mother charges, killed his father (his attempt to blackmail the judge for the Boss results in the judge's suicide); but he has also created a father, for it requires the violence of the suicide to wring from his mother, out of her love for Judge Irwin, the long suppressed information which gives Jack self-definition. The scream signalizes Jack's rebirth (symbolically, it is a scream of labor pain) in that it gives him a new mother and a new father, both of whom he can accept. It disintegrates his conception of his mother as a woman motivated by vanity and cupidity ("for years I had condemned her as a woman without heart" [458/*433*]), because it reveals to him his mother's capacity for love; and it disintegrates his conception of his father as the weak, pious Scholarly Attorney, for in Judge Irwin Jack gains a father he can accept. The scream seems to release something in him, to allow him to see the world for the first time. It allows him to understand Willie Stark, but why it does Jack cannot say. He simply knows that his knowledge of the Boss and of himself grew, finally, out of the scream, that it marked the climax of his story.

Jack's story builds toward his mother's scream in terms of his struggle to resist rebirth. At the beginning of the novel, he sees the Boss's eyes bulge as he begins a political speech and feels the "clammy, sad little foetus" which is himself, huddled away up inside himself, cringing away from "the cold hand in the cold rubber glove" (11/9) reaching down to pull him out into the cold. Jack feels that he is on the brink of a discovery about the Boss, but subconsciously he seeks the coziness of "not-knowing." His hesitation in his love affair with Anne Stanton results, in part, from the same sort of recoil from knowledge. And his dive and underwater embrace with her are an attempt to submerge himself along with Anne in a cozy womb-state of "not-knowing." (The medium will not retain them, of course, and they burst forth into their separateness.) Finally, this subconscious shrinking from a particular kind of knowledge becomes on Jack's part an attempt to repudiate his sensibility, an attempt begun as a result of his frustration in his love affair with Anne and of his dissatisfaction with his past (as symbolized by his parents). On the verge of the sexual act with Anne, he had sensed that to "know" Anne he would have to violate his image of her; he hesitates long enough to disrupt their love affair.[221]

What Jack is searching for is a womb-state of innocence in nature in which his image of Anne will be preserved. And this search becomes a dominant motif leading up to his expulsion from the womb when he unwittingly causes the death of his father. Just before his discovery that Anne has become the Boss's mistress, he sits in his office and envies the jaybird perched in the tree outside his window: "I could look down and think of myself inside that hollow chamber, in the aqueous green light, inside the great globe of the tree, and not even a jaybird there with me now, for he had gone, and no chance of seeing anything beyond the green leaves, they were so thick, and no sound except, way off, the faint mumble of traffic, like the ocean chewing its gums" (281/265). The associations with Jack's underwater dive with Anne are significant. Then, when this reverie is interrupted by his discovery of Anne's "infidelity" (of the Boss's violation of the image), Jack flies to California in an attempt to "drown himself in West." In all these struggles to lose himself in nature, there is a paradoxical struggle toward rebirth: the greater the struggle to resist rebirth, the greater the counter-struggle toward rebirth, as if Jack's nature, unformed, were enveloped by the womb of total nature, which reacts convulsively to reject him. Through his attempts to lose himself in nature, Jack is actually struggling, without realizing it, toward a discovery of his separateness in nature.

The significance of Jack's struggle to resist rebirth may be stated in these terms: Jack shrinks from the discovery of evil, of the taint in nature, of imperfection in the scheme of things. He has seen ugliness and imperfection and, with a cynical smugness, acknowledges their presence in nature, but he does not want to discover evil in himself. Subconsciously, he shrinks from the terrible knowledge that he is capable of good and evil, but until he is reborn through a revelation of the guilt he shares with humanity, he is not fully man, but rather

embryonic and amoral. This aspect of the symbol's meaning is pointed
up by a conversation Jack has with Lucy Stark about her son Tom's
alleged fatherhood of an unborn child (it is significant in terms of the
novel's structure that this conversation occurs just before Jack's rebirth):

"It's just a baby," she almost whispered. "It's just a little baby. It's just a little
baby in the dark. It's not even born yet, and it doesn't know what's happened.
About money and politics and somebody wanting to be senator. It doesn't
know about anything—about how it came to be—about what that girl did—or
why—or why the father—why he—" She stopped, and the large brown eyes
kept looking at me with appeal and what might have been accusation. Then
she said, "Oh, Jack, it's a little baby, and nothing's its fault."
    I almost burst out that it wasn't my fault, either, but I didn't. (356/335–
336)

The irony, once the symbolism is understood, is obvious. The state of
innocence Lucy has described is what Jack has been trying to discover
in his attempts to drown himself in nature. He has been trying to hide
in the dark where nothing will be his fault.[222]
    Fourteen pages later (about a week has passed), Jack is awakened
by his mother's scream, and is shocked into the revelation that it has
been his fault that his father has committed suicide. "At the moment,"
Jack says, "the finding out simply numbed me." On a literal level, he is
referring to his discovery that Judge Irwin is his father. But, symbolically, what numbs him is the disintegration of his whole conception
of himself. He has been sick with "the terrible division" of his age.
His sensibility dissociated by his repeated attempts to escape into a
womb-state of innocence, he has been living in a world out of time and
divorced from experience, a world in which his actions have been
neither good nor evil, but meaningless. Then suddenly, in one shocking
experience, this illusory world is shattered, and he cannot define himself in relation to the new world (in which Judge Irwin is his father
and a woman capable of love is his mother). When Jack's revelation
of the truth about his paternity is taken along with all the examples
in the novel of attempts to change various characters' conceptions of
the world, it can be seen that his revelation is a commentary upon
these other attempts to cure modern man of the sickness of his age.
Jack himself, as the Boss's private detective, has tried to change other
men's pictures of the world. He has tried to change Adam's by giving
him "a history lesson"; and, ironically, he has caused his father's death
by trying to change Judge Irwin's convictions about Willie Stark.
Finally, in Adam Stanton's operation on the brain of the man suffering
from catatonic schizophrenia, we have the attempt through surgery to
change the picture of the world man carries around in his head; after
the operation, Jack tells Adam, "Well, you forgot to baptize him . . .
for he is born again and not of woman" (338/319) and, ironically,

baptizes the patient in the name of the Great Twitch, symbol of one of Jack's attempts to submerge himself in nature. (Again, it is significant that this operation occurs before Jack's rebirth; Jack's wisecrack foreshadows the event and he does not realize the symbolic meaning it supports.) In one sense then, the whole novel depicts men "incomplete with the terrible division of their age" (462/436), suffering from a schizophrenia they do not understand, men whose hope lies not in change from without (through surgery, "history lessons," and the like), but from rebirth from within. And because of the nature of Jack's malady, it is plausible that it should take some time for him to formulate a definition of what has happened to him.

The beginning of his reorientation is his discovery that he is, as his mother charges, guilty of his father's death. He realizes that by killing his father he has created him, and gradually he becomes aware of the fact that all of his detective work for the Boss has been a search for a father to replace the weak, pious fool he believed the Scholarly Attorney to be. The subconscious motive for his becoming the Boss's private detective is his attempt to find a father in Willie Stark, and his fidelity to the Boss is symbolic of his having substituted him for the alleged father with whom he is dissatisfied. But when, in Judge Irwin, Jack gains a father he can accept, he no longer requires the Willie Stark father-symbol; symbolically, the very detective work he has been hired by the Boss to do results in the end in the Boss's own death. In chapter nine,[223] the day after the Judge's funeral, Jack walks into the Boss's office and refuses to do any more detective work for him. He wonders why, in fact, he does not quit the Boss's organization altogether. And, thinking of the Scholarly Attorney and Judge Irwin, he says, "True, since I had lost both fathers, I felt as though I could float effortlessly away like a balloon when the last cord is cut" (381/359). But Jack has lost not two but three fathers—the Scholarly Attorney, the judge, and, though he does not realize it, the Boss—so, still numb from the disintegration of the conception of his father, he is unable to quit the Boss's machine.

Jack remains to discover, after the Boss's assassination, that it is he himself who has set the events in motion which culminate in the Boss's own death. After the Boss has died, Jack's independent detective work uncovers the complicity of Sadie Burke and Tiny Duffy (they are as responsible as Adam Stanton for the Boss's murder), but Jack discovers his own complicity too, for he sees that it is his earlier detective work that has produced the facts which led to the involvement of Anne and Adam Stanton in Willie Stark's enterprises and which made Sadie's revenge and Duffy's opportunism possible. But, ironically, the Boss has hired Jack to produce these facts. The Boss has engineered his own assassination. Guilt for the slaying seems to spread throughout the novel among all the characters. What shocks Jack is the discovery that his crime (as opposed to those of Sadie Burke, Tiny Duffy and

Adam Stanton) is that his actions have been meaningless; the others have intended to kill the Boss, whereas he has intended to be the hired research man in search of objective fact, as faultless and amoral as Sibyl Frey's unborn baby. This perception of his spiritual sterility occurs when Jack is unable to go through with "the perfect duplication of what Duffy had done" (that is, effect the murder of Duffy by putting the idea in Sugar-Boy's head); Jack sees that he is as guilty as Duffy, that his murder of Duffy would, ironically enough, be as meaningless as Jack's unintended murder of the Boss. Jack is appalled by this discovery that he has been "caught in a monstrous conspiracy . . . I hated everything and everybody and myself and Tiny Duffy and Willie Stark and Adam Stanton . . . They all looked alike to me then. And I looked like them" (442/417).

But what saves Jack from this loathing for himself and the world is another discovery that grows out of his rebirth—the discovery of his capacity for love. When he learns that his mother is leaving the Young Executive, the scream is brought back to him in such a way that he is able to formulate a partial definition of its meaning; it releases him from his disgust with the world: "The first hint was in the wild, silvery scream which filled the house when the word of Judge Irwin's death was received. That scream rang in my ears for many months, but it had faded away, lost in the past and the corruption of the past, by the time she called me back to Burden's Landing to tell me that she was going to go away. Then I knew that she was telling me the truth. And I felt at peace with her and with myself" (458/433).[224] His mother's leaving (in that it is evidence of her love for Judge Irwin) makes him capable of loving her, and of loving the world (as his marriage to Anne indicates).

Jack Burden's reorientation grows out of a combination of events that begin with Judge Irwin's death. And after he has seen his friends die and his mother leave the Young Executive, he can see a justice in the injustice of a nature that man can never fully know. Like Cass Mastern, Jack has discovered that man cannot escape guilt, and he has discovered too that it is only through an acceptance of the evil in his nature that man can achieve good. He can even say that in his "own way" he is not certain that he does not believe the theological harangues of the Scholarly Attorney (symbol, perhaps, of the Christian tradition in the modern world). Through his rebirth, Jack has caught sight of the limits, and likewise the potentialities, of human knowledge. He had lived a long time in terms of a false conception of his paternity, and, through killing his father, had discovered his ignorance. He learns that man can never be sure of his knowledge: one can never fully know one's father. (There can be a pun in Warren's father-symbolism that equates man's knowledge of his temporal father with his knowledge of the Heavenly Father.) The only knowledge that Jack can be sure of is that tragic waste grows out of the limitations of human knowledge; therefore, man must strive constantly for that state *least* wasteful of human good. And so, as the novel ends, Jack Burden speaks of going into the "convulsion of the world" (the everchanging nature wherein he may be saved from the illusion of the absolute power of human knowledge) "and the awful responsibility of Time" (man's moral responsibility for the illusion of nature he creates).

2.

Jack is qualified to tell Willie Stark's story because it, too, is a story of rebirth, and, although Jack does not call it that in so many words, the terms he uses to describe it are significant. Huddled over his law books, Willie is "in a room, a world, inside himself where something was swelling and growing painfully and dully and imperceptibly like a great potato in a dark, damp cellar" (27/24), and "inside him something would be big and coiling and slow and clotting till he would hold his breath and the blood would beat in his head with a hollow sound as though his head were a cave as big as the dark outside. He wouldn't have any name for what was big inside him. Maybe there wasn't any name" (31–32/28). And, like the knowledge Jack gains through rebirth, the Boss's knowledge comes to him with the shock of revelation. When Willie realizes (before he has become the Boss) that the Harrison machine is using his naïve political idealism to exploit the voters, it is—as Jack puts it—as if Willie had been on the road to Damascus and had seen a great light. When he says this of Willie at the time of Willie's great disillusionment, Jack is not aware of how apt his illusion is, and even after the years that separate his telling of the story from the event, he is not certain what name he should give Willie's "blind, inner compulsion" ("Maybe there wasn't any name."), but[225] through his own rebirth, Jack gains an insight into the meaning of the Boss's life.

The Boss's story starts with a revelation and ends with a revelation. At the beginning of his story, it is revealed to him (through his "luck") that man must run counter to amoral nature and that man must create human good out of human bad. (Willie learns this when the crooked politicians in the state try to "run it over him like he was dirt" [66/61]). But when Willie tries to spread the light among his countrymen, when he tries to awaken them to an awareness of their responsibility as human beings to separate themselves from exploitable nature, he is frustrated by their failure to understand. They roar their applause, but they do not see, actually, what is behind the bulging eyes and the forelock of hair. They are as ready for Willie to run it over them like they were dirt as they were to be exploited by the Harrison outfit. Nevertheless, the Boss's conviction, gained through a sort of revelation, impels him to persist stubbornly throughout the novel in his attempt to achieve a political state based on the assumption that

men are all, potentially at least, like himself—capable of seeing the
light. He becomes "the cold hand in the cold rubber glove" trying to
wrest men from their submergence in brute nature. But in trying to
enforce on them from without a knowledge he gained from within himself, the Boss is trying to usurp the work of the mysterious principle
which brought him his knowledge. It is the same principle which
operates through Jack Burden to cause his rebirth and, finally, through
the Boss to kill him. But in the death of the Boss the knowledge he has
tried to live by is reaffirmed; Willie realizes that what has killed him is
his own failure to believe in the knowledge of his earlier revelation.
So the Boss's story ends with a revelation ("It could have all happened
different, Jack"), and the Boss is reborn in the sense that he regains,
on his death-bed, a conviction in the validity of the knowledge which
has made him the Boss.

Whereas Jack Burden's story starts out with his attempts to submerge himself in nature, the Boss's story begins with his attempt to separate himself from nature. It is as if he were trying to prove, by exploit-
ing it as it had never been exploited before, that the human in nature
will finally react to resist exploitation and prove itself capable of self-
realization, just as Willie had reacted when they tried to run it over
him like he was dirt. Throughout his career we have Nature standing
in animal-and-plant-dumb commentary upon the Boss's actions: the
stoic cows standing in the mist along the highway staring dumbly at
the soaring Cadillac, the 'possum and the moccasin trying to cross the
Boss's path only to be run down and churned thumpingly to death
against the underside of the fender. And the domestic animals are
absorbed into the symbolism: the family dog Buck in the first chapter,
whose uncooperative carcass is a latent hint of the recalcitrancy of the
unpredictable, uncontrollable, natural factor not only in animal but
in human nature as well (Buck is equated with Old Man Stark in
terms of the politically exploitable in Willie's past). Also, in many of
the images, there is an equating of Willie's constituency with brute
nature: "the gangs of people who looked at me with the country-
man's[226] slow, full, curious lack of shame, and didn't make room for
me to pass until I was charging them down, the way a cow won't get out
of your way until your radiator damn near bats her in the underslung
slats" (82/76). This is the nature in which Willie Stark seeks affirmation of the knowledge that isolates him.

Willie's apparently brutal and vindictive treatment of Byram B.
White, erring State Auditor, reflects the Boss's grinding, probing attempt to prove to himself that man can detach himself from brute
nature. It is more than a simply graphic metaphor that we get in
Warren's description of Byram's bodily reaction to the Boss's verbal
abuse: Byram draws himself "into a hunch as though he wanted to
assume the prenatal position and be little and warm and safe in the

dark" (140/*132*). The Boss is trying to force Byram's rebirth. And when Byram has left, the Boss tells Jack:

> "I gave him every chance ... Every chance. He didn't have to say what I told him to say. He didn't have to listen to me. He could have just walked out the door and kept on walking. He could have just put a date on that resignation and handed it to me. He could have done a dozen things. But did he? Hell, no. Not Byram, and he just stands there and his eyes blink right quick like a dog's do when he leans up against your leg before you hit him, and, by God, you have the feeling if you don't do it you won't be doing God's will." (142/*133–144*)

The same impulse that makes him vilify Byram in an attempt to make the man separate himself from nature drives the Boss to try to talk Adam Stanton into a realization that he can never detach himself from nature in an absolute sense. Adam and Byram represent opposite extremes of modern man's condition; they symbolize attitudes the Boss's revelation has shown him to be false.

Ironically, what makes the Boss's political success possible is the fact that his countrymen create in him a hero, an alter ego, and the Boss is unable to get through that alter ego to them. He wants to show them the light he has seen, to prove his knowledge (to himself as well as to them) by changing the picture of the world they carry around in their heads. But his downfall is a result, finally, of his inability to break down the false conceptions of him held by the various members of his machine and by his constituency, by his failure, in other words, to make them understand the principle on which his actions are based. One of the greatest ironies of the book is that the Boss thinks that among all his men Jack Burden alone really understands him. When the others have left them alone, the Boss confides in Jack as if Jack will understand where others have not. But in one sense Jack is simply a more complicated and highly developed version of Byram B. White and of the people who make up the Boss's constituency, who want "the nice warm glow of complacency, the picture that flattered him and his own fat or thin wife standing in front of the henhouse" (348/*328*).

Willie is a symbol of man's struggle toward integration in terms of his whole nature. This integration is symbolized by the successful control and cooperation he maintains in his political machine. All the Boss's men working in harmony symbolize an integration of a sort within the Boss. Separately,[227] each is a symbolic correlative for an aspect of the Boss's nature. When the Boss begins to try to operate independently of any one of them, the integration begins to crumble. When he tries to build his hospital without the cooperation of Tiny Duffy, he is trying to insist upon the idealistic aspect of his nature at the expense of the animal-gross and -predatory in his nature. And Tiny Duffy, symbol of this aspect of the Boss's make-up, and Sadie Burke, symbol of the indivisible bond between brute and human nature, participate with Adam Stanton, symbol of the exclusively idealistic in the Boss's nature, to kill him. By allowing these aspects of his nature to get out of hand, to function as isolated impulses, the Boss kills himself. Yet in his death there is a form of salvation, for through disintegration of his personality he is reborn to a realization that man cannot violate the essential complexity of his nature with impunity.

But what Sadie and Adam are trying to kill is an image of the Boss each has created in terms of his own ego—the Boss's integration has been doomed to fall because it has rested on an unsound base. Although the Boss's own choices are responsible for his fall, his incapability of maintaining his integration in the world is a commentary on "the terrible division" of his age. After his death "all the king's men" cannot put him together again; without the principle upon which the Boss's control was based, they do not add up to the microcosm maintained by the Boss's integration. An understanding of the way in which the Boss's men stand as correlatives for aspects of his nature is a key to his characterization.

Sadie and Sugar-Boy are symbols of adjustment to nature in terms of an abstract code. When Sadie informs him of the fraud perpetrated on him by the Harrison outfit, she "made him what he is" (she is the mother of his rebirth), and it is significant that she has developed a sort of honor-among-thieves code of retaliation based on her reaction to her pock-marked face and her besotted father. And Sugar-Boy's relation to nature has been the result of his limitations, too. His stuttering and his puniness at school made the big boys try to "run it over him like he was dirt." So he has developed a code which gives him mastery over his deformity and over other men. Sugar-Boy stands for a kind of counter-predatoriness, which is in harmony with the other elements of the Boss's nature as long as it is held in check. After the Boss's death, Sugar-Boy is set adrift, has no usefulness.

If there is an affinity between the Boss and Sugar-Boy, there is no less an affinity between the Boss and another of the men upon whom he heavily depends early in his career—Hugh Miller of the "clean hands, pure heart, and no political past." There is sincere regret in the scene of their parting: "You're leaving me all alone," the Boss tells him, in semi-comic woe, "with all the sons of bitches. Mine and the other fellow's" (147/*138*). Hugh Miller is a part of Willie's nature that he never relinquishes, just as Tiny Duffy is a symbol of "that other self of Willie Stark, and all the contempt and insult which Willie Stark was to heap on Tiny Duffy was nothing but what one self of Willie Stark did to another self of Willie Stark because of a blind, inward necessity" (105/*98*). Adam Stanton is a symbol of the Hugh Miller aspect of Willie Stark's nature, and Willie's[228] visit to Adam is motivated by his desire to convince himself of the truth of his self-knowledge.

Ironically, Jack Burden stands for what finally frustrates the Boss's attempt to achieve integration of his whole nature; Jack stands for a malignant skepticism that the Boss puts to work to disintegrate the other characters' conceptions of the world, and which ends in disintegrating the Boss's own conception of himself and of the people around him.

The Boss's affair with Anne Stanton symbolizes Willie's attempt to find in nature some means of achieving good through triumph over the gross and brutal in nature (the Tiny Duffy aspect of his nature). Anne's sculptured, stylized beauty, as opposed to Sadie's pock-marked, blemished face, points up the symbolic contrast between the Boss's two mistresses. It is significant that what brings the Boss and Anne together is her plea to him for assistance in her welfare work, symbol on a smaller scale of what Willie is attempting in his hospital project. Anne's disillusionment about her father and Willie's about his ability to control his son's destiny seem to determine the relationship between Anne and the Boss, as if their affair were a natural outcome of their search for a satisfactory attitude toward nature.

Tom Stark, the Boss's son, is a symbol of human incorrigibility; he is a living rebuff to his father's necessity to find proof in nature that somehow man is controllable. He is continually making not only his father, but himself too, vulnerable to exploitation. To save Tom from marriage to Sibyl Frey, Willie agrees to play ball with the opposition. In his attempt to rectify his son's blunders, the Boss is indulging a sort of parental pride that is in conflict with the code by which he is trying to live. With his eye set on the abstract political objective, the Boss is committed to give up certain of his "necessities" as a human being. But something will not allow him to relinquish his parental pride: this something is the assertion of an essential part of his nature.

The hospital scene produced by Tom Stark's injury brings Sadie, Anne and Lucy together and points up symbolic contrasts already established. Sadie, Anne and the Boss have no defense against the agony of raw grief, but Lucy, guided by her faith in human goodness and love, is able to maintain control of herself and assist her husband, unmanned by his suffering, to leave the waiting room. This is not to say that Lucy becomes the prim heroine of the novel. She does not regain her husband in the end, and we last see her clinging to a faith which makes her capable of adopting a child whose paternity is highly questionable on the long chance that it may be Tom Stark's son, and, symbolically, on the longer chance that Willie may be reborn through it. But Lucy does symbolize a faith which pronounces commentary on the Boss's faith in himself, and on Sadie's faith in her eye-for-an-eye code. Lucy's is a faith in a power before which man is helpless; and it enables her to endure the loss of her husband and of her son; ironically, it affirms the same sort of belief in the potentiality of man as that affirmed by the Boss's dying statement.

Sadie, on the other hand, has no defense against her loss of the Boss. She cannot stay away from the hospital while Tom, whom she has never liked,[229] is suffering. Finally, when she realizes that the Boss is going to leave her permanently, she cannot discipline her attitude toward the loss in terms of her code. She kills the Boss, but, after the murder, she is unable to harden herself to the crime; Jack discovers her in a sanatorium in a state of collapse: "So I continued to sit there for quite a while, holding Sadie's hand in the silence which she seemed to want and looking across her down toward the bayou, which coiled under the moss depending from the line of cypresses on the farther bank, the algae-mottled water heavy with the hint and odor of swamp, jungle and darkness, along the edge of the clipped lawn" (436/411). We have in the landscape a juxtaposition of the brute natural and uncontrollable and the rational and man-controlled, the elements which have gotten out of hand in Sadie's nature. But this is not to say that Sadie Burke is the villainess of the novel any more than that Lucy Stark is the heroine. Both Lucy and Sadie operate as dynamic symbols to qualify the central theme. Sadie is frustrated because she tries to live in terms of a code inappropriate to her nature. But she gains self-knowledge through her collapse, and in her letter to Jack after her recovery there is the implication that she has achieved a sort of mastery over herself in terms of this self-knowledge.

The Boss's downfall is a result of his losing sight of the relationship between man and nature. Highway 58 is a symbol of what Willie Stark achieves in terms of his knowledge that good must be built out of the bad in man. Crooked politics result in Highway 58. Throughout the novel sections describing the highway are repeated to develop a symbol of the precariousness of this relationship between man's aspirations to idealism and the inescapable, irrational, gross aspect of man's nature, an aspect he shares with the dense, uncontrolled natural world along the highway: the jungle at the edge of the clipped lawn. As long as he realizes that he is cutting across nature (Sugar-Boy realizes this with a vengeance when he swerves dexterously to run down the 'possum), he may maintain his separateness. But the "ectoplasmic fingers of the mist" reach out of the swamp, "threading out from the blackness of the cypresses" (54/49) to snag them—an eerie foreshadowing of the climactic catastrophe of the novel.

For Willie Stark loses sight of nature's resistance to complete control. When his son is killed, Willie's story comes to a climax. In the face of this blow, Willie loses sight of the inseparability of good and evil; he determines to fight back and force upon nature man's ability to achieve absolute good; so he sets out to build his hospital solely out of the "good" in man (Tiny Duffy and Gummy Larson are to have no hand in it). In spite of Lucy's insistence that the hospital—"those things"—does not matter in the face of their son's death, Willie sees it as a symbol of man's undaunted march toward triumph over disease and accident; through surgery, man will control accidents of the sort which killed his son. He begins by banishing Gummy Larson, the crooked contractor, and Tiny Duffy, whom he had promised an interest in the undertaking. But he is so hypnotized by his determination to impose his will upon the nature which has taken his son that he loses sight[230] of the fact that he is running roughshod over Tiny and Gummy and Sadie Burke, as his Cadillac has run over 'possum and moccasin; he becomes hypnotized like the driver who, in an image in the opening page of the book, loses control of his car, crashes over the shoulder of the highway into the weeds, and is killed. Gummy, Sadie and Tiny Duffy have all made him what he is, represent essential parts of his make-up. And, finally, Adam Stanton, symbol of idealism divorced from the brute natural, pulls the trigger. Willie has been struggling toward integration in terms of his whole nature, but the integration among his henchmen breaks down when he tries to divorce idealistic aspirations from their basis in his own pride and selfishness. His downfall is a symbol of the disintegration brought about by modern man's attempt to control the external world through will unguided by understanding. But the Boss's downfall is his "luck"; for through his own disintegration he gains faith in the potentiality of integration in man: he learns that something within man destroys him when he ceases to act as man.

3.

Warren's point of view requires that all the imagery of the novel grow out of Jack Burden's mind, and, although it is beyond the scope of this paper to try to do more than suggest the psychological motivation for Jack's reveries, something should be said about the way in which the symbolism considered here is produced by Jack's state of mind.

At the time of the telling of the story, Jack is like a man recuperating, learning to walk again, or like a man whose mind has been liberated from the effects of a drug. He is feeling his way back over territory he had thought familiar, re-exploring it in an attempt to master the knowledge brought to him through his rebirth. Earlier, as a man sick with the "terrible division" of his age, he had seen the world through a diseased sensibility. His feeling of betrayal after the disruption of his love affair with Anne had made him turn on his sensibility as if it had betrayed him, for it had brought between them the image of Anne floating in the bay, had seemed to make him incapable of going through with the sexual act. Jack had tried, after this frustration, to develop a protection against further betrayals, had done so by seeking a "realistic" attitude toward the world. Prior to his rebirth, his speech and actions in the presence of others had shown him to be a man subordinating sentiment to the requirements of the political world in which he worked (and in this respect he had felt he was like the Boss), but in moments of inactivity, he had lapsed into reveries that took the form of ambiguous overflows of sentiment: "You see a cow standing in the water upstream near the single leaning willow. And all at once you feel like crying" (82/76). After his rebirth, as he looks back on those reveries and reconstructs them, Jack can see that they were symptoms of a disease, but he cannot put a name to the sickness; and, as he tells the story in retrospect, he seems to reproduce those reveries with an almost loving and morbid relish. So what we get in the novel in Jack Burden's "style" (which cannot be equated with Warren's style) is a marked alternation between[231] passages of straight, laconic reporting (Jack Burden describing Jack Burden the ex-reporter) and passages lyrical, rhetorical and often sentimentally ironic (Jack Burden trying to reproduce Jack Burden the ex-romanticist). By more than simple juxtaposition this alternation involves a mutual qualification; one Jack Burden qualifies the other and gives us the whole character: a man whose incorrigibly active sensibility is still resisting his attempts to subordinate it to the requirements of his adopted cynical view. In this alternation the conflict (the struggle toward and against rebirth) which is Jack's hope is dramatized. But the tension and conflict produced by this alternation do more than characterize Jack Burden. They bring to focus several meanings and implications that sharpen our perception of the total intention of the novel; these meanings and implications are brought to focus by the quality such passages possess of functioning in a number of ways simultaneously.

For example, passages produced by his unchecked flow of sensibility occur when Jack "relaxes." Lolling in a hammock while the Boss paces the yard pondering a political problem, Jack sees the leaves about his head and reflects:

I lay there and watched the undersides of the oak leaves, dry and grayish and dusty-green, and some of them I saw had rusty-corroded-looking spots on them. Those were the ones which would turn loose their grip on the branch before long—not in any breeze, the fibers just relax, in the middle of the day maybe with the sunshine bright and the air so still it aches like the place where the tooth was on the morning after you've been to the dentist or aches like your heart when you stand on the street corner waiting for the light to change and happen to recollect how things once were and how they might have been yet if what happened had not happened. (37/33)

What starts out as an apparently casual, almost languid speculation about the leaves develops into a vague, aching nostalgia. By a process of association Jack arrives at a sardonic *carpe diem* theme from which he is awakened by the crack of Sugar-Boy's automatic from behind the barn where the gunman is practicing fast draws.

We have here a reverie framed by our awareness of the Boss pacing the leaves and Sugar-Boy practicing his skill (both described in terms Jack Burden the self-styled hard-boiled henchman would use: "Well, it was his baby, and he could give it suck" and "It was Sugar-Boy off down in the lot playing with his .38 Special again"). The irony of the juxtaposition grows out of the terms in which Jack describes the three activities. He feels that he shares no responsibility for the Boss's problem: he is simply doing what he is paid to do. So he relaxes in the hammock in a sort of luxury of irresponsibility, allowing his mind to drift in a vague lack of purpose like the leaves he is contemplating; he is, in his withdrawal, trying to submerge himself in the womb of total nature, but his reflections on the leaves lead him to a contemplation of the inevitability of change. The leaves fall, the tooth deteriorates, the traffic light changes, and suddenly Sugar-Boy's automatic cracks the silence. The critical problem is this: How aware is Jack Burden, at the time of his telling of the story, of the irony of this juxtaposition—Boss pacing, Jack brooding, Sugar-Boy practicing?[232] Certainly, at the time the events took place, Jack was unaware of any irony in the fact that while he mused on the futility of human action Sugar-Boy was diligently practicing a highly developed technique of human action. The fact that Jack forgets the leaves, listens for a while to Sugar-Boy's target practice, then dozes off in the hammock is evidence that he missed the irony completely at the time the events occurred. At the time, much later, of his report of what happened, Jack reconstructs the events in a way that suggests that he is still unable to define the irony of the scene. But the reader, through his insight into Jack's subconscious state of mind, can see how the whole sequence has functioned to point up three conflicting attitudes toward nature which produce the basic conflict in the novel.

Again, in his reverie just prior to his revealing the evidence of her father's participation in crooked politics to Anne Stanton, Jack subconsciously struggles with the conflict produced by his sensibility:

A month from now, in early April, at the time when far away, outside the city, the water hyacinths would be covering every inch of bayou, lagoon, creek, and backwater with a spiritual-mauve to obscene-purple, violent, vulgar, fleshy, solid, throttling mass of bloom over the black water, and the first heartbreaking, misty green, like girlhood dreams, on the old cypresses would have settled down to be leaf and not a damned thing else, and the arm-thick, mud-colored, slime-slick moccasins would heave out of the swamp and try to cross the highway and your front tire hitting one would give a slight bump and make a sound like *ker-whush* and a tiny thump when he slapped heavily up against the underside of the fender, and the insects would come boiling out of the swamps and day and night the whole air would vibrate with them with a sound like an electric fan, and if it was night the owls back in the swamp would be *whoo*-ing and moaning like love and death and damnation, or one would sail out of the pitch dark into the rays of your headlights and plunge against the radiator to explode like a ripped feather bolster, and the fields would be deep in that rank, hairy or slick, juicy, sticky grass which the cattle gorge on and never get flesh over their ribs for that grass is in that black soil and no matter how far down the roots could ever go, if the roots were God knows how deep, there would never be anything but that black, grease-clotted soil and no stone down there to put calcium into that grass—well, a month from now, in early April, when all those things would be happening beyond the suburbs, the husks of the old houses in the street where Anne Stanton and I were walking would, if it were evening, crack and spill out into the stoops and into the street all that life which was now sealed up within. (257–258/*243*)

We have in such imagery a complex of references to the basic symbolism. In the water hyacinth metaphor, for example, we have the principle of natural change and rebirth which is uncontrollable ("throttling mass"), miraculous ("spiritual-mauve," the connotations of the ecclesiastical robe), gross and irrational (the "obscene-purple" suggests the membrane in which the foetus huddles; "violent, vulgar, fleshy, solid," the bestiality of lust), and in the face of which man seems helpless. We have the "obscene-purple" played off against the "spiritual-mauve" to produce a tension which reflects Jack's conflicting impulse to worship and loathe nature, to find mingled hope and despair in[233] natural fruition (the "misty green" of the cypress is a summons to idealism, to hope in an ultimately "good" end toward which natural process tends; but the "misty green" turned "leaf and not a damned thing else" seems to turn the hope to despair, like fragile girlhood optimism frustrated in the adult experience of womanhood). The image of the car running over the moccasin symbolizes man running counter to brute natural process (the passage of the highway through the dense, uncontrolled nature is antagonistic to the passage of the moccasin impelled by the season to cross the road): part of man's nature separates him from brute animal nature. Yet his idealism is rooted in the mysterious, uncontrollable, gross and irrational process which determines his environment. The undernourished cows are reminders that nature is, if not inimical to man, at least so organized that it has no regard for his welfare: the lush fruition of the season produces insects, snakes, owls, hyacinths, but it barely supports the domestic animal upon which man depends. One could probe the passage further and discover new connotations which function to point up the total meaning of the novel. It is enough here to point out that the passage creates an atmosphere in which the reader's sensibility is focused on the mystery which furnishes the basis for the novel's theme.

It is to such passages as those just considered that critics must return for a proper evaluation of *All the King's Men*. And those passages must be read as the product of Jack Burden's mind. Warren's choice of his particularly oblique point of view is an index of his rigorous and thorough-going ontological approach to the mystery of good and evil. We have in *All the King's Men* the story of how Willie Stark was assassinated at the peak of his political career, but what we experience is that story happening inside Jack Burden's head. The legend of political power is brought to us through a medium which dramatizes the limits and validity of human knowledge. In fact, one might say that the whole strategy of Warren's technique thwarts any attempt to find the simplified, clear-cut answer to the question of political power; the form of the novel forces the reader to take the Willie Stark story as a mystery—a mystery thoroughly explored in the psychological terms of Jack Burden's experience.[234]

Varied Approaches

A STUDY IN POPULISM

Malcolm O. Sillars

All the King's Men, Robert Penn Warren's novel of the Southern demagogue and the men and women around him, has been examined from many points of view. It may be worthwhile to examine some of the too often overlooked socio-economic implications of the novel. All the king's men, and the king himself, can be clearly seen to represent the great American tradition of Populism that swept the poorer agricultural areas of the Middle West and the South in the late 1930's. It is surely far more than the narrow context of the life of Huey Long, as too many have mistakenly supposed. The spirit of Willie Stark has reared itself in many states and in many forms; in Bloody Bridles Waite of Colorado, Sockless Jerry Simpson of Kansas, William Jennings Bryan of Nebraska, Alfalfa Bill Murray of Oklahoma, Kissin' Jim Folsom of Alabama and many others. The political elements of *All the King's Men* are rooted in the past and yet are all, in one way or another, degenerative of the tradition they represent.

There are four such elements which should be isolated and their interrelationships known in order to see more clearly the novel's meaning. The hill people of the South represent a particular economic group who are now, as they were in the days of Willie Stark, and earlier

Malcolm O. Sillars, "Warren's *All the King's Men:* A Study in Populism," *American Quarterly,* IX (Fall 1957), 345–353. Reprinted by permission of the author and the publisher.

in the days of Pitchfork Ben Tillman, set apart from the more aristocratic and proper conservative people of the flatlands. Willie Stark is an example of the leaders produced by the hills to do battle on their behalf. The political position of the aristocrats of the Delta illuminates Stark's rise and fall. Jack Burden is an aristocrat who loses, then finds himself in trying to bridge the gap between the hills and the Delta.[345]

I

    Essential to the understanding of Willie Stark is an understanding of the social construct which produced him. The hill people are a crucial phenomenon in the economic and social structure of middle-western and southern agricultural areas. The geographical dividing line between hills and black belt only serves to draw into sharper focus, in the South more than elsewhere, the economic battle. These hill people are holders of small plots of poor red farmland from which they eke out an existence with the assistance of amazing stubbornness, and an evangelical Protestant code of ethics. They see themselves as the chosen people who do battle with the more prosperous, and evil, Delta planters. They are fiercely individualistic.
    They were less inclined to favor the Civil War because they had less interest in Negro slavery. They were more susceptible to Populism with its interest in freeing the small farmer from the control of the bankers, railroads, elevator operators and other more well to do elements of the society. They were more likely to break from Al Smith on the issues of Catholicism and Prohibition because the economic issue was less pronounced in 1928 and so provided them with a chance to vote religion and liquor. They supported the New Deal and in the election of 1948 they endorsed the Democratic party more than did the Delta, which found the politics of the New and Fair Deals threatening their power position by raising the standards of the Negroes and the rednecks of the hills.[1]
    The same Populist sentiment was strong in the Corn Belt and for similar reasons. In the South it was rocky red soil; in Kansas and Nebraska it was rainfall. In the late nineteenth century there was real correlation between the amount of rainfall and the intensity of Populist fervor in western Nebraska.[2] *All the King's Men* is the product of a socio-economic vortex which reduced a proud people to desperate action.

---

[1] Perhaps the best explanation of this condition is found in V. O. Key, "Alabama: Planters, Populists, 'Big Mules,' " *Southern Politics* (New York: Alfred A. Knopf, 1949), chap. iii.
    [2] John D. Hicks, *The Populist Revolt* (Minneapolis: The University of Minnesota Press, 1931), pp. 30–35.

The hill people have a concept of good and evil by which they see themselves as the chosen people who have had their birthright stolen. To the Populist, as to most liberals, good and evil are concentrated. One attribute is found in one group and one in another. Or, the individual is good and governments, or corporations or bankers or what have you, are evil. Thus, reasons the liberal, return the society to its natural owners and there will be peace in the land. The hill people, with Presbyterian rigidity, see the inhabitants of the Delta living a riotous life of drunken orgies, during which[347] time they spend on booze and vain, heartless women, the money that the tax collector, the banker, the railroad agent and the grain elevator operator steals from the children of the hills. Their strong religious backgrounds also cause them to be more susceptible to the Messiah. And this Messiah, they believe, will always rise from among them (a false conclusion if we examine the backgrounds of the men who have actually acted positively for these people—Jefferson, Jackson and F. D. Roosevelt).

One of the lessons to be learned from *All the King's Men* is that these conditions still exist and this latent evangelical liberalism is always present. In 1948 Henry Wallace (a curious combination of populist and aristocrat) tried to exploit this agrarian liberalism with his "Gideon's Army" and his promises to the "little people." His liberalism had lost its roots, however, and the stronger urban liberalism which dominated the Wallace campaign was not acceptable to rural people. Further, in 1948 Wallace had in Harry S. Truman, an opponent who better fit the picture of the hill people's leader. The conditions—economic, social and religious—which formed the amalgam producing Willie Stark are a significant part of American history. They should be studied in a dispassionate light for insights into our future.

I I

Willie Stark, the leader produced by the conditions and prejudices of the hill people, is the second of the important social elements in Robert Penn Warren's novel, for while Willie Stark is an individual, he is also an institution. He has all the background and beliefs of the hill people mentioned earlier. As county treasurer he sacrifices his political life in a fight to see that the courthouse gang in Mason City does not make the new schoolhouse a political plum. His opponents tell the people that the company submitting the lowest bid would bring in Negroes from the lowlands and thus deprive the local people of jobs. Incidentally, they tell the people that the Negroes would be the semi-skilled workers and the hill people that were hired would be the common laborers. Essentially this is the point at which the hill people always break with the Negroes. They do not have as many to contend with as in the flat country and so do not fear their political power as the aristocrats do. But when the Negro threatens them economically, race becomes an issue. Willie fights but loses. Other real life Willie Starks are destroyed politically in just such a manner.

The fire escape of the schoolhouse, built of inferior materials, falls during a fire drill and three children are killed. Willie is thus made a political power. He had warned them about what the courthouse gang was trying to do and he was right. With this he advances to the second step in the rise of the redneck leader, what Professor V. O. Key calls the "friends[347] and neighbors" politician.[3] In the hills around Mason City he is a political power. His is the protest for the inarticulate people of the area.

His rise to statewide prominence comes when Willie again sacrifices himself politically. Convinced of his popularity he is induced to enter the race for Governor by Tiny Duffy, the perfect stereotype of the smalltown political boss. During the campaign, Stark discovers that he has been nominated to take votes from MacMurfee, a candidate who is also popular in the hills. Willie goes to the political rally, rather symbolically pushes Tiny Duffy off the platform and reveals his part in the act. He tells the people to vote for MacMurfee and not for him. He tells them to sit in judgment on MacMurfee and remove him if he is wrong. MacMurfee wins the election. Willie, by this sacrifice, becomes a state-wide figure. He fits the standards of honesty that the hill people want and becomes their champion. He was duped as they had been, time and time again.

Probably of interest here is the change in the spoken rhetoric of Willie Stark. Previous to this time Stark talked about issues, about specific problems of taxes, education and roads. His speeches were clearly dull and unemotional. When he speaks at the rally he speaks to the emotional needs of the hill people. One might reflect that this was Willie's awakening, or rebirth if you will, to the realities of political power and the first step to his destruction. I do not, however, place such an interpretation on the act. Willie is here telling the truth and in the language the Hills understand.

MacMurfee, of course, fails to live up to the promises of the election and the inevitable wave of the future sweeps Willie into the Governor's Mansion. But Willie is different from the rest. He cannot be bought by political machines. Instead he forms his own machine and like too few others who rose in a similar manner, he actually goes about attempting to solve the problems of the hill people. He builds highways, schools and hospitals. He raises the taxes of the rich (the lowland aristocrats) and defends the hill people in the courts.

The greatest fight is the one which Willie goes through in relating his past to the realities of politics. He finds out that there is both good and evil in all men. Byram B. White, as State Auditor, dips his hand into the till and Willie is shaken up. The little man from the hills is

<hr />

[3] Key, *Southern Politics*, p. 37.

just as capable of evil as the folks of the lowlands. Not that putting one's hand into the till is so bad—for Willie had come now to realize that this is an essential part of the machinery of political power, but White does it behind Willie's back. In short, he is disloyal to the cause which Willie represents. And White's willingness to write an undated resignation deepens Stark's realization of his power over men.[348]

"I gave him every chance," the boss said glumly. "Every chance. He didn't have to say what I told him to say. He didn't have to listen to me. He could have just walked out the door and kept on walking. He could have done a dozen things. But did he? Hell, no. Not Byram, and he just stands there and his eyes blink right quick like a dog's do when he leans up against your leg before you hit him, and, by God, you have the feeling if you don't do it, you won't be doing God's will. You do it because you are helping Byram fulfill his nature." (142/*133–134*)

Out of his experiences there grows the conclusion that life is not just a clash of good and evil but rather (returning selectively to his fundamentalist Sunday school) all evil. As Willie Stark puts it, "Man is conceived in sin and born in corruption and he passeth from the stink of the didie to the stench of the shroud" (54/*49*).

This conviction influences Willie's concept of progress profoundly. His real concern is with the problem of producing that which is good. He reveals this in his exchange with the intellectual and idealistic Dr. Adam Stanton.

"There is one question I should like to ask you. [Said Stanton.] It is this. If, as you say, there is only the bad to start with, and the good must be made from the bad, then how do you ever know what the good is? How do you even recognize the good? Assuming you have made it from the bad. Answer me that."
"Easy, Doc, easy," the Boss said.
"Well, answer it."
"You just make it up as you go along."
"Make up what?"
"The good," the Boss said. "What the hell else are we talking about. Good with a capital G." (273/*257*)

His political philosophy thus completed, Willie runs roughshod over everyone who gets in his way.
Indicative of his change in philosophy, there is a degeneration in Willie Stark's oral rhetoric. The genuine Populist cry for justice is dissipated into demagoguery. Observe Theodore Bilbo in actual life as cited by V. O. Key in *Southern Politics.*

In 1934, Bilbo brought into play his genius for rough-and-tumble campaigning. He wore, from an earlier campaign, a scar won in his oratorical battles for the people. He had been rapped over the head with a pistol butt by an opponent whom he had described as a "cross between a hyena and a mongrel ... begotten in a nigger graveyard at midnight, suckled by a[349] sow, and educated by a fool." In the 1934 campaign as in others, Bilbo—who had earlier done a little Baptist preaching—salted his oratory with bastard King Jamesian orotundities, long familiar to his audiences from the sermons of their evangelical preachers: "Friends, fellow citizens, brothers and sisters—hallelujah.—My opponent—yea, this opponent of mine who has the dastardly, dewlapped, brazen, sneering, insulting and sinful effrontery to ask you for your votes without telling you the people of Mississippi what he is a-going to do with them if he gets them—this opponent of mine says he don't need a platform ... He asks, my dear brethren and sisters, that you vote for him because he is standing by the President. . . . I shall be the servant and Senator of all the people. . . . The appeal and petition of the humblest citizen, yea, whether he comes from the black prairie lands of the east or the alluvial lands of the fertile delta; yea, he will be heard by my heart and my feet shall be swift, . . . your Senator whose thoughts will not wander from the humble, God-fearing cabins of Vinegar Bend, . . . your champion who will not lay his head upon his pillow at night before he has asked his Maker for more strength to do more for you on the morrow ... Brethren and sisters, I pledge ... "[4]

There is further degeneration in Willie. It is exemplified by his infidelity to his wife, Lucy. Lucy, the prime mover in Willie's earlier high moral purpose, is relegated to the position of a publicity piece. She is used for the furtherance of the Governor's political ends. For sexual satisfaction Willie turns to a collection of women who are not the product of the hills. In short, Willie falls into the very pattern of life in his personal affairs which the hill people have hated (or perhaps envied) in the people of the lowlands—heavy drinking and infidelity. In the end it is Anne Stanton's brother Adam who kills Willie when he finds out that his sister had been Willie's mistress. Thus, Willie's failure to do the impossible and fulfill the picture which the redneck has of his leaders caused his downfall.

Despite Stark's actions, the wool hat boys never desert him. Even more significant, the clear-thinking Lucy doesn't either. When their wild-living son Tom is paralyzed in a football accident—a symbol of Willie's attempt and failure to construct a pleasant world—Lucy is there to help Willie on with his coat and take him home. After the deaths of Willie and Tom, Lucy adopts a child born to the promiscuous Sibyl Frey with a conviction born of faith that it is Tom Stark's illegitimate son. The name for the boy: Willie—Willie Stark. With all that she has been put to personally in Governor Stark's rise and fall, she knows as the hill people know that there is something in Willie which must be preserved. Thus, as the novel ends, Lucy Stark represents the inarticulate hill people who must have faith in their Willie Stark because experience has taught them that there is no other source for their salvation. And Willie knows also, perhaps for[350] the first time clearly, on his death bed as he says—"It could have been different."

4 Key, *Southern Politics*, pp. 242–43.

Thus, in death, Willie Stark returns to his roots. There is a solution to the evils of the society in which the hill people live and the solution is in the conquest of political power by an articulate spokesman who will act. Whether or not this belief is correct is not an issue. The real point is that the hopes and aspirations of these people are genuine and Willie's attempts to meet these needs are also genuine. It is in the red dirt and man's weaknesses that Willie's failures are rooted. The fallacy of Populism, and perhaps of all liberalism then, is the fallacy of not understanding nature.

III

The third social element in the novel is the aristocracy of the Delta. Like the geographical division between the hills and the plains, the aristocracy of the deep South is more clearly defined than in other sections of the country. On the plains of the deep South, the plantation owners have built a tradition of aristocratic conservatism. They use political power to protect a social system which is grounded in stability and respect for law. It is from this area that most of the great leaders of the South have come to contribute to American government in the fields of finance and foreign policy. But with all of their respectability they have almost always been lax in their willingness to help the poor farmers of the hills. They are the evil which the hill people see and react to. Because of the code and tradition of these people they do not understand Willie Stark. In *All the King's Men* Judge Irwin of Burden's Landing is the personification of this school of thought. Judge Irwin is the best of his tradition. He, unlike many of the more complacent men and women of the area, sees a need for social improvement. However, the judge is in a dilemma. The society which he represents will not allow change without the overt pressure of Willie Stark. Thus, there is no conservative way to solve problems, it seems. There is only Willie Stark's way and this is unacceptable to the judge.

Robert Penn Warren goes beyond this weakness, however, to show that even the people of the plain, when the hard crust of conservative respectability is removed, are not without corruption. Judge Irwin, while he was Attorney General, was involved in a kickback scheme which eventuated in the suicide of Mortimer L. Littlepaugh, Counsel for the American Electric Power Company. Governor Stanton had known of the action and shielded Irwin. The rectitude which is so lauded in the aristocracy is really only a façade. They are not above corruption when they find it necessary. This element dramatizes the sin of the aristocracy. Their real sin is their failure to recognize and alleviate the economic conditions of the poorer[351] people of the hills. Thus, in the South as well as elsewhere, the aristocracy has a respectable legal conservatism. They contribute greatly by giving powerful and intelligent leadership to the nation. But their conservatism is seldom respectable in dealing with the real socio-economic problems of the area and their legality is constructed to control such socio-economic improvement.

I V

The fourth element in the novel is Jack Burden. From the standpoint of the political nature of the agrarian areas he is significant as a touchstone moving between the hills and the black belt. Jack Burden is a product of the aristocracy. His early association with Judge Irwin makes a great impression on him. His youth is spent with Anne and Adam Stanton. All the elements of his life are linked to the Delta, but his realization that there is something unsatisfactory in this self-satisfied existence sets him adrift. Given the chance to work for Willie Stark, he accepts and quickly falls in with all the activities which characterize Willie. His actions in working to find ammunition for Willie's plans eventually bring him to attack the very roots from which he sprang. Through his revelation of Judge Irwin's and Governor Stanton's actions he destroys the very people who had previously meant the most to him, Adam Stanton, Anne Stanton and Judge Irwin. Anne Stanton becomes Willie Stark's mistress, Adam Stanton kills Willie and is killed himself by Willie's bodyguard and Judge Irwin commits suicide.

Burden seems lost in his conviction that there is no code of ethics or morals but only the "big twitch." Although Willie feels that Jack is the only person who really knows him, Jack realizes that he does not understand Willie at all. Perhaps the products of the aristocracy can never really understand the hill people and their kind of leadership.

As the novel draws to a climax, Jack Burden looks through the cloud of action without purpose in which he has been existing and begins to see clearly. He does, in the end, bridge the gap. There can be, he seems to know, a connection between the hills and the Delta. There can be respect for law and at the same time socio-economic progress. As the novel ends he is telling the reader that he may get back into politics. If so, it will be to help Hugh Miller who resigned as Attorney General when Governor Stark refused to fire Byram B. White. Miller is the symbol of the very leadership which is necessary, a man of respectability who wishes to use the law to help the people.

v

In surveying the rise and fall of a Populist politician and the people who support and oppose him, *All the King's Men* leaves the reader with the[352] hope of Lucy Stark. Another Willie will come along and he will not fall into the snare of demagoguery, blackmail and thuggery. Contemporary politics would seem to show us that this is possible. George Norris in Nebraska and Bob La Follette in Wisconsin are clear examples of this tradition. And in the South, examples of respectable Populism like John Sparkman and Lister Hill of Alabama prove that agrarian democrats can be law abiding. Further, the enlightened conservatism of such men as Fulbright of Arkansas adds awareness to respectability. It is also true that shortsighted conservatism still exists in the agrarian areas in the personages of Thurmond, Byrnes, Byrd and the like. It is further true that Populism has gone sour of late not only in Huey Long and Theodore Bilbo but most recently in Joseph McCarthy of Wisconsin. But the gap can be bridged either by a Populist who climbs up or an aristocrat who bends down. This is the essential lesson of *All the King's Men* and perhaps of America.[353]

A STUDY IN NIHILISM

Newton P. Stallknecht

Long ago, I had a friend, a militant atheist, who one day surprised me by taking sides in a lively and almost technically theological discussion concerning the relation of faith and morals. When I pointed out the manifest personal inconsistency involved in his so doing, he remarked with emphasis that he was indeed an atheist, but, he would have me know, a *protestant* atheist—almost I thought, as I regained my equilibrium, a Scotch Presbyterian atheist. Such loyalty is impressive. It indicates that more than agnostic intelligence is required to kill a tradition, just as more than dogmatic intelligence was required to create it. This something that goes beyond formal doctrine is often open to the artist more completely than to the professional philosopher. It is apparent in an almost spectacular way in Mr. Penn Warren's novel.

Mr. Warren, to be sure, is not an atheist, although he does otherwise resemble my friend in his loyalty to ancient ways of thought and feeling for which he must find new support. As a matter of fact the term *atheist* has long lost its edge. The older atheists, those, let us say before Nietzsche, were transitional figures. They belonged to a false dawn, or a false twilight, which we can now recognize for what it was.

From John Crowe Ransom and others, *"All the King's Men:* A Symposium," *Folio,* XV (May 1950), 2–22. Reprinted by permission of the author and the Indiana University Department of English.

They hardly guessed, as Nietzsche did, the extremes of dissolution of which the acids of modernity are capable. These men were, after all, humanists and they often found the dignity and autonomy of human nature enhanced in an atheistic cosmos. They had no notion that the skeptical denial of God might be followed by something far more devastating, namely, the "abolition" of man himself. This abolition or abdication of man has appeared both in theory and practice, in philosophy, in art, and conduct. As a result the humanities, both moral and esthetic, are in grave danger of following theology into the discard as systems of unintelligible myth.[18]

Such *nihilism* is often thinly disguised as pragmatism, or even as a sort of realist common sense. It is sometimes superficially humanitarian, sometimes satirical, sometimes sadistic, sometimes strictly descriptive, but always empty. There is, after all, no speculation in those alert and calculating eyes, no sense of man as a being for himself, or as an end in himself. The quality of man is obscured when human freedom, or the dominion of self-consciousness over sensation and instinct, is ignored. Man is left without his soul, almost without his imagination. Unable to assign a meaning to his own existence, he loses sight of himself. In such an *impasse*, art must become strictly impressionistic or abstractionist. It cannot honestly comment on life. Philosophy is even more helpless. Since there is no significant comment on life, we are left in morals, politics, and religion without standards and without authority, and in all fields propaganda takes the place of education. The sincere thinker is at the mercy of the Sophist.

Nothing is then left of human nature, as Mr. Warren sees it, but the Great Twitch, i.e., the nervous system responding to pressure, and occasionally, although paradoxically, a detached consciousness that recognizes the Great Twitch for what it is, hence the great nausea, or at best a desperate resignation. Mr. Warren presents this moral in a brilliant panorama of modern American life, that is almost Elizabethan in intensity of feeling and violence of action. Even so, his thoughtful melodrama is quite at home in the drugstores, cocktail-lounges, and smoke-filled rooms of a southern metropolis.

Like my friend, the protestant atheist, Mr. Warren is a *nihilist* with qualifications. He is a Christian *nihilist*. One is reminded of Dostoevsky but even more of Coleridge's *Ancient Mariner*, a figure whom Mr. Warren himself has, in his capacity as historical critic, interpreted astutely. For him the modern world, and with it modern man, has suddenly lost its substance. Each one of us stands alone, oppressed by an unintelligible world. The "sky and the sea, and the sea and the sky," which should have been the "round ocean and the living air" of Tintern Abbey, have become intolerable strangers to us. We stand like the mariner on a ship, manned by the dead who were once our fellow men. We find ourselves loathing the sea now rotten with slime, and cursing the harmless water snakes upon it, and all the while hating ourselves for loathing[19] and cursing. Somehow we feel responsible for the "dead" with whom we cannot communicate and we are burdened with a sense of guilt, for we know that through some error of our own, perhaps through some desire to escape responsibility, our world has perished. And so we look nothingness in the eye, a blazing and nauseating nothingness which consumes even the beauty of nature.

Jack Burden, hero of *All the King's Men,* is a sort of modern Mariner. He has not as yet made port—but he seems to remember the lighthouse, the harbor, and the kirk. He cannot describe these clearly but he does make them seem real again, even if still beyond our reach, and thus largely undefined.

For one who has witnessed and comprehended the abolition of man, it is no easy task to redefine human nature, its objectives and responsibilities. Weary of its blindness, a wicked and an adulterous generation crieth out for the truth, and there shall no answer be given it—at least no answer that it does not frame for itself. It is the task of the mid-twentieth century to frame this answer in terms that the skeptic cannot ridicule, the sentimentalist disfigure, or the scoundrel exploit. Here we stand alone, forlorn in our anxiety. The past will, to be sure, teach us something. In his day Dante faced some such problem and Shakespeare seems to have been aware of it—certainly Mr. Warren's finest characters are Hamlets in modern dress and he quotes Dante very aptly—but the worlds of the Middle Age, of the Renaissance, of the American liberalism of the thirties, lie prostrate like shattered Humpty Dumpties. The king's horses and the king's men cannot repair the damage of time even if they were to try. So we must look elsewhere. But Mr. Warren is too honest a thinker to hope to call a philosophy into being out of nothing, just as he is too much a scholar to expect to find our needs supplied ready-made in an historical philosophy. Thus we find him turning, or on the point of turning, toward that most interesting blend of modernism and traditionalism, the philosophy of Christian existentialism. Kierkegaard, Unamuno, Gabriel Marcel, or the more cautious and academic Jean Wahl, come continually to mind as we reflect upon the many philosophical passages in *All the King's Men.* Even Sartre, the "atheist," is by no means irrelevant, although his ideas are translated back into a religious context. Thus Sartre's way of seeing[20] things, partially inspired by the fiction of Hemingway and Faulkner, returns to America in the consciously philosophical fiction of Mr. Warren.

The two most formidable versions of a non-existentialist philosophy, determinism and the theory of an all-seeing providential deity, seem to be repudiated in favor of a theory of radical freedom. "It might have been all different, Jack, you got to believe that" (461/*436*). This statement, on the lips of a dying "King-Fish," is the spiritual turning point of Mr. Warren's novel. We *must* believe in our freedom of choice or acquiesce in the abolition of man.

Man's existence *is* his freedom. Such freedom is often a painful burden, a source of evil and of guilty suffering. But it is none the less real. So conceived, man is neither a puppet of predestination nor of the Great Twitch. He is, for all his shortcomings, a creature worthy of his maker.

> The creation of man whom God in His foreknowledge knew doomed to sin was the awful index of God's omnipotence. For it would have been a thing of trifling and contemptible ease for Perfection to create mere perfection. To do so would, to speak truth, be not creation but extension. Separateness is identity and the only way for God to create, truly create, man was to make him separate from God Himself, and to be separate from God is to be sinful. *The creation of evil is therefore the index of God's glory and His power.* That had to be so that the creation of good might be the index of man's glory and power. But by God's help. By His help and in His wisdom. (462–463/437; my italics)

Jack Burden accepts the theology of this passage provisionally by admitting that "In my own way I did believe what he had said."

Man is created in the image of God. As an existentialist would say, this image with its resultant freedom, is forced upon him. It is at once the cross and the crown of human existence. Man may caricature or repudiate his freedom. If he does so he is a contemptible misfit in his world. But if he accepts this burden laid upon him alone of all creatures, he realizes his humanity and achieves a genuine if tragic dignity.

It is characteristic of our times that increasing numbers of thoughtful people can accept so austere and somber a philosophy with something like enthusiasm. We find them hoping desperately that it may be true. Then there are others[21] of us, who fear that we have, in our haste to escape *nihilism* and its terrifying ennui, surrendered too eagerly to this uncompromising individualism with its horizon of pessimism. It is hard to say whether existentialism is one of the final symptoms of dissolution or a desperate remedy. In this it resembles ancient Stoicism. We can find critics arguing for either interpretation. Which one of these interpretations Mr. Warren prefers, it is a little difficult to say. Certainly he has not committed or engaged himself with finality to an existentialist life of individualist decision. If he is an existentialist, he is indeed an admirably sober one.[22]

WARREN AS PURITAN

Norman Kelvin

In that speculative and suggestive study, *The Mind of the South* (1941), W. J. Cash writes of a contradiction which beset Southerners during the nineteenth century. Speaking of the advance among them of religious and other movements and ideas, he says that "the triumph of the Evangelical sects . . . involved the triumph of the Puritan ideal" but that the victorious struggle for its establishment was carried on "coincidentally with the growth of that curious Southern hedonism which was its antithesis." Cash does not believe that Puritanism and hedonism ever met, during the nineteenth century, in "open and decisive conflict," but neither does he say that the issue was finally resolved. Nor could he, for today these antithetical traditions of thought, feeling, and conduct are in stronger opposition to each other than ever they were in the past. Moreover, the conflict between them is no longer confined to the South but has thrust itself upon the nation at large and has given rise everywhere to confusion of values and agony of spirit.

Because the contention between Puritanism and hedonism has now become a national problem, Southern writers, for whom this perplexing matter is a heritage, have much to say to the rest of us, and their knowingness is a reason for their eminence today. And among Southern writers none is more articulately concerned with ideas, none has been more deeply disturbed by the antinomial claims of Puritanism and hedonism, than Robert Penn Warren. Though he has not said explicitly that he has been caught up in the struggle between these opposing philosophies, he has allowed their antithetical pulls to shape his approach to the theme he has acknowledged as his own—the meaning and nature of evil—and if we can discover how this has happened, we will be in a fair way to understand how one writer, at least, has been influenced by the dilemma, and how he has tried to resolve it.[355]

A more elaborate and precise way of describing Warren's theme would be to say that he has reiterated his belief that man's quest for something grand and pure, be it honor, justice, virtue, or love, will

From Norman Kelvin, "The Failure of Robert Penn Warren," *College English*, XVIII (April 1957), 355–364. Reprinted with the permission of National Council of Teachers of English and Norman Kelvin.

necessarily suffer betrayal by the evil in human nature. A concern with evil does not of course distinguish Warren from the many writers who have today rediscovered its existence, forced as they have been by the continuing history of moral outrage to give up their pure faith in the power of rationalism to make people good. But Warren differs from many contemporary thinkers, from those at least who have not lost their faith in humanism, in his sense of what evil is.

Most humanists see evil as the gap between moral aspiration and moral capability, as the feeling of being limited which that gap creates. With this picture they have generated the hope that the power of evil can be reduced, for if capability can be enlarged and made to approach aspiration—and humanists believe this to be possible—a sense of moral progress and relative increase in the power of goodness will be the spiritual results. Another consequence of this view, and a most important one, is that it dislodges evil from that central position in the scheme of human motives which it had held for so long. Until recently, however, Warren consistently rejected this view and its beneficent consequences, and in order to explain why his characters were destroyed, found it necessary to restore evil to its dominant power and dark glory.

To see the connection between Warren's disagreement with the humanists and the current conflict between our Puritan and hedonist aspirations, we must remind ourselves that Puritanism has traditionally believed pleasure to be the lure through which evil beguiles us into destroying ourselves. Hedonism, on the other hand, sees no difficulty in identifying pleasure-seeking with our desire to be good as well as happy. Thus, it is no accident that humanists have adopted the hedonistic creed as their own; as a philosophy suggesting a method through which the magnitude of evil in the world can be reduced. It is also not a matter of chance that Warren, who, until he wrote *Band of Angels* (1955), unequivocally charged our most pleasurable pursuits—the quest for honor, virtue, justice, or love—with being the decoys of evil, should have taken his stand on the Puritan side of the controversy. This is a dubious commitment for a writer to make when approaching a real cultural dilemma, and a close examination of Warren's writing will reveal that he paid a heavy price for his choice.... [356]

...*All the King's Men* is the story of Willie Stark, a ruthless, ambitious blackmailer. Willie is also a naive idealist: he wants personal power, but as governor of the State he also wants to do good for the people. In many ways Willie is a hedonist, a man of our century, a leader who has cut himself loose from traditional guides to conduct and who believes he can reform society into any shape he deems best. But Willie is not as autonomous as he regards himself: he is controlled by a peculiar view of Calvinist theory, by a belief that the raw materials of human nature are invariably corrupt and that a social builder must therefore fashion goodness out of badness, the only material available. As a consequence, Willie relies on blackmail as his chief instrument for directing public affairs toward his beneficent ends. Blackmail cannot fail to work, for as he tells Jack Burden, his private secretary and the first-person narrator of the story, "Man is born in the stink of the didie and he passes to the stench of the shroud," and "there is always something"—something corrupt to be found in the history of the most apparently upright of citizens. Willie also feels there can be no moral censure of his methods, for if evil is all there is, blackmail is merely the most efficient instrument available for working evil into good. In short, Willie, although a man of many good impulses, has made[358] the enormous error of thinking it is all right to exploit people for the sake of an attractive social goal. Thus, Willie Stark . . . has the makings of a tragic figure. . . . However, Warren loses control of his story, and the conclusion to *All the King's Men* unfortunately ignores its own beginnings.

To understand why this is so, we must briefly review what has happened in the story. Willie, after having destroyed other men in his zeal to create a magnificent social order which would be his monument, was shot down by Adam Stanton, who was a brilliant surgeon, the director of the Willie Stark Memorial Hospital, and the brother of Anne Stanton, lately in love with Willie. Adam's action . . . was touched off when an informant told him that Anne was sharing Willie's bed and that Adam's own appointment as director of the hospital had merely been a move on Willie's part to get closer to Anne. The second half of this tale was untrue.

Because Adam is the man who brings Willie down, the conflicting and opposing forces in the novel ought to have been caught up in these two men, and Warren, through his narrator, Jack Burden, asks us to believe that such was the case. Yet when we look again at Adam Stanton to see just why he was chosen to stand against Willie, we get the uncomfortable feeling that something has gone amiss. Willie's crime, after all, was ruthlessness toward his political opponents, and however reprehensible it is that Willie, a married man, has fallen in love with Anne Stanton, there is nothing in the part of the novel leading up to his murder—the major part—to suggest that Warren wanted us to consider Willie's affairs with women the great evils in his career. What seems to have happened is that Warren, after laboring long and successfully to create a story about political morality, suddenly swept away the edifice he had been carefully building and substituted a new story, one concerning the outraged sensibilities of an inflexible doctor whose sister had engaged in illicit love—a doctor who had very little to do with the politics in the previous story.

It is therefore amazing to hear Jack Burden say that Adam and Willie *had* to be instruments of each other's death (Adam was killed by one of Willie's henchmen); to hear him say that together they represented the "tragic separation of our times"—the separation of the man of ideas from the man of facts. This may be the tragedy of our times, but it has nothing to do with Willie and Adam as Robert Penn Warren created them. The Willie Stark we met in the novel was as much a man of ideas as was the puritanical, compulsive Dr. Stanton. They merely held to *different* ideas, and while some of Willie's were outrageous, so were some of Adam's. If Willie had an immoral idea in thinking there is only bad in the world, Adam had an equally wrong and wicked one in thinking that all the corruption in the State was concentrated in rising riff-raff like Willie and that there was none in old Southern gentlemen like Adam's father. On the other hand, both Willie and Adam had moral, or good, ideas. Willie believed in the efficacy of political action to relieve a part of human suffering, and Adam believed in the reality of integrity and personal honor.

Thus, what Warren calls the "tragic separation" between Willie and Adam has nothing really to do with the opposition of "facts" to "ideas." The real separation, the one which exists in the novel, is between a man of political action and an aloof, isolated patrician. What Warren has told us is that he believes the life of action to be irreconcilable with the maintenance of integrity and personal honor, that human action necessarily allows the triumph of the evil inherent in man. He has, by electing Adam Stanton to be Willie's judge and executioner—Adam Stanton instead of some politically more significant figure like Hugh Miller, the decent[359] attorney-general—condemned Willie not for being a man of facts but for being a man who believed in ideas which lead to action.

Would it not have been more to the point in a novel about political morality to begin with a belief in the validity of ideas which lead to action (what else should a politician believe in?) and then to show that there are moral and immoral ideas of this kind and that Willie's are immoral because they encourage a violation of human dignity? Such a procedure would have allowed Warren to make Hugh Miller, who has as much integrity as Adam Stanton but who, unlike Adam, believes moral government can help people to the good life, the meaningful opposition to Willie. Although, as *All the King's Men* is written, Hugh is relegated to a minor role, it is significant that Jack Burden, after Willie's death, announces he will return to politics and that this time he will serve Hugh Miller. But Jack tells us his resolve at the very end of the novel, so a story about Hugh and what he stands for is really a sequel to *All the King's Men,* not part of it. Unfortunately, Warren has not yet seen fit to write that sequel. . . .[360]

WARREN AS MORALIST

Seymour L. Gross

It is admittedly difficult for a reader to respond favorably to a piece of literature which grows out of a philosophical position quite different from his own. I believe it was Allen Tate who said that there are two kinds of people—those who believe in original sin and those who believe in the ultimate perfectability of mankind. When reader and writer[361] fall into two such inimical philosophical camps, as is the case with Robert Penn Warren and a recent commentator of his novels, Mr. Norman Kelvin, the problem of sympathetic response is heightened to the extreme. Mr. Kelvin certainly has the right not to like Warren's novels; he perhaps also has the right to berate Warren for not being a humanist and to suggest how Warren's novels ought to be written; but both of these rights demand that Mr. Kelvin accurately explicate what Warren is trying to do in his fiction. I believe that even a summary review of Mr. Kelvin's assumptions and assertions about Warren's work, especially as these condition his reading of Warren's finest novel, *All the King's Men,* will demonstrate how limited (and unfair) his evaluation of Warren is.

In Mr. Kelvin's view, Warren is a "Puritan," who, because he sees our "hedonist aspirations" as being "the lure through which evil beguiles us into destroying ourselves," consistently in his fiction "reiterates his belief that man's quest for something grand and pure, be it honor, justice, virtue, or love, will necessarily suffer betrayal by the evil in human nature." Nor is there in Warren's fiction, as Mr. Kelvin sees it, any possibility of Grace lighting the dark ways man must walk in, for by 1946, in *All the King's Men,* Warren had embraced completely "the extreme Calvinist position which sees man so at the mercy of an unaccountable Divine Will as to make puny and pathetic his hope that he ever can be capable of right choices in life."

It is more than a little difficult to reconcile this portrait of a moral nihilist (the term is Mr. Kelvin's) with Warren's remarks before a Columbia University audience in 1954: "Every soul is valuable in God's

Seymour L. Gross, "The Achievement of Robert Penn Warren," *College English,* XIX (May 1958), 361–365. Reprinted with the permission of the National Council of Teachers of English and Professor Seymour L. Gross.

sight, and the story of every soul is the story of its self-definition for good or evil, salvation or damnation. Every soul is valuable in God's sight. Or, with the secularization of things, we may say: every soul is valuable in man's sight."[1] Surely, at least in these remarks, Warren posits an ultimately coherent universe in which man's capacity for making right (or wrong) choices is the crucial factor in his existence. The fiction written before this address similarly demonstrates that Warren's writings are not conditioned by "Puritan negation or worse" (Kelvin).

Although Warren believes that original sin (or ineradicable imperfection) is a constant factor in human life and that men such as Thomas Jefferson, at the beginning of *Brother to Dragons,* or Adam Stanton in *All the King's Men,* or Jeremiah Beaumont in *World Enough and Time,* are destroyed or nearly destroyed by their refusal to acknowledge it, nowhere in Warren is there the "unequivocal" assertion that honor, justice, virtue, or love are merely "decoys of evil," as Mr. Kelvin has it. True, Adam and Jeremiah are defeated in their search for honor and glory; but they are not defeated because honor and glory are doomed "by the evil in human nature," but rather because neither man is willing or able to make the right choice. (Jefferson does and is saved.) Because both Adam and Jeremiah are driven by self-generated absolutistic ideals that have no relationship to reality— each believes that Good and Evil are undiluted, unrelated essences— they are doomed to destruction by a reality which will not be ordered to fit their impossible ideals. But to maintain, as Mr. Kelvin does, that in Warren's world goodness and moral choice are doomed by a ubiquitous evil is to deny the existence of many other characters in Warren's fiction. For example, in *All the King's Men,* Hugh Miller is the soul of honor and justice and Lucy Stark is the essence of compassionate love. Similarly, Mr. Kelvin's statement that Warren exhibits "an indifference to the relation between choice and morality" is not consonant with the facts. There is, for example, Jack Burden, who changes from a "sad little foetus that wants to lie in the dark and not know" to a morally mature man who is willing to accept "the awful responsibility of Time"; or Willie Stark, who in his dying moments can unflinchingly judge his own spiritual corruption; or Lucy Lewis (in *Brother to Dragons*), whose own failures in love and kindness ultimately teach her that love is the most valuable of human traits.[2] At

---

[1] "Knowledge and the Image of Man," *Sewanee Review,* LXIII (Winter 1955), 182–192.

[2] Mr. Kelvin "proves" that Warren does not believe in love by quoting Jefferson's speech on love as being "a mask to hide the brutal face of fact, / And that fact is but the immitigable ferocity of self...." But since this speech, as Prof. Frederick P. W. McDowell points out in his brilliant study of *Brother to Dragons* (*PMLA,* LXX [Sept. 1955], 573), is the product of an "agonized pessimism" (which the total poem refutes) that is as uncritical and dangerous as Jefferson's earlier optimism, Mr. Kelvin's argument is without validity.

the end of *All the King's Men* there occurs a tract written by the Scholarly Attorney, which, in some ways, is the most succinct summation of Warren's view of the relationship between good and evil. (That the tract is of importance can be seen in the fact that not only is it strategically placed but a morally renovated Jack Burden, whose final spiritual synthesis can be taken as[362] Warren's own,[3] admits that in his own way he believes what it says.) "The creation of man whom God in His foreknowledge knew doomed to sin was the awful index of God's omnipotence. For it would have been a thing of trifling and contemptible ease for Perfection to create mere perfection. To do so would, to speak truth, be not creation but extension. Separateness is identity and the only way for God to create, truly create, man was to make him separate from God Himself, and to be separate from God is to be sinful. The creation of evil is therefore the index of God's glory and His power. That had to be so that the creation of good might be the index of man's glory and power. But by God's help. By His help and in His wisdom" (462–463/*437*). This is neither "pessimism" nor "nihilism." Evil is not the coiled serpent which will *inevitably* poison all of man's noblest aspirations: it is rather the descriptive term for man's necessarily limited and imperfect condition, out of which, and despite which, he will create the goodness which is his "glory and power." This tract, as I will try to show later, adumbrates the central theme of *All the King's Men.*

Mr. Kelvin, however, reads the novel differently. Conditioned by his *a priori* conviction of Warren's nihilism, he sees *All the King's Men* as the depiction of the idea that "the life of action [is] irreconcilable with the maintenance of integrity and personal honor, that human action necessarily allows the triumph of the evil inherent in man." Willie Stark, then, is seen as "a ruthless, ambitious blackmailer," who, although a "naive idealist," is so caught in the grips of Warren's "peculiar . . . Calvinist theory" that "evil is all there is" that he "feels there can be no censure of his methods" in working evil into good. The novel is also thematically inept because Willie is brought down by Adam Stanton, "a doctor who had very little to do with the politics in the previous story," so that Warren's assertion that these two men had to kill each other because they represented "the tragic separation of our times"—the separation of the man of "facts" from the man of "ideas" is a spurious one. "The real separation, the one which exists in the novel, is between a man of political action and an aloof, isolated patrician." Mr. Kelvin suggests that "some politically more significant

3 Both Jack and RPW, the baldly autobiographical figure in *Brother to Dragons*, sum up their experiences in almost the same terms. RPW: "I opened the sagging gate, and was prepared / To go into the world of action and liability." Jack: "now we shall go out of the house and go into the convulsion of the world, out of history into history and the awful responsibility of Time."

figure like Hugh Miller" should have been Willie's "judge and executioner."

Such a view of the novel might perhaps have *some* validity if *All the King's Men* were only a political allegory. But I believe most readers would agree with Warren that the novel "was never intended to be a book about politics. Politics merely provided the framework story in which the deeper concerns ... might work themselves out" (Modern Library intro., 1953). If we look at the novel in terms of these "deeper concerns," the thematic confusion which Mr. Kelvin finds will, I think, disappear.

I think it is more nearly accurate to say that *All the King's Men* is "about" man's attempt to formulate a moral perspective on the facts of good and evil in a world in which the traditional guides to moral conduct have been obscured by various disruptive forces. In three of the more thematically significant characters—Willie, Adam, and Jack Burden—Warren investigates three calamitous approaches to the achievement of spiritual security in the ethical turmoil created by science, naturalism, determinism, and power politics. But out of the pain and defeat and death there emerges, in the final pages of the book, a positive moral synthesis. What a changed Thomas Jefferson says towards the end of *Brother to Dragons* might serve as an epigraph to *All the King's Men:* "We shall be forged/Beneath the hammer of truth on the anvil of anguish."

First of all, although Willie Stark is for much of the novel a ruthless politician, it is a mistake to assume that his career is meant to demonstrate the impossibility of wedding personal integrity to political action. Such an assumption is repudiated both by the presence in the novel of Hugh Miller, a courageous and impeccably honest man, who, with Jack Burden, returns to politics after the death of Willie, and by the tragic consequences which come from Willie's having divorced integrity from political action.

Willie Stark is not a naturalistic portrait of a totally corrupt and cynical politician. After he discovers that a purely idealistic approach to social betterment is useless because it does not square with the facts of human nature, he gets hold of a more accurate and usable world picture: to help people you must be willing to get your hands dirty with their selfishness and cruelty. For a time, Willie maintains the precarious balance between the creation of good (symbolized by Hugh Miller) out of the evil in man's nature (symbolized by Tiny Duffy) because he still believes in the good of the people as a valuable "idea" (or directive ideal).[363] In time, however (it begins with the Byram White episode), Willie becomes so obsessed with the evil in human nature and with his power to manipulate it, that he stops believing in goodness as an absolute entity. No longer is he a kind of "Jesus Christ scourging the money changers" out of public life, but an almighty God the Father, a law unto himself, for whom the distinctions between right and wrong are something which "you just make ... up as you go along." It is significant that when Willie decides to save White's crooked hide both his wife Lucy and Hugh Miller—who together constitute a kind of moral norm in the novel—repudiate him. They repudiate him because they recognize that in setting himself up as the sole standard of ethical values, Willie has freed himself (like Kurtz in "Heart of Darkness") to take any steps he wishes to make his now corrupted vision prevail. Willie's transmogrification is made manifest in a passage towards the end of the book. Jack, who has always seen the face of "Cousin Willie" (what was originally fine and honest in Willie) behind the "other face," suddenly discovers as he listens to the Boss orate that "it did not come now." What he sees instead is an image of raw, egotistic power: "I saw the face. Enormous ... The big jaw. The heavy lids laid together like masonry. The eyes burning and bulging powerfully." Or if we interpret Willie in terms of the tract already quoted, he achieved a valid world-view when he caught hold of the fact that goodness had always to take evil into account, but he desecrated it when he cast off the restrictive stipulation—"But by God's help. By His help and in His wisdom."

Adam Stanton, not Hugh Miller, is Willie's moral opposite, for Adam is the man of pure "idea"—idea divorced from all the demands of pragmatic reality. For Adam the creation of good is, indeed, the index of man's glory, but he would have that creation absolutely free of any concourse with evil; more accurately, he cannot believe that goodness can have any concourse with evil and still remain goodness. Such a view, as Jack recognizes, is a fanatic romanticism that is ultimately destructive: "[Adam] is a romantic, and he has a picture of the world in his head, and when the world doesn't conform in any respect to the picture, he wants to throw the world away"—which is precisely what Adam does when he learns that his idolized father once committed a dishonest act and that his sister is having an affair with Willie. Preferring annihilation to the acceptance of a world in which a good father and sister might, under the pressures and temptations of their imperfect humanity, do something evil, Adam can only kill and be killed. Adam and Willie are "doomed to destroy each other" because each is incomplete "with the terrible division of their age." That is, in Willie we see how the "fact" which has lost its directive "idea" is doomed to corrupt itself; in Adam we see how the "idea" which divorces itself from the "fact" cannot long endure in a world separate from Perfection.

In Jack Burden, Warren investigates still another approach to the problem of good and evil. Whereas Adam and Willie have distorted images of the moral order upon which they are willing to act, Jack tries desperately to have no image at all and to withdraw from all human commitment. Repelled by what he thinks is a "tainted and horrible" past (he thinks his mother loveless and his father weak),

Jack tries to shrink into a foetal-like state of amoral safety. Afraid to admit the reality of moral choice and consequence lest it bring self-judgment and incrimination, Jack retreats from the terrors of moral responsibility by the various escape mechanisms open to modern man: a distorted form of philosophical idealism ("it does not matter what you do ... because it isn't real anyway"); a deliberate courting of oblivion ("The Great Sleep"); and determinism, which he dubs "The Great Twitch" ("nobody has any responsibility for anything and there is no god but the Great Twitch"). But, as it turns out, Jack's moral cowardice is as deadly as Adam's and Willie's distortions: his "objective research" causes his real father, Judge Irwin, to kill himself; his refusal to commit himself to his love for Anne Stanton delivers her over to Willie, Willie over to Adam, and Willie and Adam over to both their deaths.

But the pain and violence of *All the King's Men* do not end in the hopeless despair that comes of contemplating "the triumph of evil inherent in man." Although Adam dies morally blind, other characters do not live and suffer for nothing. Jack's mother discovers after Irwin's suicide that she always loved only Jack's real father, and this knowledge frees her from years of pretense and wins back her son's love. Jack's supposed father, after years of living with the anguishing knowledge that his wife and best friend have been adulterers, finds the "truth" (which he writes into the tract) that brings peace to his last days. And Willie recognizes that he "has spilled his greatness on the ground" and tries to recapture, albeit too late, the "idea" that once lighted his tortuous road to power.[4][364]

But for Jack knowledge does not come too late. The men that he has seen live and die "in the agony of will" give him a "new picture of the world," which, I think it fair to say, is Warren's picture as well. Jack learns that unless a man commit himself to "the convulsion of the world" and accept the infinite responsibilities of that commitment, he will squander his capacity to create that goodness which is his glory and his power. But in a world in which good and evil are in everlasting relationship to each other, to believe in one and not the other, is to become either "the man of fact" or "the man of idea," and to doom oneself to incompleteness and death. Only the man who can accept with the love and understanding that comes of a sense of personal in-

---

4 Willie begins to change after his vicious son Tom is paralyzed in a football accident (a kind of symbolic comment on Willie's own life). Seeing at last what he has become, Willie tries to regain his vision by going back to his wife and repudiating his deal with the corrupt Gummy Larson even at the risk of political suicide. "You have to start somewhere," he tells Jack. But it is too late: the forces that his corrupted spirit have let loose come back to him in the shape of Adam's bullet. Yet his final words to Jack—"It might have been all different, Jack. You got to believe that"—are at once an anguished summation and a tragic triumph of the spirit which can finally see itself for what it is and what it might have been.

volvement the good and evil in himself and in "his million fathers" will be able to achieve that dynamic spiritual insight, which, though it labor in pain, will bring forth its harvest of human happiness and fulfillment. So it is that Jack, who though he knows that he has "squandered happiness, . . . killed his father [and] delivered his two friends into each other's hands and death," can yet retain enough faith in the ultimate possibilities of life to commit himself to marriage with Anne, finish his book on Cass Mastern, and return to politics with Hugh Miller. So it is that Warren's masterpiece ends not in negation but in hope.[365]

WARREN'S TELEOLOGY

James Ruoff

Since the Pulitzer Prize novel *All the King's Men* is coming to be recognized as the most comprehensive statement of Robert Penn Warren's philosophy and art,[1] it might be worth while to remark upon a very general misconception regarding the title of the novel. Now, ordinarily, of course, a title is not a matter of any great significance, but in this case it is important because it constitutes a symbolic expression of some of the author's basic ideas. It is, in fact, a Pandora's box which opens up to reveal the profoundly spiritual nature of Warren's convictions about the broad themes of man and God; and once we have properly understood the title in its relation to the context of the novel, we shall be in a position to see exactly what the author intended when he remarked recently of *All the King's Men:* "The book . . . was never intended to be a book about politics. Politics merely provided the framework story in which the deeper concerns, whatever their final significance, might work themselves out."[2]

According to the generally accepted interpretation, "the King" in

James Ruoff, "Humpty Dumpty and *All the King's Men:* A Note on Robert Penn Warren's Teleology," *Twentieth Century Literature,* III (October 1957), 128–134. Reprinted by permission of the author and the publisher.

[1] See James Magmer, "Robert Penn Warren's Quest for an Angel," *Catholic World,* CLXXXIII (1956), 178–83; Robert White, "Robert Penn Warren and the Myth of the Garden," *Faulkner Studies,* III (1954), 59–67; J. Letargeez, "Robert Penn Warren's Views of History," *Revue des Langues Vivantes, XXII* (1956), 533–43.

[2] Introduction, *All the King's Men* (Modern Library, 1953), vi.

All the King's Men is the protagonist Willie Stark, an interpretation which derives from the fact Willie is governor of the state, a man the other characters in the novel refer to as "the Boss." "The King's Men," on the other hand, are assumed to be all the people who in one way or another serve the Boss—Jack Burden, Willie's research man; Tiny Duffy, the lieutenant governor; Sugar Boy, Willie's bodyguard, etc. Then, too, there are "the King's women," the mistresses of the governor's palace—Sadie Burke, Anne Stanton, Willie's wife Lucy. As tidy as this interpretation undoubtedly is, something more than a casual reading of the story will show Willie Stark was never intended to be "the King" in *All the King's Men,* and that the title of the novel has a meaning more significant than critics have hitherto realized.

There are a number of reasons why Willie Stark cannot be "the King" in *All the King's Men.* There is, first, the nursery rhyme from which the title was derived: Willie is Humpty Dumpty, not "King." Like Humpty Dumpty, Willie "sat on a wall" when he rose to become governor and "had a great fall" when shot down by Adam Stanton. Willie is, like his legendary counterpart, a synthetic creation, a grotesque composite of the abstract needs of the people who have shaped him. As Warren has pointed out, Willie's "power was based on the fact that somehow he could vicariously fulfill the secret needs of the people about him."[3] Hence the principal characters in *All the King's Men,* like Mr. Munn in Warren's *Night Rider* (1939), attempt to find themselves by merging their identities with another person. In Willie Stark[128] the people of the state satisfy their craving for justice—hence Willie's easy political slogan "Your need is my justice"—while to the narrator, Jack Burden, Willie fulfills Jack's need of a father, his need of the purpose and direction and decisive authority which have been lacking in his aimless life. To Adam Stanton, "the man of idea" who eventually destroys him, Willie represents the concrete power to accomplish the idealistic, humanitarian good which Adam has dedicated his whole life to achieve. In short, it is an obvious truism to say that to Sadie Burke, to Anne Stanton—to virtually every character in the novel —Willie Stark represents the fulfillment of some secret compulsion, some indigenous shortcoming or incompleteness, and in this sense, most of all, Willie is Humpty Dumpty—an artificial composite of the needs inherent in the society which has created him. After Willie's assassination Tiny Duffy performs the futile ritual of attempting to put Humpty Dumpty "back together again" when he seeks to employ Jack Burden, Sadie Burke, and Sugar Boy, Willie Stark's political aides.

But if Willie Stark is Humpty Dumpty, who then is king? In view of the nursery rhyme it is difficult to see how Willie can be Humpty Dumpty and king, too. Part of a solution to our problem is to be found in Warren's introduction to the Modern Library Edition, where

---

3 Introduction, p. i.

he states that in *All the King's Men* he tried to "avoid writing a straight naturalistic novel, the kind of novel the material so readily invited." By the phrase "straight naturalistic novel" Warren apparently intended the bleakly deterministic and materialistic novel which portrays its characters as being merely biological organisms attracted and repelled by hereditary or environmental forces over which they have no control. As we shall see, the "material" of *All the King's Men* "readily invited" a novel of this description, for there is a temptation to think of Willie Stark as an ineluctable demi-urge riding the beast of the people to their moral collapse while the rider himself is pulled to destruction by a gloomy necessity. And yet one of Warren's main problems in writing *All the King's Men* was, I think, to avoid any implications of determinism, to establish a sure balance between the fact of Willie's diabolic attraction for others and the fact of their free wills; for it was essential to Warren's moral purpose, to his whole concept of man, that his characters exercise free will, that Willie Stark remain, after all, only Humpty Dumpty and not king—not Necessity, not God. In Warren's teleology only God is King, and we are all of us "all the King's men."

God is not only King but absolute monarch informing every moment of life with His purposive Will, and this predestination, which under Warren's hand becomes something quite different from determinism of a theological order, is "the material" that "readily invited" what Warren calls "the straight naturalistic novel," the novel which, in the tradition of Zola and Crane and Dreiser, is informed by biological necessitarianism and psychological behaviorism. This naturalistic tradition is emphatically repudiated in *All the King's Men* when determinism, a chief characteristic of "the straight naturalistic novel," is sardonically labeled "The Big Twitch" by Jack Burden, who abjures it as totally inadequate to explain the events that take place in the story. The philosophy Jack Burden does come to accept, however, is one which has to do with the enigmatic paradox of Christianity—the omnipotence of God and the moral[129] responsibility of man. And if at the end of the novel Jack's acceptance of this view of life is not without some reservations, we must remember that the paradox is baffling, is one that derives not from a spontaneous rational acquiescence but from a hard discipline of faith.

If omnipotent God has power over everything, how can man be said to have responsibility for anything? *All the King's Men* confronts this question cautiously, with a full cognizance of the critical tensions created by Darwin, Marx, Freud, and the holocaust of two world wars. From these spirit-shattering, enervating experiences, we must preserve, Warren tells us, what is most distinctive, significant and compelling about man, his consciousness and spirituality. According to Warren, man has moral choice, lives in an "agony of will," but, paradoxically, he has no choice, no power whatever, in the consequences of his moral life. To put it another way, in Original Sin—which looms darkly in the background of all Warren's novels from *Night Rider* to *Band of Angels*—Adam and Eve devoured a fruit of agony when they ate of the Tree of the Knowledge of Good and Evil, for in that fatal act they took upon themselves the knowledge of what was right and wrong, and consequently the responsibility for their actions; but they were denied the divinity which Satan had promised them, the power to transcend time and perceive, as God perceives, the ultimate consequences of good and evil. (In Milton's *Paradise Lost*, for example, a travesty on those supernal powers promised to Adam and Eve by Satan is implicit when Michael comes to inform them of the Atonement, of the *real* consequences of the Fall which only God can know.)

Ironically, then, the Fall simultaneously gave man moral vision and struck him blind: it gave him an immediate, a priori knowledge of good and evil as it related to any moral decision, to any incoherent fact, but it left him blind to the ultimate purpose or direction or consequences of the fact. As an individual, he is the master of his soul in a moment of crucial moral decision; as a species, he is a pawn in a cosmic game the ultimate meaning or purpose of which he can never know. In *All the King's Men* Hugh Miller expresses the human viewpoint, indeed the only view man has capacity for, when he remarks at the end of the novel that "History is blind, but man is not."

This concept of history as a fleeting montage of seemingly purposeless causes and effects, of good and evil events so complex and confoundingly intermingled that man cannot perceive the *ultimate* good or evil of anything, is profoundly confirmed in *All the King's Men*. Several years before the story of Willie Stark unfolds, Judge Irwin accepted a bribe which Irwin's friend Jack Burden uncovers in one of his investigations as Willie Stark's research man. This bribe, a completely voluntary act, sets off a chain reaction of mediate causes and effects. First, her discovery that her father concealed Irwin's crime so disillusions Anne Stanton that she becomes Willie Stark's mistress, while her brother Adam so modifies his militant idealism that he agrees to accept Willie's offer of the directorship of the Willie Stark Memorial Hospital. When Adam learns of Anne's affair, he assassinates Willie. But Irwin's bribe has even more far-reaching consequences. Jack's discovery of the bribe leads to Irwin's suicide, to Jack's realization that Irwin is his real father, to a reconciliation of Jack and his estranged mother. Was Judge Irwin's crime an evil? Although Warren is neither a weak-headed immoralist[130] nor a sentimental relativist, his answer remains ambiguous. For his crime Irwin suffers guilt, repentance, absolution by atonement, just as do the other characters, whose particular crimes have been the indirect result of Irwin's: Jack Burden for uncovering Irwin's bribe, Anne Stanton for her adulterous relationship with Willie, Sadie Burke for her malicious jealousy of Anne and betrayal of Willie, and Lucy Stark for her pride of virtue and weakness of mind. Irwin's crime is evil because it results in the destruction of Willie, of Adam, of Irwin himself, and yet it has the undeniably good effects of saving Mrs. Burden's soul, of uniting her with her son, of bringing together Anne and Jack, and finally—if the reader chooses to remain skeptical of Willie's deathbed assurance that "things might have been different"—of freeing the people of the state from the grip of an unscrupulous demagogue. Hence Judge Irwin's crime and its results confirm what Jack Burden describes as the "moral neutrality of history." As an isolated, incoherent fact it is evil, but as a part of history, as one stitch in a complex, variegated tapestry, it has shades of both good and evil.

Willie Stark expresses a profound truth when he insists through- ⁁ out the novel that good must come from evil because "evil is all you have to work with," while Adam Stanton, the more conventionally "noble" of the two, lives a dangerous error when he arbitrarily separates people and events into moral categories. The point is made by Jack Burden at the conclusion of the story: "As a student of history, Jack Burden could see that Adam Stanton, whom he came to call the man of idea, and Willie Stark, whom he came to call the man of fact, were doomed to destroy each other, just as each was doomed to try to use the other and to yearn toward and try to become the other, because each was incomplete with the terrible division of their age."[4] Willie brings about his own destruction when he tries to be like Adam, when, like "the man of idea" that he is not, he sets out to create something which is completely devoid of evil. Inconsistent with his own philosophy that any good there is must come from evil, Willie dreams of building a magnificent hospital that will stand as the purely good achievement of his political administration, and yet, unknown to Willie, the hospital is tainted by evil in the moment of its conception, for the idea of the hospital is really the result of Willie's unconscious effort to compensate for the guilt he feels in protecting from prosecution his corrupt state auditor, Byram B. White. The hospital becomes an instrument of Willie's downfall when he refuses to permit the venal Gummy Larson from having the contract to construct it, when he refuses, in other words, to allow the good he dreams of achieving to be contaminated by evil, and this refusal prompts Tiny Duffy to inform Adam of Willie's affair with Anne. In shooting Willie Stark, Adam becomes himself "the man of fact," acknowledging Willie's

---

4 Page 462. In a recent article, Norman Kelvin argues that there is no basis for Warren's distinction between Willie as "the man of fact" and Adam Stanton as "the man of idea": "The Willie Stark we met in the novel was as much a man of ideas as was the puritanical, compulsive Dr. Stanton. They merely held to *different* ideas, and while some of Willie's were outrageous, so were some of Adam's." But this appears to be a very literal reading of what, after all, is only a pair of arbitrary metaphors. It matters not, really, what phrases Warren employs to describe Willie and Adam so long as we recognize his meaning.

dictum that the end justifies the means, but more than that, he proclaims by his act that he has God's knowledge, a final knowledge of good and evil. In his arrogant effort to usurp divinity, Adam repeats the folly of the Fall.

The fact that Willie's hospital is never built underscores man's tragic limitations. Confined to a tenuous reality of isolated facts, hemmed in by illusory absolutes of good and evil, man cannot perceive the transcendent reality, the ultimate moral purpose and direction of life. Willie, "the man of fact," thinks he knows how things really are, and Adam Stanton, "the man of idea," thinks he knows[131] how things ought to be, but both are incomplete, both presumptuous. So man lives on one moral level of reality, where he suffers an "agony of will," of personal responsibility, and God exists on another, the level of "history" or "direction," a level unknown to man, who yearns toward the fulfillment of some ideal good which in the "moral neutrality of history" has no objective existence.[5] On God's level, good and evil are not as inseparable as man persists in making them. What man conceives as a completed moral action is, in God's omniscient comprehension, merely another phase in man's continuous struggle to create some good in a fallen world he only faintly understands. Warren's concept of man as a fallen, debased, limited, and therefore heroic, creature working out moral decisions in an "agony of will" yet oblivious to the eventual good or evil of those decisions is one which recalls St. Augustine and medieval nominalists like Duns Scotus (the analogues of Warren's Puritanism), who stressed God's awful power and mystery, and man's irrationality and impotence. Like these medieval nominalists who reacted against the liberal rationalism of the Scholastics, Warren has repudiated the optimistic rationalism of the liberal reformers, just as he has repudiated their scientism and materialism—what Jack Burden refers to as "the dream of our age."

In *All the King's Men* man finds solace not in the liberal experience, not in the nineteenth-century dream of power through reason, but in the more ancient Christian experience of humility, repentance and hope; for Warren sees this world as a Dantesque purgatory where man works out his salvation by a process of transgression, acknowledgement of guilt, and contrition. Every character in *All the King's Men* who is worth saving eventually submits to this tortuous ritual of life: Cass Mastern, Judge Irwin, Willie Stark, Jack Burden, Mrs. Burden, Sadie Burke, and Anne Stanton. Tiny Duffy, like his friend Gummy Larson, is a mere shade, an abstraction, while Adam Stanton,

---

[5] In a very interesting article ("The Meaning of Robert Penn Warren's Novels," *Kenyon Review*, X [Summer, 1948], 417), Eric Bentley describes Warren as "utterly empirical." This is of course true; nevertheless, Professor Bentley does not appear to be sufficiently aware of how in Warren's novels the facts of experience and Christian orthodoxy coalesce. Of how, in other words, empiricism confirms Warren's essentially Christian philosophy of life.

paradoxically the "noblest" character in the novel, is, by the fact of his fierce and intransigent pride in virtue, quite beyond all hope of redemption. For the remainder of the characters in *All the King's Men*, however, the epigraph to the novel applies. Appropriately, the epigraph to *All the King's Men* is Manfred's tortured cry of hope in Canto III of Dante's *Purgatorio:* "Mentre che la speranze ha fior del verde."

As if to turn back at the end of the novel to interpret his story, Warren spells out these ideas about God and man in a religious tract dictated to Jack by Ellis Burden:[6]

> The creation of man whom God in His foreknowledge knew doomed to sin was an awful index of God's omnipotence. For it would have been a thing of trifling and contemptible ease for Perfection to create mere perfection. To do so would, to speak truth, be not creation but extension. Separateness is identity and the only way for God to create, truly create, man was to make him separate from God Himself, and to be separate from God is to be sinful. The creation of evil is therefore the index of God's glory and His power. But by His help. By His help and in His wisdom. (462–463/*437*)

Jack Burden tentatively concurs in Ellis Burden's credo. "I did so to keep his mind untroubled," he says, "but later I was not certain that in my own way I did not believe what he had said." Jack's statement, although not an unqualified affirmation, is nevertheless a long step away from his earlier cynicism and philosophical determinism.[132] It signifies a gradual awakening of Jack's spirituality, the beginning of an unconscious application of Cass Mastern's story to his own tragic experience in life. In his diary, which Jack had studied but could not understand until his own experiences confirmed its views, Cass Mastern had written: "I do not question the Justice of God, that others have suffered for my sin, for it may be that only by the suffering of the innocent does God affirm that men are brothers in His Holy Name" (199/*187*). Cass Mastern sees the world as a vast spider web of intersecting lives: "Your happy foot or your gay wing may have brushed it ever so lightly, but what happens always happens and there is the spider, bearded black and with his great faceted eyes glittering like mirrors in the sun, *or like God's eye,* and the fangs dripping" (200/*189;* italics mine).

Because the Cass Mastern episode was printed as an independent story before the publication of *All the King's Men*, some critics have been quick to regard it as an extraneous feature, as a brilliant but

---

6 I am not suggesting that Ellis Burden is a mouthpiece through which Warren expresses his views, nor that this religious tract is a violation of the novel's dramatic integrity. Ellis Burden is a fully developed, integrated character, and his tract does have a certain dramatic inevitability. Nevertheless, Ellis Burden and, to a less extent perhaps, Hugh Miller function in a way reminiscent of a Sophoclean chorus: they may have their etiology in Warren's pseudo-Greek drama *Proud Flesh*, which, written in 1938, was the germinal beginning of *All the King's Men*.

irrelevant *tour de force,* and yet, as Eric Bentley has pointed out, it is really Warren's effort to "put the whole theme of a work into one short and strongly symbolic interlude."[7] It supplies not only an inverted contrast to Jack's own story, a contrast between a crime of commission and one of omission, but plainly underlines the dominant themes of the omnipotence of God, and the utter helplessness and brotherhood of men. Cass Mastern tripped the gossamer threads of the spider web when he seduced his best friend's wife; Judge Irwin when he accepted the bribe; Willie Stark when he refrained from prosecuting Byram B. White; and Jack Burden when he revealed the truth about Irwin. That Jack comes to accept Cass Mastern's view of the world is suggested when he observes toward the end of the story that "each of us is the son of a million fathers" (462/436), but more pointedly, when Jack, who has always been lashed by a compulsion to seek and reveal the truth, tells his mother an outright lie rather than impart to her the cause of Irwin's suicide, and when he lies to Sugar Boy rather than name the man who was indirectly responsible for Willie Stark's death. On both occasions Jack's prevarication, like Marlow's lie to Kurtz's Intended in Conrad's *Heart of Darkness,* is an honest man's acknowledgement and atonement. Now sharing Cass Mastern's vision of the world as a web of humanity, Jack dares not assume responsibility for awakening the drowsy spider. He has come to see the brotherhood of men and the universality of guilt.

To assume, then, that Willie Stark is "the King" in *All the King's Men* is to ignore the meaningful symbolism of the title, to lose sight of Warren's basic idea. As I have attempted to show, *All the King's Men* portrays a world which Willie could not have ruled; for in that world of Warren's thoughtful creation there is but one King and we are all of us "all the King's men." From first to last, Willie Stark is but Humpty Dumpty, whose fall is a form of triumph for those who survive him. As Ellis Burden states in another context, "Separateness is identity," and with the death of Willie those who involved their identities in him must find completion within themselves or not at all. As in any great tragedy, there is loss, there is gain: they have lost Willie but have gained the power to find themselves. It may not be a coincidence, therefore, that the conclusion to *All the King's Men* is reminiscent of the ending to another great tragedy as Jack Burden

<hr>

[7] "The Meaning of Robert Penn Warren's Novels," 415–16. It ought to be mentioned, however, that the Cass Mastern episode is not completely successful. For one thing, it invites comparison with the adulterous relationship between Irwin and Mrs. Burden rather than with the Platonic romance of Jack and Anne. Hence at the end of the novel Warren felt it necessary to have Jack Burden point out that Judge Irwin bears no resemblance to Cass Mastern: "For Judge Irwin and Cass Mastern do not resemble each other very closely. If Judge Irwin resembles any Mastern it is Gilbert, the granite-headed brother of Cass" (p. 464).

and Anne Stanton,[133] like Adam and Eve departing from the Garden after the Fall, prepare to leave Burden's Landing forever to "go into the convulsion of the world, out of history into history and the awful responsibility of Time."[134]

ROMANTICISM AND REALITY

Joseph Frank

Robert Penn Warren is a highly self-conscious writer, not only a novelist of elemental power but one of our best literary critics as well. It can be taken for granted, then, that when Mr. Warren chose a fragment from a famous poem as the title of his latest novel, *World Enough and Time,* he did so because there was more than a casual relation between the two; and perhaps the best way to approach the book is to examine the poem for a moment. The poem, of course, is Andrew Marvell's "To His Coy Mistress," and the title is from the first line: "Had we but world enough, and time." In the poem, a lover tells his coy mistress that he would, if he could, devote an impossible eternity to her courtship:

> An hundred years should go to praise
> Thine eyes, and on thy forehead gaze;
> Two hundred to adore each breast;
> But thirty thousand to the rest.

However, he argues quite cogently that death would intervene in this happy arrangement before the courtship would have any palpable results; and this being so, he urges his mistress to recognize the facts of life: "Now let us sport us while we may."

The poem, thus, is based on the antinomy between the desire for an impossible ideal of courtly love—a properly Romantic ideal—and a recognition of the implacable barriers in our poor human lot that make this ideal self-defeating; it reveals the contradiction, the necessary conflict, between the world and the idea. This is the conflict at the heart of Mr. Warren's latest novel, and it is because the protagonist cannot

From Joseph Frank, "Romanticism and Reality in Robert Penn Warren," *Hudson Review,* IV (Summer 1951), 248–257. Reprinted by permission of the author and the publisher.

face it with the good-humored worldliness of Marvell that Mr. Warren has subtitled the book: a Romantic novel.

To be sure, this is not the first time that Mr. Warren has been occupied with Romanticism. The literary group out of which he sprang, the Southern Agrarians, fought a constant critical battle against both the theory and practice of literary Romanticism; and Mr. Warren in particular, in a well-known essay, spoke out in favor of an "impure poetry" capable of assimilating the tough complexities of experience. Poetic unity, Mr. Warren argued, should not be achieved by glossing over those obstinately "unpoetic" aspects of reality that are an inevitable part of human experience. The Romantic poet, in Mr. Warren's view, tries to "strain nature out of nature," abstracting one aspect of an experience—for example, the spiritual aspects of love—and calling this the[248] total experience. Against Shelley's "I arise from dreams of thee" Mr. Warren cites the garden scene from *Romeo and Juliet*, in which Mercutio utters ribald obscenities as the lovers declaim their passion in pure Platonic accents; and we can take this passion seriously, according to Mr. Warren, only because it can survive the corrosive effects of Mercutio's "realism." As an artist, Mr. Warren is deeply concerned with "the context in which, and the terms by which, faith and ideals [can] be earned." In a much larger framework—a framework no longer of esthetic but of ethical and, ultimately, of metaphysical commitments—the same concern plays a major part in Mr. Warren's novels.

This is not the place, however, to examine all of Mr. Warren's novels from such a point of view. But without going back beyond *All the King's Men,* we can see how this notion of Romanticism has already entered Mr. Warren's work. In this book, Adam Stanton is explicitly called "a Romantic"; he "has a picture of the world in his head, and when the world doesn't conform in any respect to this picture, he wants to throw the world away." It is the cynical and worldly-wise Jack Burden who makes this comment, but in his own hard-boiled way Jack Burden is just as much of a Romantic as Adam Stanton. For even though Jack is up to his neck in the off-color politics of Willie Stark, the measure of his Romanticism is precisely the extent of his ironical detachment from the events in which he takes part. He refuses, in other words, to accept the full responsibility of his participation; no more than Adam Stanton can Jack Burden—at least until the very end of the novel—accept in any true sense the "impure" reality of the world that confronts him; but while Adam Stanton, the pure Romantic, revenges himself on reality by committing murder and being murdered in turn, Jack Burden succeeds in forming a "new picture of the world" which, in leading him to accept his own guilt, simultaneously causes him to forgive the guilt of others. By transcending his Romanticism in this way, Jack Burden "earns" the faith and ideals—however chastened and unassuming they may be—which permit him once more to "go into the awful convulsions of the world."

In *All the King's Men*, the character of Willie Stark poses the problem of Romanticism and "conversion to the real," so to speak, in still other terms. Willie Stark is defined as the "man of fact," who, presumably, manipulates the "impure" reality of the world with a fine disregard for the moral problems that weigh on both Jack Burden and Adam Stanton; but Willie becomes this "man of fact" only after he finds he has been played for a sucker, and that high ideals are not enough to combat political corruption. This is what impels Willie to abandon his wide-eyed innocence about political realities—also a form of Romanticism—and makes him decide to beat the politicians at their own game. And so Willie, too, is converted to the "impurities" of the real; his tragedy is that, at least until it is too late, he accepts it without self-reflection,[249] without the humility and the guilt that make Jack Burden's acceptance a true reconciliation of the dualism between "pure" and "impure" reality. We have, then, in *All the King's Men* three levels of relation between Romanticism and reality: the total rejection of Adam Stanton, the total acceptance of Willie Stark, and the transcendence of the dualism in the moral evolution of Jack Burden. . . .[250]

THE CONSERVATIVE QUEST

Chester E. Eisinger

In *All the King's Men*, Warren emerges from apprenticeship and brings his many characteristic themes together in one of the most distinguished novels of the period. Politics is the framework for his story, and amid the thrust and surge of the public scene where a great, virtually omnipotent political boss takes and wields his power Warren weaves his complex of beliefs. The end of man is to know, he demonstrates. What man seeks is the knowledge of good and evil, and the knowledge of truth, and out of these, self-knowledge. But man's way is hard, not simply because truth is elusive, but because it has

From Chester E. Eisinger, "Robert Penn Warren: The Conservative Quest for Identity," in *Fiction of the Forties*. University of Chicago Press, 1963. Pp. 198–229. Reprinted by permission of the author and the publisher. © 1963 by Chester E. Eisinger.

different shapes for different men, who are all the victims of the modern world and of their own self-division. Man's way is hard because he must come to the painful recognition of what he is as man, which takes him apart from and enables him to transcend nature. Since man exists in time, however, he has history, and history may help him to find the truth and to understand the world. The past may reclaim for a man the present and give him a world he can understand and live in. The past may give a man his father and his mother, and giving them, it may release him to live in the world and understand himself.

If these are the themes to be discovered in the novel, we are prepared to consider sympathetically Warren's contention that Huey Long did nothing more than suggest Willie Stark. Yet I suspect that Warren's comment was prompted by tactical considerations: he wished to give the authority of his own voice to the repudiation of a purely political reading of his novel. A sound enough purpose. But the social scene, Warren and his *Sewanee Review* champions notwithstanding, has the largest kind of meaning for this novel. I do not speak of the class tensions that are present and exploited by Willie in the conflicts between aristocracy and rednecks. Nor even of Jack Burden's treason to his own class at Burden's Landing when he allies himself with Willie,[214] the cocklebur candidate whose economic policies are a threat and an affront to the well-born and the well-to-do. (Although Jack's dilemma, the conflict in social and political loyalties, is instructive, because the resolution of such a dilemma is a step on the road toward self-knowledge. . . .) What I am saying is that the social-political scene, aside from its intrinsic value for movement and interest in the novel, is the indispensable background for working out the view of man's character and destiny that Warren wishes to set before us. All the ideas in the novel, then, are in a sense socially oriented, for they have their reality, not as abstractions which emerge as valid for Warren or Jack, but as strands in the fabric of social interaction. The obvious should not be overlooked: men in life are political creatures, living in society among other men and by institutions created by men and according to moral standards conceived by men and preserved for their use as a social heritage; and it is equally obvious that the actions and beliefs of such men are the raw materials of fiction. *All the King's Men*, to be sure, is not the story of a dictator. But that story, like the story of Jack's social dilemma, takes its place in the novel to say something about the nature of man, about man and human history, about man's morality, so that what Warren finally achieves is an integrated view of man *and* the world he lives in.

The totality of that view can be formulated in terms of the Hegelian dialectic. Men are good, like Adam Stanton, Hugh Miller, the Scholarly Attorney, or Lucy Stark; these characters may stand for thesis. And men are totally bad (depraved would not be an inaccurate term here), like Tiny Duffy and Byram White; these characters are the antithesis. And men are mixed, like Willie Stark and Judge Irwin, and finally Jack Burden himself; they are the synthesis. Everyone in the first two groups, with one possible exception, is incomplete. In the last group Willie, with the potentials of indivisibility within his grasp, gives way to a fatal yearning for absolute good, in violation of his intrinsic character and beliefs. Judge Irwin dies to preserve the successful synthesis as he had lived by it. Jack, alone of the last group, survives to embody the final understanding and acceptance of this position, this acceptance of good and evil, this burden of an optimum condition of life which is at best only a set of provisional resolutions.[215]

Adam Stanton makes the fullest statement of the thesis. He is a brilliant surgeon and the son of a former governor. He wants to do good. But he is appalled by the world when it does not conform to his picture of what it ought to be. Since for him all politics is dirty, he holds aloof out of a spirit of moral fastidiousness that is absolute. The structure of his moral ideas, while it is simple, is nonetheless appropriate to the rational and scientific mind. Morality, for him, is as orderly, straightforward, and predictable as physical laws. Because he cannot stay aloof and because he cannot, in his simple-minded morality, cope with the evil in the world, he consummates his life in violence, which is usually the end of uncompromising principle and undeviating rationalism (a lesson Warren might have learned from the French Revolution as Burke did). Faced with the charge that he was made director of Willie's hospital because Willie is sleeping with his sister, Adam's only possible response is murder. He kills Willie in the capital and is in turn shot down. They were doomed to destroy each other, Warren says, because they were two halves of each other: Adam the man of idea and Willie the man of fact.

Hugh Miller, Willie's attorney general, also takes a straight-line view of morality. He believes that if a man is guilty of malfeasance in public office, such a man should be prosecuted and condemned. When Willie saves Byram White, who is certainly guilty, Hugh resigns. Willie saves Byram because he has to use the Byrams of this world and because he cannot permit the opposition to use Byram, i.e., to bring his administration into bad odor by revealing Byram's corruption. Willie has to stay in power in order to bring his conception of good to his people and his state. He is acting in accordance with a moral idea, but it has not the rigidity of Hugh's absolutism. Hugh has the satisfaction of intact principles, but he surrenders the public arena in which he might display them. Willie is still in power fighting to bring into effect his vision of good despite the evil that surrounds it.

The Scholarly Attorney, Ellis Burden, is another good man who, unable to cope with the evil of the world, withdraws from it. When he discovers that he is not Jack's father, he leaves his wife. He becomes a religious fanatic and undergoes a perpetual debasement of the self, losing his individuality in the lives of others. His position is ultimately life-denying and cowardly, resting[216] as it does on the failure of the world to conform to his subjective notion of reality.

Lucy Stark disturbs a little the schematization here established, for if she is incomplete in her attachment to the simple verities, she is nevertheless close to irreproachability. She and Miller represent two varieties of simplistic morality; hers is a naïve, stubborn, biblical, folk honesty which has all the strength, and some of the limitations, of Hebraism. She tells Willie that if he protects Byram White she will leave him, and she is as good as her word. When her son promiscuously fathers a child, she takes it unquestioningly, exchanging her love for its innocence. When her son is seriously injured, she rejoins her husband, understanding that the great crises of parenthood, the crises of life and death, supersede differences in moral evaluations. Before her adherence to a given code, an adherence where the cost in pain and responsibility is always hers and no one else's, loyalty to Willie's realistic, ambiguous morality must blush.

The characters who are evil are nothing, as Percy Munn was nothing. Willie says of Byram White that he is a thing, less than a man. He has no inner essence, but is, in his being, what Willie tells him to be. The same is true of Tiny Duffy, who, as Willie's campaign manager during the first gubernatorial campaign, was a part of the double-cross that victimized Willie. After Willie breaks the Harrison organization to which Tiny had belonged, he permits Tiny to join him. He makes Tiny his creature so that Tiny's success is a measure of Willie's. Tiny is the complete politician, the very stereotype of the pig in the trough; as Willie's other self, Tiny provides an outlet for Willie's self-contempt. It is Tiny who, frustrated in the pursuit of that graft which is natural to his species, sets Adam on Willie. The irony is that a man who is nothing should kill the man who gives him substance and animates him. But I must say, parenthetically, that Tiny is not alone in this, for like the death of the Swede in "The Blue Hotel," many people must share that responsibility.

Among them, Willie himself. Warren is not altogether fair to Willie when he describes him, in the "Introduction" to *All the King's Men,* as "the politician [who] rises to power because of the faculty of fulfilling vicariously the secret needs of others, and in the process . . . discovers his own emptiness." What Willie so[217] fatally discovers is the lure of the absolute. All through the novel, from the time of his great drunk during his first campaign to the moment when he decides to build his hospital, Willie lives with the stern knowledge that good must come out of evil, and the evil it comes out of is man, who is conceived in sin and born in corruption and passes from the stink of the didie to the stench of the shroud (for Willie, it must never be forgotten, went to a Presbyterian Sunday school). Willie knows that men cannot go into the world without getting the dirt of the world upon them or the poison of it under their skin. He knows that the government of his state is made up half of slaves and half of sons of bitches. But he tells the mobs, who listen raptly, your will is my strength, your need is my justice, and he is not at all sure that this is demagoguery. Warren gives us in Willie a brooding, thoughtful man of destiny with a sense of the mystery of life. He is a man who, as he sat studying law, felt growing inside himself, painfully and imperceptibly, his own world. Out of his reflection comes a conception of good and an understanding of how at least limited good can be imposed on people. And of how means, even evil means, must be adapted to good ends. Knowing all these things, Willie inexplicably sets them aside. He decides to build a hospital that shall be a memorial to purity and a justification for his political chicanery. It is his expiation. It is the sacrifice he offers to placate the stern Hebraic God whom he cannot, after all, escape. This inconsistency—the knowledge that good comes out of evil but the refusal to let Duffy (who is certainly evil) negotiate the usual crooked deal in the construction of the hospital—leads to Willie's death. Warren has said that Willie was corrupted by power, even power exercised against corruption. The statement is true enough. But it seems to me also to be the case that Willie could not live with the truth he had discerned. He could not accept finally the mixed nature of man and things.

Judge Irwin, in many ways Willie's most formidable political opponent, is the living demonstration of Willie's theories about the nature of man and ethics. His aristocratic appearance of unimpeachable probity does not deter Willie from ordering Jack to get something on the judge, because there is always something. Jack finds it. Irwin had once taken a bribe when he was broke. When Jack tries to use this knowledge to force the judge to call[218] off a political offensive against Willie, the judge commits suicide. He does not swerve from his principles when confronted with an impossible situation. He does not use the fact that he is Jack's father to persuade Jack to call off the attack. He had been a good judge and he had done good. But he knew, like a Russian that Warren may have had in mind, that you have to break eggs to make an omelette. He had been a strong man and he had broken plenty. He had cuckolded his friend and betrayed his own wife. He had taken a bribe and driven a man to suicide. Warren's point is that good and evil are intertwined, but it must be pointed out that there is no necessary connection in the judge's case between the good he does and the evil. Irwin is simply an illustration of the proposition that, in the nature of things, man achieves good despite himself.

The only completely successful synthesis is achieved by Jack Burden. It is not simply that he survives, but that he is reborn, as Norton Girault has so cogently argued. Or that, to use Joseph Frank's formulation, Jack transcends the good and evil of reality to reach a dualism which caps his moral evolution. Jack succeeds in reconciling good and evil because his synthesis is on a grand scale: he brings together history and time, knowledge and self-knowledge, apparent truth and real truth. His synthesis is his maturation as it is Warren's resolution of the problems raised by the novel.

Jack is the narrator of the novel, and very close to the beginning he gets at its ironic center. "The end of man is knowledge," he observes, "but there is one thing he can't know. He can't know whether knowledge will save him or kill him. He will be killed, all right, but he can't know whether he is killed because of the knowledge which he has got or because of the knowledge which he hasn't got and which if he had it, would save him ... the end of man is to know" (12/9). Jack's struggle is to know himself, but in order to do this he must work out a means of knowing and he must understand the past. In college he believes in Idealism, which holds that if you did not know a thing or recognize it, it did not exist. He persists in this epistemological sub-jectivism well into the novel. If you think you are sorry, then you are, he tells Anne Stanton, and that's an end to it. He will discover that objective truth exists, and when it is uncovered, he will know with[219] finality whether he is sorry or not. When he discovers the truth about his father, that makes a real difference in how he thinks and feels. Warren is concerned to show that part of the maturation of Jack is the shucking off of this Idealism, which is the heresy of the self and which cripples the human capacity to deal with reality.

As a student of history, Jack makes two extensive excursions into the past. The first, a failure, is a doctoral dissertation which convinces Jack that if the human race never remembered anything it would be happy. He will revise this judgment when he comes to understand the meaning of his materials. These are the adultery and expiation of Cass Mastern during the Civil War. And the meaning is that the world is one, and to be in the world is to be evil, for evil is a function of living. What is seen in the story of Cass is seen and reinforced in Jack's story.

The second investigation into the past is the one that reveals Judge Irwin as a bribe-taker and Governor Stanton, the judge's friend, as an accessory to the crime. It is successful in the sense that Jack finds what Willie has asked him to find. It is successful because it yields Jack a father and a mother. When the judge kills himself, Jack's mother, a woman he has despised, tells him that Irwin was his real father. Jack has, then, in one blow, found his father and killed him. These are the fruits of the pursuit of truth. Later, his mother summons Jack to Burden's Landing. This much-married lady tells him she is leaving her present husband because she knows now that she always loved the judge. When she does this, she gives Jack back the past, "... which I had before felt was tainted and horrible. I could accept the past now because I could accept her and be at peace with her and with myself" (458/432). In killing his father, accepting and loving his mother, Jack is liberated. He is freed for love and marriage to Anne; together they may go forth into the convulsion of the world, shed of their innocence, like Adam and Eve walking hand in hand out of Milton's paradise.

For the past and the future are forever tied together, and "we can keep the past only by having the future" (329/311). Self-trust gives us the confidence to live in the future; having such confidence, we need not live in the past. Warren wants his characters to take account of the past but not to be bound to it. This attitude toward the[220] past, linked to Jack's growth toward self-knowledge, is illustrated in the episode at Burden's Landing when Jack undresses Anne in his room but fails to sleep with her. He fears to destroy the meaning of the idyllic summer that they have had; in fact, he is afraid for their total past as companions. Such a need for the past exists for the immature man who does not understand himself and does not know where he is going. The sentimental view of the past paralyzes action. And not knowing who he is, he does not know how to act. The deepest meaning of this episode lies in the paralysis it reveals. But another meaning may be discerned as Jack rationalizes his behavior, hiding from his own identity. With Anne lying on his bed, he suddenly says, we can't, it isn't right. His explanation for his failure is that he was noble. But if he had slept with Anne, they would probably have been married, and then she would not have become Willie's mistress later on. My nobility, he says, had as dire a consequence as Cass Mastern's sin. I suspect that Warren wants us to see the irony here as a valid manifestation of the ambiguous relationship of good and evil and at the same time to see Jack's rationalization for what it is.

The maturation process in Jack consists in large part in his learning to accept and absorb such ironies in which apparent evil comes out of apparent good, to accept the notion that the discovery of the truth is more often than not calamitous. Early in the novel, in a conversation with Anne, he is confident about grasping the plain truth, as he talks about why Ellis Burden, his putative father, left his mother. In the event, it turns out that Jack did not know the reason or have the truth at all. The truth about Jack's father, when it is discovered, leads to the death of his father, as I have already said. Pursuing the truth about Judge Irwin, Jack reveals to Adam and Anne that their father had helped Irwin to take the bribe. Later, when Jack asks Anne why she is sleeping with Willie, she says because she loves him and because there was no reason not to once she had heard about her father. The truth has destroyed an image of moral integrity by which Anne had lived. Jack thinks, I only told her the truth, and from this truth has come this sin, this adultery.

Hard-boiled Jack Burden, armed with a mucker-pose, finds it excruciatingly painful to deal with the complexities he has uncovered. He throws up a series of defenses, all of them escapes[221] from the self-knowledge that will ultimately be forced upon him, or obstacles to it.

These are the ways, Girault says, in which he resists being reborn. These are the Great Sleep, the Great Twitch, and the flight to the West. Jack's response to crisis is withdrawal—when, for instance, he loses his job; or flight—when he learns that Anne is sleeping with Willie. But he always returns, to consciousness or to home. The Great Sleep is an induced and deliberate failure of consciousness which makes it impossible to continue pursuit of the truth; it may be a withdrawal to the womb out of an inability to face life. When he runs away to California, he discovers the Great Twitch, which is, I take it, a philosophy of nihilism, a belief in a purely mechanistic view of man and nature. He thinks for a while that he has uncovered knowledge which will give him power, but he soon surrenders this empty belief as he had surrendered Idealism. In the West responsibility is meaningless and life is an illusion. Jack is momentarily soothed and believes he can return home with a defense adequate to his need. He is to learn that he must return home, there to find the truth that will release him to a life of responsible action.

The maturation process in Jack includes also his rejection of a role as alter ego. The masks that hide the self in *At Heaven's Gate* are transmuted into a technique of alter egos in this novel, whereby a personality is complemented or completed by another personality. As in the earlier novels, so too here, Warren makes the point that self-definition cannot be achieved through another person. Cass Mastern knows this. It is part of Willie's failure that both Tiny and Adam represent elements in his personality—irreconcilable elements. Near the end of the novel, Jack finds himself in a position to be like Duffy in order to kill Duffy. Such action would be the perfect revenge for Duffy's having unleashed Adam against Willie. By this time, however, Jack is strong enough to resist this kind of complement to his selfhood.

The synthesis Jack makes is reflected in the structure of the novel. If all things are in time, and time is a continuum, then it is necessary to peel back layer after layer of experience in any individual life to reveal how an event came to pass and why it had precisely the impact it had. It is necessary to move deeper and deeper into the past, exploring contingent lives, if time makes all things one. If one theme of the novel is that man must possess[222] and believe in his history in order to live in the present and look forward to the future, then there must be constant movement in time in the novel. There is such movement, and the manipulation of time levels becomes an informing device both structurally and thematically. The scheme of the book therefore reinforces the theme; the structure is carefully adapted to the end. Despite the time shifts, the first chapter begins at what is essentially the beginning—Burden's Landing where Jack comes from and Mason City where Willie comes from—and in neat circularity it suggests and contains the ending, which is the death of the Boss and Adam and Judge Irwin, and the consequent freeing of Jack. Furthermore, abandoning straight chronology permits Warren to show the irregular and abrupt stages of self-revelation in Jack Burden, as any given episode leads him into the past.

This novel is Warren's finest work to date. No writer in our time except Faulkner has given us a book that speaks so eloquently with a conservative voice; no writer has so well anatomized the modern world, showing it to be the product of history expressed in those social terms we call politics.... [223]

Three Recent Assessments

THE DIALECTIC OF SELF

John Edward Hardy

More than ten years ago, Robert Penn Warren defined the pre-eminent position of William Faulkner among modern American novelists. His judgment—that Faulkner's books, "for range of effect, philosophical weight, originality of style, variety of characterization, humor, and tragic intensity are without equal in our time and country" —remains unchallengeable. Almost all the Faulkner criticism that has been written in the meantime, a near surfeit of it, indeed, has been purely appreciative, something as if called forth by Warren's essay simply to confirm and strengthen his insights. And the work of no other novelist, new or of Faulkner's own generation, has been put forward by any critic of importance to rival his claims to such attention.

But if any American novelist of the generation just younger than that of Faulkner and Hemingway has seemed likely to attain a stature sufficient to make him the successor, if not the rival, of Faulkner, it is Warren himself. And it is precisely in the essay on Faulkner, more-over, that we find one of the best commentaries on his own vision and purposes as novelist.

One must hesitate yet to predict the final direction of Warren's

John Edward Hardy, "Robert Penn Warren: The Dialectic of Self," in *Man in the Modern Novel*. Seattle: University of Washington Press, 1964. Reprinted by permission of the author and the publisher.

development, and the chances of his producing other novels of the scope and strength of *All the King's Men* and *World Enough and Time*. *Band of Angels*, *The Cave*, and *Wilderness* are certainly weaker performances. It is quite possible that his final reputation as novelist will have to depend on the earlier work. But however this may be, it seems to me sufficiently interesting for the moment to try defining something of what he has accomplished in his art, and what his critical work—for our specific example, again, the essay on Faulkner—has to do with both the scope and the kind of that accomplishment.[194]

For it has been at once his strength and his weakness that Warren is a critic (and professor and poet) as well as a novelist. One must think of him, perhaps, primarily as novelist, of the novel as the single form, or medium, in which he is most effective. But the effects of his other activities are everywhere apparent in the fiction, and ultimately inseparable from whatever total effect any one of the novels, as such, may achieve. In opposition to the recurrently fashionable, simplistic theory that the practice of criticism, especially academic criticism, is necessarily a hindrance to the novelist or poet, I would insist first on the strength that Warren as artist has derived from his critical awareness. If anything, the comparative shallowness and failure of control in the three latest novels would seem to have gone hand-in-hand with his slackening interest in strictly literary criticism and his temporary retirement from teaching. But the principal point to be established is that, for better or worse, the novels are not fully understandable without reference to the criticism—that the two minds, of the poet-novelist and the critic, are identical.

Warren, in short, is first of all the artist of intellectual self-awareness and sophistication. This is his essential difference from Faulkner.

What the essay on Faulkner amounts to is a definition and defense of regionalism. It was inevitable that Faulkner's work be discovered, sooner or later, as the supreme embodiment of the virtues of the Southern regionalism for which Warren has long been one of the principal theoretical spokesmen. But it is also important to realize that he was, in fact, "discovered," and that it was, not sooner, but later; that Faulkner developed his art quite independently of the Fugitive and Agrarian movements, and in an entirely different intellectual atmosphere. Faulkner, back home in Oxford after the war and the brief flings at the expatriate artist's life in New York, New Orleans, and Paris, simply was—became, as it were, without thinking about it—what the Vanderbilt intellectuals were theorizing about.

It is not that Faulkner is any sort of "unconscious" artist, neither the rude, unlettered bard, nor the divine madman, that some commentators have made him out. He has, obviously, a better education than many, even quite recent and sympathetic,[195] critics have given him credit for; and he is the most intensely careful of craftsmen in his writing. But (there is a difference between "unconsciousness" and "unselfconsciousness") he is intellectually naïve, naïve, specifically, as regionalist, in a way that probably no novelist, no Southern novelist, beginning his career as Warren did even one decade later, and certainly no one of Warren's intelligence, could be again.

Faulkner is not simply regionalist, but thoroughgoing pastoralist. For him (at least in the novels of his great period—the later things, from *Intruder in the Dust* on, are another matter) the region is pure myth, fable, a world whole and entire in itself, in which as artist he can live without ever the remotest desire to inquire into other, possible modes of existence, the order of other, different societies in other places. His novels achieve their universality of significance precisely, if paradoxically, by virtue of their intense and exclusive concentration on the regional society. There is only Yoknapatawpha County—and, vaguely of a piece, the world outside. The region of the myth is threatened by history, by intrusive influences from the outside world, but there is no real sense of its being itself part and product of that history.

But Faulkner's is very probably the last such regional synthesis that we shall see in American literature, the last in any way realistic and believable representation of the Southerner as "a different kind of American," of the South as actually constituting a "region" in the sense of distinct cultural community. To the regional theorists of the Twenties and Thirties—for only a cause already consciously "lost" could have produced such a movement as Fugitivism, and the clear cogency as well as the eloquence of the essays of *I'll Take My Stand*— the South was all too obviously back in the current of history. And this historical awareness, the awareness that regionalism could be adhered to now only as idea, is apparent from the first in Warren's development as novelist.

The essay on Faulkner does, as I have said, furnish a commentary on Warren himself. The critical study probably represents a background of interest and acceptance of influence that goes back farther than the writing of *All the King's Men*. And he could derive from his appreciation of two essential[196] truths of Faulkner's art—that of the relationship between the realism and the legend in Faulkner's treatment of the "South," the way in which Yoknapatawpha County functions as the world's stage, and that of his handling of time relationships, the fact that for Faulkner "the 'truth' is neither of the past nor of the future ... [but] of both"—principles of order for his own fiction. But they were principles that had to be readapted, to the purposes of the new historical consciousness.

Several aspects of Warren's practice might be explicated in these terms, each one of which probably calls for a separate essay. For one thing, there is the characteristic grounding of the fiction in some matter of more or less public, historic record, whether of past or near-present. The whole problem of the relationship between historical and fictive (or poetic) truth is one that has a kind of direct and immediately conscious fascination for Warren that it never has for Faulkner. There is the generally more cosmopolitan variety of types among his characters, and, related to this, even in the fictions that recreate the more remote past of the South, a sense of the comparatively easy accessibility of other regions. There is the distinctly un-Faulknerian manner in which he, the author—whether in the mask of a Jack Burden or more openly in the commentaries counterpointing Jeremiah Beaumont's diary entries—puts himself directly "on stage." There are various features of the stylistic practice—in which, of course, the structure of attitudes is necessarily involved—including, in addition to what he accepts from the great regionalist, certain influences from the writer who with his expatriate, journalistic internationalism and deliberate poverty of language is Faulkner's most direct opposite among the novelists of the post-World-War-I generation, Ernest Hemingway. There is the conscious and deliberate, almost scholarly adherence to traditional principles of structure, as for example in the striving for an authentic tragic form in *All the King's Men* that Robert Heilman has pointed out. There is—related, obviously, both to the tragic sense and to the historical awareness, the heightened, post-Faulknerian consciousness of the breakup of the regional culture—his central concern with what might be called the public dimension of human affairs, and with the relationship between the public and[197] private selves of man. This concern is most apparent, most at the surface, in *All the King's Men;* but it is actually of no lesser importance in any of the other novels.

But the problem I want specifically to take up here, with a brief reconsideration of the structure of *All the King's Men,* illustrates perhaps better than any other that self-conscious intellectuality of which I have spoken as distinguishing Warren from the naïve fabulist, Faulkner. This is the problem of his dialectic sense.

The theme that has principally exercised his imagination is that of the incompleteness of man, the struggle to reconcile the idea and the need of unity with the facts of multiplicity in human experience. He has, on the one hand, an immense fascination with the varieties of human possibility, with man becoming. But, opposed to this—Warren's formulation of the problem is, I think, basically a moral one—there is the old Hawthornean, post-Puritan hatred of hypocrisy, the profound feeling that man, a man, should *be* what he seems. And it is from this opposition that the peculiar tension of his fiction derives— the conflict between the psychological and merely sensual, human richness of the story, with its endless complications of mere plot, that threatens continually to get out of hand, and the continually and rather desperately reimposed philosophical order, the precarious balancing of antinomies.

If *All the King's Men* must share honors with *World Enough and Time* as Warren's finest work, the earlier novel still remains the better known; and I have chosen to discuss it for this reason, that being so it is the more readily available for treatment in a short essay. But we might well begin consideration of the theme of the dialectic with some reference to that element of the work which was the principal ground of its great popular success—what Warren himself called its "journalistic relevance"—and to the ultimate exploitation of this in the film based on the novel.

The most significant thing Hollywood "did to" the book in preparing a movie script was to subordinate the role of Jack Burden. Burden is all but a supernumerary character in the film, largely the ghostly voice of the narrator offstage, now and again[198] fitted with a form and face to appear briefly as one of the crowd around Willie Stark.

In short, the moviemakers cut the design of the work neatly in half, reducing it to a straightforward story of Willie Stark as man of action, indeed to what the cover blurb of one paperback edition calls it: "the world-famous American novel of power and corruption, and the meteoric rise and fall of Willie Stark—politician."

But in so doing, they accomplished something really impossible. For without Jack Burden, Willie is not the same man. Somewhat consciously after the example of Conrad, say, in *Heart of Darkness,* and of Fitzgerald in *The Great Gatsby,* Warren created in the two of them, Willie and Jack, a composite hero—the man of action *and* the man of reflection—neither side of whom is intelligible apart from the other. It is precisely the occasion of the tragedy, the tragic aspect of the age which the book represents, that the hero should have to be divided into the two persons.

This, if anything, is the large, central theme of the novel: the familiar theme of the dissociation of sensibility, the split of consciousness, in modern man. It is stated, of course, succinctly, in the allusive title. "Humpty-Dumpty sat on a wall / Humpty Dumpty had a great fall / And all the King's horses and all the King's men / Couldn't put Humpty together again." And with reference to this miniature of the classic situation of tragedy—the hero raised to a height of success and honor, and then falling, from the "wall" of some precarious balance between opposed purposes or motives in his career—it is both Willie and Jack, we must realize, who are Humpty.

And, indeed, the hero, this Humpty-Dumpty, Shem-and-Shaun, is not simply doubled, but doubled and redoubled. Behind the two principals are other, more or less two-dimensional characters whose oppositions shadow the primary antithesis.

There is Tiny Duffy, the lieutenant governor, whom Willie keeps with him as a reminder of what he himself could become if he loses the direction of his purpose. Jack at one point speaks directly of Duffy as Willie's "other self . . ." and of how[199] ". . . all the contempt and insult which Willie Stark was to heap on Tiny Duffy was nothing but what one self of Willie Stark did to the other self because of a blind, inward necessity" (105/*98*). And again, in a variation on the nursery-rhyme imagery:

The Boss ... had busted Tiny Duffy and then he had picked up the pieces and put him back together again as his own creation. He must have taken a lot of pleasure in looking at Tiny's glittering rig and diamond ring, and thinking that it was all hollow, that it was a sham, that if he should crook his little finger Tiny Duffy would disappear like a whiff of smoke.... In a way, Tiny's success was a final index of the Boss's own success. (104–105/*97–98*)

And, earlier, in the description of the first election campaign—when Willie has finally discovered that he is being used by one political faction as a decoy candidate, to split the opposition—there is an hilariously pathetic episode in which the fat Duffy, pushed off the speaker's platform by the drunk and revengeful Willie, teeters precariously for an instant on the edge of the stand before crashing to the ground—enacting here, obviously, a slapstick comic version of the Humpty role.

Behind Jack, on the other hand, is the idealistic doctor, Willie's assassin, Adam Stanton. Adam represents, in extreme and ultimately impossible purity, the ideals of personal integrity and selfless humanitarianism which Jack has held onto under his mask of breezy cynicism, and which he risks in his association with Stark. It is Adam whom Jack himself sees as the antagonist of Willie. Speaking of himself in the third person, Jack records, toward the end of the narrative, how

he had seen his two friends, Willie Stark and Adam Stanton, live and die. Each had killed the other. Each had been the doom of the other.... Adam Stanton, whom he came to call the man of idea, and Willie Stark, whom he came to call the man of fact, were doomed to destroy each other, just as each was doomed to use the other and to yearn toward and try to become the other, because each was incomplete with the terrible division of the age. (461–462/*436*)

But the narrative, so to speak, needs these secondary characters, Jack Burden needs them, in order to project in an[200] abstractly simplified form for analysis, the problems of his own relationship with Willie. The situation he describes, of Adam's and Willie's doomed opposition, their mutual attraction and repulsion, their complementary incompletenesses, is simply a condensed, as it were disinterested, view of the way Jack and Willie stand toward each other.

There are certain complications of the scheme that need to be taken into account. In order, for example, to keep the composite, Humpty-Dumpty identity of Willie and Jack intact, Jack must be made finally to identify, in some sense, with Tiny Duffy. He must see, as he does when he has first been tempted to put the finger on Duffy as Willie's betrayer, or later, to take a more subtle pleasure of vengeance in withholding the information he has, that in condemning Duffy he inevitably condemns himself, that they are "twins . . . bound together forever." And in the first passage I have quoted concerning the relationship of the Boss and Tiny, how Willie had "busted him . . . and then picked up the pieces and put him back together again as his own creation," there is a prophetic, moral irony at Willie's expense. We are to see that it is not Warren, but Willie, with his distortion of Puritan morality, who has made a two-dimensional character of Duffy; and that in so doing, in assuming the godlike role of destroyer and creator, in failing to recognize Duffy's fellow-humanity, he projects his own doom. But, although this point is enforced again and again—in Burden's later reflections on Tiny, his several times renewed surprise in discovering that "the Boss's poodle . . . the funny fat man . . . the cartoon character" is human—the reinforcement is a little too insistent to be dramatically convincing, and the fact remains that Duffy (as well, I think, as Adam Stanton) never emerges as a full, fictive personality, but only as a more or less variable "term" in the "argument" of the book.

In the representation of the two main characters, of course, psychological realism, probability, requires a complexity of personality that necessarily obscures the philosophical dialectic, so that the latter must be shadowed forth on the screen of the action of the minor figures. There is something, consciously, of the man of reflection in Willie himself, certainly, as in the comparable figure of *Heart of Darkness*, Kurtz, something of the[201] man of eloquence, as well as the man of action. Thus it is not altogether by "blind necessity" here, but by a more deliberate and knowing sympathy, that he is attracted to Jack. And in Burden there is a similar, conscious yearning for participation in the world of action—evidenced in the first place by his having turned his power of language to the uses of journalism instead of going on with his career as historian. Further, since the story is told throughout in the first person by Jack, he is too directly and self-interestedly involved to be represented convincingly as able to analyze his relationship to Stark without some means of objectifying, mirroring it, in other relationships.

(One might legitimately be tempted at this point to undertake some reflections on the relationship between narrator and author, and the character of Burden as "mask" for Warren. And I offer, incidentally, for whatever it may be worth, the suggestion that in the career of Jack—the historian turned journalist-political aide whose earlier academic research can be, ironically, completed only in and through his work in the latter role—there is an image, and effort at justification, of Warren's own history of the professor turned novelist. But that, as I have said, is the subject of another essay. We have here, meanwhile, to pursue the pattern of characterization into other elements of the book's structure.)

Corresponding to the two parts of the hero are the two worlds of the novel. There is the world of the gullied red-clay hills, the cut-over pine country, of Mason City and its tin-roofed little houses "with the sad valentine lace of gingerbread work around the eaves of the veranda," the world of the red-neck farmers, the "hick" world of Willie Stark.

And there is the world of Jack Burden's origin: the quiet and mannerly world of the low country, of Burden's Landing; the aristocratic world of the Stantons and the Irwins, where people dress for dinner, and belong to tennis clubs, where Judge Irwin sits in the leather-upholstered armchair in his library and makes miniatures of medieval siege weapons, and has his whisky brought to him on a silver tray.

The "burden" of Jack Burden is to find the means of access between the two worlds—with and through, of course, Willie Stark. And the action of the story is suspended, as it were,[202] between the two worlds, on the soft-sprung wheels of Willie's Cadillac. The novel opens—as someone has pointed out, in what is by now a convention of modern Southern fiction (actually, it is a convention of modern American fiction)—upon the road, with the episode of a visit by Stark, comparatively late in his public career, to his father's home outside Mason City.

The recurrent emphasis of the imagery is upon the automobile, which operates here with an extension of approximately the same symbolic values, sexual and sociological, that it has in Fitzgerald, say, or again in Faulkner.

For this is the country where the age of the internal combustion engine has come into its own . . . where the eight-cylinder jobs come roaring around the curves in the red hills and scatter the gravel like spray, and when they ever get down in the flat country and hit the new slab, God have mercy on the mariner (4/2).

And the mood established in this first section—the account of the trip first to Stark's father's home and then, during the night, to Burden's Landing, for Willie to pay his call on Judge Irwin—symbolically defines the psychological and intellectual situation of the narrator throughout the action. (We may observe how certain details of imagery are carried over from one episode to the next to enforce the ironic connection of the two worlds, and the continuity of Burden's consciousness, as for example in his mental picture first of an hypothetical farm woman lying in the bedroom of one of the country houses of the Mason City area, and then of his mother asleep behind the jalousied windows of her elegant big house as they roll past along the bay road.)

Burden's story is a story of search, the quest for identity, again. He is always on the road, always reliving the journey. He is the Ancient Mariner. (Warren has not been content to present the automobile merely as automobile, but points up the implicit symbolism with a recurrent, nautical metaphor—the cars that "scatter the gravel like spray . . . and . . . God have mercy on the mariner," and Willie's limousine that is "a cross between a hearse and an ocean liner.") Even at the end, married to Anne Stanton and living again in Burden's Landing—but not[203] with any prospect of permanence, Jack is careful to make it clear—he is "back home," has "landed his burden," only about as decisively, let us say, as Odysseus returned to his true Penelope, lying awake all night to tell his tales.

For the end, of course—observe the Faulknerian, Fitzgeraldian, Conradian, Coleridgean, the Homeric, time-scheme of the narration—is the beginning. Jack Burden, within the rather obvious father-search pattern of his career, is in his relationship to Willie both Odysseus and Telemachus by turns. (One can hardly miss the significance of the transformation of Stark from "Cousin Willie," the "plowboy" and "teacher's pet," who was glad to meet "*Mr.* Burden" to "the Boss" who, when some years later they reminisce about the occasion of their first encounter, specifically addresses Jack as "boy.") And the traditionally opposed, symbolic values of the two worlds—the innocence, simplicity, purity, and potency ordinarily associated with the high country, and the perverse decadence and guile, the sterility of the low country (compare the relatively straightforward acceptance of the convention in Hemingway's *A Farewell to Arms*)—are exchanged and re-exchanged four or five times in the course of Burden's readjustment of his moral perspectives.

But mention of the time-structure of the novel brings us to one final set of correspondences. The two worlds of Stanton and Stark represent, respectively, the past and the present. And these in turn (to use the pair of terms that Jack chooses for defining the dialectic opposition of Adam and Willie) correspond roughly to idea and fact.

Before turning reporter, i.e., before entering the world of the present and factuality, Jack had been an aspiring historian, working on a doctoral dissertation, never completed, to be based on the private papers of his Civil Wartime "ancestor," Cass Mastern. And it is in an ironic version of this role that he undertakes, for Willie Stark, the research into the past life of Judge Irwin and the Stantons that leads him, first, to the dirt on the Judge that Willie wanted—the evidence of corruption in the politics of the old, aristocratic order that Jack had once so desperately supposed to be entirely pure and noble—and, finally, to the discovery that he himself is the bastard son of[204] Irwin, not, as he had supposed, of that one of his mother's many husbands whom he calls the Scholarly Attorney.

This, of course, is an essential part of the novel's plot. It is the means by which Jack comes to his final understanding of the relationship between the two worlds, of how "this time came out of that time," and of what has been wrong with his relationship to his mother, and so, in turn, to Anne Stanton. It is the basis of his final acceptance of "the awful responsibility of Time," and so of the completion of the traditional, tragic design in the novel, with the postclimactic, hopeful look to the future at the end. It also provides one of the essential springs to the double catastrophe—the death (with his assassin) of Willie Stark, and the suicide of Judge Irwin—in which Jack has, not once but twice, found his "father" only by killing him. If Jack had not dug up the dirt, found the blotch on the Irwin and Stanton scutcheon, then Adam would never have been provided the immediate motivation for the shooting, nor Judge Irwin that for his suicide.

But back of all this is the question of the significance, for Jack, and for Warren's total design in the novel, of the Cass Mastern story itself. The problem is extremely complex, and we can make no pretense to a treatment of it in all aspects. One thing that seems to me very important, however, and that has not been noted, so far as I know, in the published commentaries on the novel, is that this is about the only place, in this eminently Southern work, that the racial problem, as such, is touched upon.

Between the main action of the novel and the Mastern story—of the conflict of idealism and passion, of a man's betrayal of his friend to his death, of the punishment of the innocent by the guilty for their own projected guilt, of the ironic selfishness of remorse, of the hero's final self-immolation and death in the service of a public cause whose principles he cannot support—there are a number of obvious, and very interesting, parallels. But the one point I want to make here is a negative one: that, for the function of the episode in the total structure of the book, it is not a matter of first importance that the story involves the problems of the injustice of slavery.[205]

The view of the sociologically minded critic would be that any novel about the "South" which pretends to "realism" and "seriousness," any Southern novel of "conscience," must take into central account the question of race relations. But Warren's kind of regionalism, his kind of realism, makes him no more concerned to satisfy this demand than he was to be true to the "facts" of Huey Long's career, and as a right-thinking citizen of the democracy accurately to portray the evils of demagoguery—his supposed failure in which raised such howls of dismay from the liberal, Eastern critics at the time of the book's appearance.

What we get through Jack Burden's handling of the Cass Mastern story is a kind of final synthesis of idea and fact, an alteration of the formula to something like the idea *of* fact. Or, to put the matter another way, the story provides Burden with the essential metaphor for his grasp of the truth of human dependency and the moral universe, specifically, his metaphor of the world as the great web, about which he tells us Mastern learned through his sin and its consequences, that "if you touch it, however lightly, at any point, the vibration ripples to the remotest perimeter." But the whole story, actually, is metaphor, or parable—which is the precise kind of story it is, about that time and place and the circumstances of that society, in order to give Jack the farthest possible, but still personal, reach into the past, a past even beyond the time of Judge Irwin and Governor Stanton, to learn that the human condition was always the same, that "any this time came out of any that." The fact that the innocent victims of Mrs. Duncan's and Mastern's sin (and of his misdirected remorse) were Negro slaves, has neither more nor less significance than that, for example, Christ's parable of the Good Samaritan is based on a then-current and familiar situation of social prejudice among the Jews.

Rich though the novel is in its representation of the particularities of time and place, Warren is concerned primarily to present the relationship of two men, Jack and Willie, in a tragic situation of incomplete and belated understanding, a failure of communication, which is the universal situation of modern man. The fatal incompleteness of the human relationship in the white-Negro, master-slave situation, with which Jack in the parable identity of Cass Mastern is momentarily[206] concerned, is only one, not necessarily even the most important, historical manifestation of the permanent failure.

At the end of the book, Jack Burden has "adopted" old Ellis Burden—his "notfather," as we might in Faulknerian phrase call him—as the only one of his "million fathers" with whom he can live. And I suppose the final, retrospective irony is that, through his discovery that he is Judge Irwin's bastard, not the son of the Scholarly Attorney, Jack learns that Cass Mastern was not even, as he had supposed, his ancestor.

The central, regionalist preoccupation of Faulkner is with blood, with the bloodline, with the themes of incest and miscegenation. For Warren, these are characteristically only instrumental concerns, toward the final expression of an almost terrifyingly abstract moral vision, whereby the ultimate significance of the human drama is discoverable only within the shadow play of the dialectic. Whatever the affinity he felt for the man of the papers and the photograph, Jack Burden must learn, it was something at once thinner and stronger than blood.[207]

HAVING IT BOTH WAYS

Roger Sale

A funeral parlor at midnight is ear-splitting compared to the effect you get in the middle of the morning in the back room of a place like Slade's if you are the first man there. You sit there and think how cozy it was last night, with the effluvium of brotherly bodies and the haw-haw of camaraderie, and you look at the floor where now there are little parallel trails of damp sawdust the old broom left this morning when the unenthusiastic Negro man cleaned up, and the general impression is that you are alone with the Alone and it is His Move. (16/*13*)

This is the characteristic voice of Jack Burden, and in order to place it generically, here is another voice speaking about quietness:

In jail a man has no personality. He is a minor disposal problem, and a few entries on reports. Nobody cares who loves or hates him, what he looks like, what he did with his life. Nobody reacts to him unless he gives trouble. Nobody abuses him. All that is asked of him is that he go quietly to the right cell and remain quiet when he gets there. There is nothing to fight against, nothing to be mad at. The jailers are quiet men without animosity or sadism. All this stuff you read about men yelling and screaming, beating against the bars, running spoons along them, guards rushing in with clubs—all that is for the big house. A good jail is one of the quietest places in the world. You could walk through the average cell block at night and look in through the bars and see a huddle of brown blanket, or a head of hair, or a pair of eyes looking at nothing. You might hear a snore. Once in a long while you might hear a nightmare. The life in a jail is in suspension, without purpose or meaning (Raymond Chandler, *The Long Goodbye*).

These voices speak from the inside; they are usually thought of as belonging to tough guys or smart alecks. It is difficult to speak in such tones and not abuse the reader, who is on the outside and who needs to be told the way things work. The reader of the[68] average "private eye novel" has to put himself to sleep in order to be able to listen to the fancy talk characteristic of the tough guy. The narrator speaking from the inside who seeks not to be contemptuous of the reader's

Roger Sale, "Having It Both Ways in *All the King's Men*," *Hudson Review*, XIV (Spring 1961), 68–76. Reprinted by permission of the author and the publisher. Copyright 1961 by The Hudson Review, Inc.

intelligence must really know something that those on the outside would not know and he must be willing to pay whatever consequences are due because he insists on this superiority. In the passages above, it is Jack Burden who fails and Philip Marlowe, private detective, who succeeds. Marlowe proceeds straightforwardly, with a careful eye for the relevance of detail and with a refusal to get cute. He speaks with great sympathy for the jailers and the jailed, thus placing himself amongst them, of their world. Jack's tone is less controlled, his details do not lead to his conclusion, his toughness is worn on his sleeve as though he needed to prove it was there. He also feels he must detach himself from the normal inhabitants of pool halls by using big words and by being metaphysical. He enjoys being on the inside but he needs to assure the reader that he is not part of that world. Marlowe, here at least, is willing to pay the penalty for talking down to the reader; he does not try to protect himself by anticipating the reader's irony. Jack constantly hedges his bet, talks down but then dissociates himself from the consequences.

Discovering what attitude to take towards the voice of Jack Burden is the main task for the reader of *All the King's Men.* Jack speaks from the inside because he must tell us what it is like to be one of the king's men, what is involved in knowing all about state and local politics. But Jack is not simply on the inside the way Sadie Burke and Sugar-Boy are; he is special, a blue blood without portfolio. Jack is also very knowing about Burden's Landing, situated on the Gulf, far from the rednecks up north, home of former Governor Stanton and Judge Irwin. The story of *All the King's Men* is the story of the entanglement of the main figures of Burden's Landing—Jack, his mother, Judge Irwin, Adam and Anne Stanton—in the world of the capital and the provinces, and Jack is on the inside because he is the only one who is sure he understands both worlds. Burden's Landing is a world that existed once long ago, so it can be seen clearly only in memory; his description of that world is therefore static, always filled with the same details. The world dominated by Willie Stark is constantly changing, and, instead of natural description, Jack[69] provides meticulously detailed stories of the machinery of politics and completely dramatized accounts of Willie creating his public image, whether that public be two people or twenty thousand. Perhaps the finest instance of Jack demonstrating his right to speak from the inside is the account of the Case of the Upright Judge, Jack uncovering the dirt on Judge Irwin that will stick to his coat. Here he employs his knowledge of both worlds and his professional training, about which he usually is embarrassingly self-congratulatory. Not once in fourteen pages does he allow himself to abuse his position on the inside by lapsing into a sneer or a set piece. He bullies Miss Littlepaugh the way he does almost everyone else, but he does so only after he is sure that there is no other way to gain information from her. Finally, the story itself is fascinating, rivalled among Warren's many inset stories only by Hamish Bond's narrative of the African coast in *Band of Angels*.

But, as we have seen in the passage about Slade's place, Jack is not content to be knowing only about the jungles of cities and the rarefied air of Burden's Landing. He constantly aspires to demonstrate his right to talk from the inside about life. Here he is on Anne Stanton's laugh:

Her eyes were glittering like the eyes of a child when you give a nice surprise, and she laughed in a sudden throaty tingling way. It is the way a woman laughs for happiness. They never laugh that way just when they are being polite or at a joke. A woman only laughs that way when something has touched her way down in the very quick of her being and the happiness just wells out as natural as breath and the first jonquils and mountain brooks. When a woman laughs that way it always does something to you. It does not matter what kind of face she has got either. You hear that laugh and feel you have grasped a clean and beautiful truth. You feel that way because that laugh is a revelation. It is a great impersonal sincerity. It is a spray of dewy blossom from the great central stalk of All Being, and the woman's name and address hasn't got a damn thing to do with it. Therefore, that laugh cannot be faked. If a woman could learn to fake it she would make Nell Gwyn and Pompadour look like a couple of Campfire Girls wearing bifocals and ground-gripper shoes and with bands on their teeth. She could set all society by the ears. For all any man wants is to hear a woman laugh like that. (219/*205–206*)

The voice is still tough, but with a difference. Jack has a love of the natural world and cleanliness and truth. His images of the sound of Anne's laughter—he uses them again in describing her[70] on the other side of the tennis court when they were younger—are characteristic of all the fake nature writing in the novel; here they serve only to contribute to the general unreality of Anne Stanton. At the time of this scene, Jack has seen Anne only occasionally in ten years, and no reason is offered why she should laugh this way and even less why she should suddenly stop. But then Anne never is more than a soap opera figure with her natural wisdom about being in love and getting married at age seventeen and her clutching at her last chance by becoming Willie's mistress when she is almost thirty-five.

But above and beyond the gratuitousness of the passage, the leaden repetition of "a woman laughs that way," and the embarrassing collocation of the tough guy with the lover of truth and mountain brooks, is the hollowness of the assumption that Jack knows about everything. He is only vulgar in his familiar tone toward historical figures; he can make Nell Gwyn and Pompadour "relevant" just as he always knows what the great men of the past really meant: "Listen, pal, there was a man named Dante . . ." (251/*236*); "A man may forget the death of the father, but never the loss of the patrimony, the cold-faced Florentine, who is the founding father of our modern world, said, and he said a mouthful" (417/*393*). Even worse, he knows about the nature of a woman's laughter, and his patronizing use of the second person pronoun assures us that we do not. This smugness is very upsetting as it assumes that the reader, even if he has never heard this laugh or could not recognize it if he did, some day will; thus "you hear," "you have grasped," and "you feel" take on the force of "you will hear," "you will grasp," and "you will feel." Warren apparently is not content to have the narrator speak from the side of his mouth just about politics and the socially elite, and he apparently is not aware that the voice that speaks from the inside about Life always begins to sound slightly hysterical.

One of the reasons it is difficult to control the voice that speaks from the inside is that it is hard to know how to prevent the voice from sounding pompous about matters of common knowledge, and from trying to reach levels of sagacity and awareness available to no one. Jack falls neatly into both mistakes in a passage early in the novel. Willie, Jack, and Sugar-Boy leave Mason City to go to Burden's Landing to try to scare Judge Irwin. The section[71] opens with this observation: "Burden's Landing is one hundred and thirty miles from Mason City, off to the southwest. If you multiply one hundred and thirty by two it makes two hundred and sixty miles." Jack then leans back in the seat and closes his eyes, but, just as he could sense Anne Stanton's laugh metaphysically, so too he can see the side of the road while riding with his eyes closed:

Close to the road a cow would stand knee-deep in the mist, with horns damp enough to have a pearly shine in the starlight, and would look at the black blur we were as we went whirling into the blazing corridor of light which we could never quite get into for it would always be splitting the dark just in front of us. The cow would stand there knee-deep in the mist and look at the black blur and the blaze and then, not turning its head, at the place where the black blur and blaze had been, with the remote, massive, unvindictive indifference of God-All-Mighty or Fate or me, if I were standing there knee-deep in the mist, and the blur and the blaze whizzed past and withered on off between the fields and the patches of woods. (40/36)

The car then moves on, Jack muses some more on the countryside, and two paragraphs later Sugar-Boy is driving down the new boulevard by the bay in Burden's Landing. A number of things about this passage about the cow are worth noting: There is the solemn tone in which Jack says that a car will never catch up to its own headlights. There is the needless repetition of "the blur and the blaze" and "standing there knee-deep." There is Jack's telepathic sensing of the cow's mood, with or without his eyes closed. But most important, there is the complete gratuitousness of the symbol. The fact that nature is indifferent to man has nothing to do with the rest of the passage, the chapter, or anything in the novel except the most abstract statement of the theme, and, even if knowing this were a necessary part of the action, the use of the cow to communicate this truth involves an extremely awkward dragging in of an otherwise extraneous object on which meaning can be heaped.

The reasons why Warren is not content with his tough guy narrator and so involves him in these extremely damaging and usually pointless intrusions and discourses are not far to seek. Warren is apparently determined to be a philosophical novelist, one who, to use his own description of Conrad, "is constantly striving to rise to the level of generalization about values, for whom the image strives to rise to symbol, for whom images always[72] fall into dialectical configuration, for whom the urgency of experience, no matter how vividly and strongly experience may enchant, is the urgency to know the meaning of experience." Warren seems to want to have it both ways. He wants his narrator completely embroiled in and knowing about the areas of his special competence, and yet he also wants him to detach himself and strive to "the level of generalization about values." In this novel, the result of wanting to have it both ways is that finally he has it neither way; caught in this fashion, Jack often sounds absurd or hysterical.

This impulse to have it both ways is not, of course, necessarily self-contradictory; the narrator of many successful novels does speak from the inside and then rises to the level of generalization about values. But the voice changes in these novels as the irony is established, broken, and re-established from a new point of view—this is Conrad's technique in *Nostromo*—and Warren does not seem to want to commit himself to such a method. Part of the difficulty lies in the use of the first person narrator who is both character and narrator, both learning and learned, so that shifts in voice usually involve real awkwardness. But even more important, Warren seems only partially willing to be ironic about his central character, to insist on the limitations of speaking from the inside.

At the level of generalization about values, this irony is fully articulated in *All the King's Men*. Jack's development towards self-knowledge is rendered by the shifts in Jack's philosophy which result from his gradual involvement in the worlds around him. As narrator, Jack is able to achieve ironic distance from the metaphysical positions he took in the past and now sees to be wrong. For instance, when Jack adopts the idea of the Great Twitch—"nothing was your fault or anybody's fault, for things are always as they are"—on his return from California, the later Jack Burden, speaking as narrator, allows us to see what is wrong. He has already, in the Cass Mastern episode, given us the Spider Web theory and the subsequent narrative demonstrates how Jack ran to the theory of the Great Twitch because he could not face the truth he found in working on the Mastern papers. Thus the narrator dissociates himself from his own past and prepares the way for an acceptance of the Spider Web theory—"the world[73] is all of one piece"—and its concomitant—"if you would accept the past you might hope for the future."

But Warren is not really willing to commit himself to all the implications of this development. Jack's tone is kept constant throughout, and the tough guy is allowed to sound impressive even though he later will be repudiated. For instance, here is Jack when Willie tries to tell him about the new hospital:

> "I'll be dead," he said, "and you'll be dead, and I don't care whether he votes for me or not, he can go there and—"
>
> "And bless your name," I said.
>
> "Damn it!" he shook me hard, crumpling my lapel in his big hand, "you stand there grinning like that—get that grin off your face—get it off or I'll—"
>
> "Listen," I said, "I'm not any of your scum, and I'm still grinning when I please."
>
> "Jack—hell, Jack—you know I don't mean that—it's just you stand there and grin. Damn it, can't you understand? Can't you?" (247/233)

This is the little man talking back to the big man because the little man is Jack Burden of Burden's Landing. In the end, of course, Jack will come to see himself as one of Willie's scum, but he is not, despite this confession, quite willing to relinquish such an attractive position as the one he is in here. Thus we are made to sympathize with Jack even though he must turn his back on the position he takes in this scene. But this discrepancy between tone and moral position is even clearer towards the end of the novel. After the murder of Adam and Willie, Jack has learned almost all he ever will. When a photographer comes to Adam's funeral, Jack tells him: "If you live long enough, you'll find out there are some kinds of son-of-a-bitch you don't have to be even to be a newspaperman." After he finds out who Jack is, the photographer retorts: "you work for Stark and you call somebody a son-of-a-bitch" (427/403). Jack sees that the photographer is partly right, and, seeing this, he can only stare at him. This scene very consciously parallels an earlier one in which Jack gets tough with a policeman who molests him when he is walking with Anne. Here, in the later scene, we are supposed to see how much Jack has learned, how much more sense and humility he has. But this new humility does not keep Jack from calling the photographer a "squirt face." Up to the very end, Jack acts as he always has; he[74] refers to Trollope as "Anthony," he feels free to pontificate about the fate of Sugar-Boy, and he abuses Anne in their last conversation much as he did in their first.

Warren, then, does not really want ever to have to repudiate his narrator, some of whose absurdity, vulgarity, and weakness I have discussed already. Jack "learns" something, but only in an abstract way. He says he sees the world differently, but his tone never leads the reader to believe that the violence which destroyed his world really touches him. He only partly takes on the responsibilities for what he is and wants to be, a tough guy with a difference. He refrains from telling Sugar-Boy that Tiny was the one who called Adam, but he never stops talking as though he knew what had to be known about everything really important.

We have three reasons, then, why Jack fails as a narrator. First, Warren is simply uncertain about what role he wants Jack to take. This, I suspect, is the source of the endless chatter about jonquils and mimosas and mountain streams, and for the more excessive of the pasted-on symbols. Second, Warren seems to feel that to take a stance on the inside is compellingly attractive even when it involves Jack in being solemn about the obvious or pretentiously knowing about real mysteries. Finally, Warren does not really believe in his story enough, he does not see that this story of growth commits him to changes in the narrator's way of talking about the world. If Jack is just as much of a smart aleck in 1939 as he was in 1922, the whole dramatic point of the novel is evaded and finally blurred.

Although it is admittedly dangerous to speculate, I think we can say that the major source of all these weaknesses is the fact that Warren's genius lies in one direction and his bent and ambitions lie in another. Warren can be a marvelous storyteller; the main story of *All the King's Men* is not just "good plotting"; it is the testament of an imagination that always seems to have the best detail right at hand. But the nagging concern with symbol and theme, the effort to rise to the level of generalization about values, mars and finally negates much that is good in the book. To delete the network of symbols and the discourses on metaphysics would be to make the book much better and not necessarily lesser. Most of the symbols are like the one about the cow; they seem to open up the novel for richer and more elaborate exegesis, but in fact[75] they never point to anything the brute action of the story has not already made clear. It is difficult to think of one symbol in the novel, unless it is Judge Irwin's advice to Jack about duck hunting, that it is not at least a little embarrassing because of the wrench its gratuitousness forces on the narrative voice. Even the better ones, like Jack's mother's birth cry, suffer because Warren seems afraid we will miss the point and so resorts to explanation and repetition.

When we move to the later novels and *Brother to Dragons,* all the indications of a split between Warren's ability and his ambition grow more and more marked as the wonderful storyteller is gradually buried by the images which strive to rise to symbols and the symbols which strive to rise to allegory at the level of generalization about values. Seeing that Jefferson had to be the hero of the story of his cousin's fratricide was a stroke of genius; adding the choral "R.P.W." spoiled much of this brilliant perception. The same thing is true to a lesser extent of the heavy voice of the modern narrator of *World Enough and*

Time. Finally, in *The Cave,* Warren tries to return to the methods of *Night Rider* and *All the King's Men,* to ground his novel in the life of the characters, but now the story is almost completely dictated by Warren's sense of the "meaning of experience," and his tremendous technical skill is made the victim of the abstraction represented most clearly in the title. And, as always in Warren, when the urgency of the tale is not felt, the writing grows loose; the narrator easily falls into gratuitous comments on the sex-demon and the gullibility of the American Public, and perhaps worse, a good deal of the dialogue seems to exist in order to convince us that the author really knows how Tennessee hillbillies talk. The genius remains for recreating the urgency of experience, but the bent, which has grown more and more powerful over the years, is for metaphysics, and so Warren tries to have it both ways. The impulse is finally self-destructive, and *All the King's Men,* even though it is his best novel, remains, for that reason, a dishonest book.[76]

ᕼ

POLARITY OF THEMES

Elizabeth M. Kerr

The elaborate counterpoint of themes in *All the King's Men* greatly enhances the dramatic quality of the novel by a basic scheme of polarity that not only intensifies the conflict and heightens the character contrasts but also invests individuals and their struggles with universal significance. The configuration traced by the whole thematic structure manifests a comprehensive philosophic concept; interpretations based on single themes or a few themes are inadequate to represent the total meaning. The action centers in man's sin and guilt and his attempt to evade evil; the total meaning centers in the necessity of assuming responsibility and acknowledging guilt, thereby accepting evil as an inevitable part of life, "the index of God's glory and His power," and creating good, "the index of man's glory and power" (462–463/*437*). Willie Stark and Jack Burden may be compared to the opposite poles of a magnetic field, around which cluster such contrasting themes as guilt and innocence, action and idea, present and

Elizabeth M. Kerr, "Polarity of Themes in *All the King's Men*," *Modern Fiction Studies,* VI (Spring 1960), 25–46. Reprinted by permission of the author and the Purdue Research Foundation.

past. But this is an over-simplification, since most of the characters have thematic significance and are so complex that they embody conflicting qualities. The two stories, of Willie and Jack, present contrasting narrative movements, ending in defeat and victory respectively. Discussion of the themes in terms of these movements or cycles may simplify the problem without minimizing the complex thematic pattern described by characters and action.

The use of Jack Burden as the narrator dramatizes the themes: he provides the chief explicit recognition of the universal problems involved. But the choice of characters and events is the author's; Jack's awareness, though keen, is limited, and the reader will see significance often when Jack makes no illuminating comment. The literal and figurative images that distinguish Jack's style are often clues to the thematic meaning of characters and episodes not explicitly identified with Jack's own concepts. The themes which Jack consistently and explicitly develops and analytically formulates are those[25] of the pursuit of knowledge and of the philosophic stages which conclude with Jack's rebirth at the end. Jack also recognizes Adam Stanton and Willie Stark as "the man of idea" and "the man of fact" (462/436). In the absence of explicit statement of themes or identifying comments by Jack, the thematic structure, unlike the dramatic structure and style, does not depend upon the narrator device. Recognition of the whole thematic structure therefore rests upon analysis of characters and their relationships, of narrative movement and episodes, and of the imagery that, although part of Jack's style, often has implications of which he seems unaware.

Robert Penn Warren specifies some of the themes that give depth of meaning and organic relation to the naturalistic elements and the finely articulated plot. In his Introduction to the Modern Library edition of *All the King's Men,* he points out that both the initial theme of the corrupting effect of power, with its corollary themes of the scientific age and politics in the power state, and "the problem of naturalistic determinism and responsibility" which "crept in" were developed in the play *Proud Flesh,* which preceded the novel. In the novel the first theme centers in Willie Stark, the man of action and destiny. The second theme centers in his confidential agent, Jack Burden, the man of thought, who, as narrator, interprets the action.

The limitation to the point of view of Jack Burden and the complexity of the two stories of Jack and Willie serve to subordinate the corollary themes, the problems of individuals thus overshadowing the problems of society. We never see the whole operation of the power state nor the whole structure of society, but they are suggested by some of the chief symbols and episodes. The characters divide roughly into two groups: the conservative aristocrats like Judge Irwin and his friends, who have allowed the state government to lag behind the needs of society, and Willie and his political machine, who represent the common man and are making up for lost time. By birth Jack belongs to the first group, by choice to the second. Willie's principles and objectives, which guide the activity of the machine, are derived from his pragmatic philosophy that society makes up "right" as it goes along in order to survive and keep doing business. The practical program to which Willie is committed offers to the people of the state hope for opportunity, education, health, and freedom from want.

This philosophy and this program are symbolized in specific achievements of Willie's career and government. Willie began his political career by fighting the graft which subsequently turned a schoolhouse into a death-trap. The novel begins when Willie is governor, whizzing in his Cadillac along Highway 58, a recurrent symbol specifically of the roads which enabled the red-neck farmers to get their produce to[26] market and in general of modern communication and transportation, with its benefits and dangers.

The chief symbol of Willie's program and of the scientific age is the hospital, which was to be Willie's crowning achievement, his gift to the people with no strings attached. The hospital represents first the beneficent effect of science. Second, it represents the suppressed idealism in Willie: this contribution to the people is to be figuratively as pure and uncontaminated as it is antiseptic and sterile. Willie's effort to keep the hospital free of graft is a factor leading to his assassination. And third, after Tom Stark has been fatally injured, the hospital represents the emptiness of fame and the vanity of human wishes. That the multiple symbolism of the hospital is strengthened by the fact that Adam Stanton is the director will be apparent in the discussion of Adam's role and thematic significance.

Related to the hospital symbol, though not to the projected building, are two surgical operations performed by Adam. The first, a prefrontal lobectomy, represents the partial triumph of science: the patient can be given a new personality but cannot be given a new set of values. The second operation, on Tom Stark after his injury in a football game, unsuccessful because the spinal cord had been crushed, shows the limitations of science. The third operation, performed on Willie after he was shot by Adam, was successful, but science could not prevent the infection from which he died. The fact that Willie was shot by Adam, the embodiment of science and intellect, signifies the destructive effect of science when it is not animated by human understanding. As will be apparent, these episodes have other symbolic meanings.

Figures of speech and images dealing with machines are motifs reflecting the theme of the scientific age. A remarkable image begins with Jack's meditation on a literal train and small town but transmutes train and town into symbols of civilization: the train, the impermanence of scientific civilization and the restlessness and insecurity of its people; the town, a more primitive civilization, looking "improvised, flung down, ready to be abandoned," but perhaps representing some "secret knowledge" from which there is no need to run away (81/76). John Hart notes that the town represents the "farmhouse way of life," contrasted with the new age.[1] Jack's later recollection of the incident, when he thinks he too has a "secret knowledge," emphasizes its thematic significance (332/313). The political machine is an obvious symbol, given an original twist when Willie justifies political graft, in a double image, as a necessary loss of energy and as the grease[27] which keeps the wheels from squeaking (417/393). Another particularly effective double image is used to describe Willie's restless pacing when he first runs for nomination for governor. First Jack compares him to a caged beast, hunting for a place to get out; then the feet are like plungers in a machine trampling on you, "the thing in the vat." "The plungers didn't care about its being you, or not being you, in the vat. But they would continue until there wasn't any you, and afterward for a long time until the machine wore out or somebody switched off the juice" (75–76/70). The blind compulsion driving Willie toward fulfillment of his destiny is thus imaged in terms of both nature and machine. Numerous minor images deal with machines. The fact that the story does not deal notably with even the familiar mechanical aspects of life, except automobiles, makes the use of symbols and images reflecting those aspects the more essential and impressive.

Involved with the themes centered in the stories of the two main characters, the corrupting effect of power and the problem of responsibility, are other themes which are more abstract, even more universal, more sharply contrasted; beneath the intricately woven texture of character, event, movement, and images a pattern of polarity is discernible.[2]

Though it is impossible to deal with themes chronologically, a brief statement of the chronological order of events, from which the narrative order often deviates, may be useful. The story of Willie Stark is that of a farm boy who becomes governor, too easily accepts corrupt methods to achieve worthy ends, involves in his personal corruption the idealistic and aristocratic Anne Stanton, and is assassinated by Anne's even more idealistic brother, Adam. The story is told by Willie's confidential agent and Anne's and Adam's best friend, Jack

[1] John Hart, "Some Major Images in *All the King's Men*," *All the King's Men: A Symposium* (Carnegie Press, 1957), pp. 68, 70. This article was written before the *Symposium* was published. Any use of the *Symposium* in revision is specifically indicated. ·

[2] The following articles were useful in identifying and tracing the themes specified: Norton Girault, "The Narrator's Mind as Symbol," *Accent*, VII (Summer 1947), 220–234: the theme of rebirth; Robert Heilman, "Melpomene as Wallflower; or the Reading of Tragedy," *Sewanee Review*, LV (January 1947), 154–166: general polarity, kinesis and paralysis; John L. Stewart, "The Achievement of Robert Penn Warren," *South Atlantic Quarterly*, XLVII (October 1948), 562–579: flight and return.

Burden. Under Willie's orders, Jack discovers that a discreditable episode in the life of Judge Irwin had been concealed by Governor Stanton; this discovery leads to the situation that causes Adam to kill Willie. The inexorable working of cause and effect forces Jack to alter his basic attitudes and to recognize his own share of responsibility in what has happened.

The characters can be roughly divided into men of action and men of thought, with the movement swinging from the kinesis of the men of action to the paralysis of the men of ideas, from participation to withdrawal. Willie Stark, the man of action, is motivated by fine ideas of service to the people but yields too easily to expediency and[28] delegates too much authority and action to those whose ends are purely selfish. Of the political figures clustered around Willie, Tiny Duffy personifies political power: he is the political machine incarnate. In revenge for Willie's announced intention to cancel the hospital deal with Gummy Larson and thus cut Duffy out of some graft, Duffy informs Adam Stanton of Anne's relationship to Willie and falsely says that that relationship is the price of Adam's appointment as head of the new hospital. But because, as in this instance, Duffy does not perform the deed himself but pulls wires, makes deals, uses pressure, he is imaged as the bloated politician of the cartoons or as a drowned body. Sadie Burke, the woman of action who has risen from the gutter by her own efforts and who uses her political acumen to aid Willie, becomes the mistress to whom Willie always returns. Her activity and passion are symbolized in terms of electric energy or steam pressure. In a fit of insane jealousy at Willie's intention to end his extramarital affairs and return to his wife, Sadie gives Duffy the information upon which his lie to Adam is based. "But what she had done had been done hot. What Duffy had done had been done cold" (436/411). Sugar Boy, with, but not really of, the machine, is pure action: he can express himself and serve Willie only through his two great skills, driving a car and shooting his .38 Special. The deft use of thematically relevant but realistic detail, presented with no sense of its ironic significance, is well illustrated in Chapter One, when Jack dozes off while Sugar Boy practices shooting. On this same day Jack is ordered to get something on Judge Irwin; as a consequence of this order, Sugar Boy's final demonstration of skill is the shooting of Adam.

Willie's lack of balance between action and idea is apparent, in his personal life, in his handling of his son, Tom. Tom becomes the man of action, the football star and car-and-drink-crazy youth. The injury of Caresse Jones, in a car crash with Tom, Willie hushes up by pressure on her father. Tom's later affair with Sybil Frey, whose father was inaccessible to pressure, brings about the situation which forces Willie to give the hospital contract to Gummy Larson. After Willie literally causes Tom's fatal injury by putting action above principle and insisting that Tom be put back in the game, regardless of eligibility rules, Willie cancels the deal with Gummy and arouses Duffy's anger. Duffy's lie to Adam sends Adam gunning for Willie. Thus the father kills the son and the son kills the father because action has not been balanced and controlled by right ideas.

Thematically, and often literally, opposed to this group of characters are those in whom ideas and ideals predominate. Hugh Miller, "clean hands, pure heart, and no political past" (104/97), becomes Attorney General and finds satisfaction in taking political action against evil. But when he can no longer countenance Willie's methods, he[29] resigns. Adam Stanton, the man of ideas, acts solely as a scientist. His only personal human feelings are for his sister Anne and Jack Burden, the Friend of his Youth when he was capable of affection. With scarcely the ordinary comforts and no luxury except his piano, he lives in a shabby apartment where closeness to other lives supplies the warmth he lacks in his own. His error is expressed in the question Jeremiah Beaumont asked himself: "So . . . what becomes of the idea, if we place it apart from our warm world and its invisible fluids by which we live?"[3] Adam limits his passion for doing good to his action as a scientist. He has withdrawn from other aspects of life because of his romantic mental picture of the glorious and noble past, inhabited by such perfect men as his father. As Jack puts it, "when the world doesn't conform in any respect to the picture, he wants to throw the world away. Even if that means throwing out the baby with the bath. Which . . . it always does mean" (262/247).

Jack changes this picture by the information that Adam's father had connived at the Judge's acceptance of a bribe and to protect the Judge had been unjust to others. In bitterness Adam accepts the position offered by Willie, thus abandoning his idealistic withdrawal and participating, for the sake of doing good on a wholesale scale, in a government program of which in general he does not approve. But he does so only when he is assured by Willie that no taint of politics will touch him. He seeks fulfillment in the sterility of science as Jeremiah Beaumont sought "communion only in the blank cup of nature, and innocence there" (*World Enough and Time,* 459). But the sterility of science can either preserve or destroy life. When Adam kills Willie, idea and act are one: vengeance on corruption for the destruction of innocence. Warren, as R. P. W., says in *Brother to Dragons:* "destruction's but creation gone astray."[4] Creation goes astray because in Adam's mind and heart there is no room for understanding and forgiveness, for reconciliation to the imperfect human form of the abstract and perfect idea.

[3] Robert Penn Warren, *World Enough and Time* (Garden City, New York, 1951), p. 459. Quotations from works by Warren which were written after *All the King's Men* serve to verify interpretation and confirm significance of thematic ideas in *All the King's Men,* not to present a comparative study of themes.

[4] (New York, 1953), p. 99.

As Jack Burden comes to realize, "Adam Stanton, whom he came to call the man of idea, and Willie Stark, whom he came to call the man of fact, were doomed to destroy each other, just as each was doomed to try to use the other and to yearn toward and try to become the other, because each was incomplete with the terrible division of the age" (462/*436*).

That terrible division divides Jack Burden himself from his past[30] and from a purposeful life. He is the man of idea, the spectator, withholding judgment and refraining from participation except as he carries out orders. Jack's idealism, unlike Adam's, is rooted in early disillusion, and he uses it as a shield to defend himself from further injury. But unlike Adam, Jack is cynically and ironically aware of his position. Self-knowledge prevents Jack from acting frantically and fatally as Adam did. When Jack learns that Duffy is really responsible for Willie's and Adam's deaths, he wants to avenge them. Telling Sugar Boy the truth would amount to a death sentence for Tiny Duffy and would rid Jack of a sense of guilt: "I felt free and clean, as when you suddenly see that, after being paralyzed by ignorance or indecision, you can act. I felt on the verge of the act" (436/*411*).[5] After telling Tiny what he has learned and leaving him to worry, Jack says: "I felt like a million.... I was a hero. I was St. George and the dragon, I was Edwin Booth bowing beyond the footlights, I was Jesus Christ with the horsewhip in the temple" (440/*415*). But Sadie Burke, who reads him like a book, deflates him by her neat description: "... you got some high-faluting idea you are an Eagle Scout and she [Anne] is Joan of Arc" (441/*416*). Sadie generously would spare Anne the consequences of publicity. But what really keeps Jack from telling Sugar Boy, and perhaps destroying him also, is the realization that he himself was a "party to that conspiracy... which had committed Willie Stark and Adam Stanton to each other and to their death" and that he and Duffy are "twins bound together more intimately and disastrously than the poor freaks of the midway" (442/*417*). Duffy is *his* other self as well as Willie's, and when Jack in his mind's eye sees Duffy wink at him "like a brother" he cannot duplicate Duffy's treachery; instead of telling Sugar Boy the name, Jack says, "I was kidding" (446/*421*). By allowing himself to be involved in action initiated by others and not by his own principles and ideas and by being morally neutral, Jack has been as guilty as if he were a Duffy, acting selfishly and greedily.

Anne is the other main character who represents ideas and ideals. She lives by her ideals and by her illusions, but with a desire for

---

[5] The parallel to Hamlet's "Now might I do it pat" soliloquy is one of several possible comparisons with *Hamlet*. Since similarities to such characters as Hamlet, Oedipus, and Telemachus, though interesting in themselves, tend to obscure the more consistent and significant polarity of themes with which this study is concerned, parallels will be noted only incidentally when relevant to central ideas of this paper.

participation. Having refused to marry Jack because he has no purpose in life, she devotes her lonely life to charity work. In an attempt to save Adam from cutting himself off from human feelings, she acts to change the picture in his mind. Her action destroys both Adam's and her own ideals; after learning that her father was less noble than she thought, she becomes Willie's mistress: "There wasn't[31] any reason why not then" (345/325). Adam's second disillusionment is the result; Anne's action thus destroys both Willie and Adam. Jack's failure to live up to Anne's sound ideal of a life of purposeful action condemns her to a life of inaction, when no other channel for her emotions opens up for her, and delivers her over to Willie, the man of purpose and action.

As Anne represents the desirability of transmuting Jack's ideas into action, so Lucy represents the desirability of modifying Willie's actions by ideals. After futile protests against corruption in politics and against Willie's spoiling Tom, Lucy leaves Willie but does not divorce him. As events finally change Jack so that he finds a purpose and way of life in harmony with Anne's, events change Willie so that just before his death he is about to return to Lucy and to try to make his methods conform to the ideals which he had originally shared with Lucy but had abandoned.

The implications are clear: ideas and action must achieve a balance. Wrong action produces paralysis and death: the paralysis and death of Tom and the deaths of Willie and Adam all stem from the wrong actions of Willie after he limits his ideals to his ultimate goals. Because he dislikes the means Willie uses, Judge Irwin refuses to participate in Willie's government or to lend Willie the support of his influence. But the one time when the Judge failed to withdraw from action contrary to his ideals, when he accepted a bribe to save his property, proves fatal: this wrong action is the "single act of perfidy," to use Cass Mastern's phrase, from which the suicide of the Judge and the deaths and suffering of others eventually result.

Conversely, wrong ideas produce paralysis and failure to live.[6] Adam's incomplete life, Jack's irresponsible life, and consequently Anne's unfulfilled life result from having the wrong picture of the world. Jack's wrong picture was caused by the sin and deception practiced by Judge Irwin, Jack's father, and Jack's mother, which robbed Jack of his real parents and his heritage. The positive, desirable relation of ideas and action is seen in Jack at the end. The consequences of the wrong relation of ideas and action serve to change Jack's picture of the world; realizing his own complicity and accepting responsibility,

---

[6] An extraneous episode underlines some of the themes. George, a ward of Ellis Burden's, is psychologically paralyzed by the death of his wife while performing an "angel" act in a circus. George's paralysis, his dreams of falling, the angels he makes of masticated bread, all suggest, in the larger context, the themes of paralysis, withdrawal, and innocence. His wife's aerial act symbolizes flight and innocence.

Jack becomes the integrated man of action and ideas, ready for the first time to participate in life.

Prominent among the ideas which inhibit action or motivate wrong action are evasion of responsibility and denial of guilt. At the end[32] only Jack and Anne, of the main characters, have an opportunity to embrace the opposite ideas and, through their acceptance of responsibility and admission of guilt, to build a future. The movements of flight and return home symbolize the attempt to cling to innocence. Concepts of good and evil are inevitably involved with those of innocence and guilt.

Willie evades responsibility for the corruption of his political machine by pronouncing his Calvinistic philosophy of original sin: man is inherently evil, the truth is always sufficient to threaten a man with, and goodness must be made of badness "because there isn't anything else to make it out of" (272/257). But Willie's corruption derives not from belief in this traditional doctrine but from his Machiavellian application of it to sanction his utilization of the worst elements of human nature in working towards his goals. The sophistry of his reasoning he tacitly admits when he resolves that his hospital is to be untainted by the corruption which he has justified as necessary in other government projects and when he refuses to let Tiny Duffy make a deal with the hospital contract. Jack wonders why Willie gets "so heated up just because Tiny's brand of Bad might get mixed in the raw materials from which he was going to make some Good" (276/260). The answer is, of course, that Willie retains elements of his original high ideals, though he discards the naive innocence of his youth. Willie's corruption extends to his personal life: his heavy drinking, his affairs with women, his lack of moral standards for his son—all evince his general moral deterioration. In addition to his specious Calvinism that merely serves his Machiavellian policy of expediency, Willie has another dangerous idea that justifies him in his own eyes. He is the Man of Destiny.

This concept is a theme in itself, beginning when Willie looked at Tiny Duffy as a celestial messenger delivering a divine call to greatness. The animal or mechanical pacing which Jack heard in the hotel room symbolizes the blind compulsion which had driven Willie from the time of his solitary broodings in the farmhouse, when he was groping his way toward discovery of his powers. Beneath Jack's cynicism there is a note of sincerity when he refers to Willie as having been on the road to Damascus and having seen a great light, and there is an ironic prophecy, in the same episode, in Willie's calling Duffy a Judas Iscariot. But the true Judas, of whom Duffy is a kind of *Doppelgänger,* is the evil side of Willie himself. Jack finally decides that the real reason why Willie kept Duffy in politics is that "Tiny Duffy became, in a crazy kind of way, the other self of Willie Stark, and all the contempt and insult which Willie Stark was to heap on Tiny Duffy was nothing but what one self of Willie[33] did to the other self because of a blind, inward necessity" (105/98). Jack decides this because Duffy is *his* other self too.

Willie's sense of destiny, which is part of his genuine gift and a source of his power over people, blinds him to the very truth which inspired his first appeal to the public: he is one of them, a hick and a red-neck. But when he gains power, he comes to regard the masses as brutes, as hogs to swill, and to regard men like Byram White as mere things. What one does to brutes and things does not matter.

In light of the theme of evasion of guilt and the symbolism of return home as a search for innocence, the first chapter takes on great significance. When Willie speaks at Mason City, on his way home, he concludes quietly, with the statement that he hears voices saying, "Come back boy. So he comes back." The abrupt ending, the simple naturalness, unlike the previous phony "plain folks" tone of the demagogue, have a note of sincerity. But Willie's return proves to be chiefly a publicity stunt. The farce of the picture of Willie and the dog shows the lack of genuine feeling. Jack's bit of whimsy, when he imagines that the linoleum rug might rise and sail out of the door with the King and his men on it, leaving "Old Man Stark sitting there as if nothing had happened," also symbolizes the falseness of this return home. The family reunion is not genuine; Lucy and Willie are separated, and Lucy and Old Man Stark are the only ones with a strong bond of sympathy, drawn together by what they once shared. Though Willie shows no deep desire to recapture the lost innocence symbolized by Lucy and his father, he still evades guilt.

But at the end of Willie's life, when he sees that no utopian state of innocent happiness is to be attained by Machiavellian tactics, he is truly ready to go back to Lucy, to return home in the only way open to the mature man: he assumes responsibility for the evil he has done and he desires to atone. He begins political housecleaning by breaking the contract with Gummy Larson, after the injury to Tom alters the situation; as he says to Jack, "You got to start somewhere" (411/387). When Adam shoots him before he can carry out his intentions, Willie says to Jack, just before he dies: "It might have been all different, Jack. . . . And it might even be different yet" (425/400). So the man of action ends with ideas that, had he lived, might have motivated right action and have made him a leader who could, without too great irony, be likened to Saul on the road to Damascus. Certainly we are intended to believe, with Lucy and Jack and Anne, that Willie had greatness in him, that the bad never wholly destroyed the good, and that in acknowledging his guilt he regained a measure of his lost innocence.

Willie embraced a political philosophy which stimulated action and absolved him of responsibility and guilt, men being what they[34] are; Jack embraced personal philosophies which inhibited action and allowed him to evade responsibility and guilt, the universe being as it is. The love story Jack recalls, in Chapter Seven, shows the strength of his ideal of innocence, symbolized in Anne, and the flaw which stood in the way of their happiness. Jack grew up without thinking "about right and wrong very much in connection with anything" (313/296). But he was unable to destroy Anne's innocence when his vision of her, floating in water that symbolizes innocence, fused with the scene in his room. He blamed his society for the fact that his nobility, as he came to think of it, had the same disastrous results as Cass Mastern's act of perfidy. But Anne's real reason for refusing to marry Jack was his lack of purpose. If they had been caught in compromising circumstances, she would have been quite capable of still refusing to marry him. Jack cherished the ideal of innocence but evaded the responsibility of offering Anne a life she could accept.

The first philosophy by which Jack justifies his moral neutrality and detachment, his lack of participation, is his brass-bound idealism, dating back to his college days, but due to his deep-rooted dissatisfaction with his parents. To the idealist, "it does not matter what you do or what goes on around you because it isn't real anyway" (33/30). In that mood Jack listens to Sugar Boy's target practice, which anticipates the shooting of Adam. Aimless as a person, Jack does the bidding of Willie, even to digging up the dirt on the Judge, Jack's old friend. Jack has this excuse: he could not prevent the truth from being discovered, and if he does it himself he can exercise some control over how the truth is used. And he hopes that he will find the Judge innocent and be able to go to the Boss and say, "No sale, Boss. He is washed in the Blood" (229/215).

But Jack watches without protest the progress of Willie's corruption, and that corruption destroys Jack's dream of innocence, the picture of Anne, floating inviolate, her face outlined against the stormy sky. Facts Jack dug up for Willie release Anne's moral inhibitions. But in a more culpable way Jack exposes her to corruption by Willie: he has left her free and allowed her to waste her youth when, had he united idea and action, she would have married him, even if she had had to live in a shack and eat red beans.

So, having lost his dream of innocence, Jack flees from his responsibility for its destruction and goes West. He comes back with a secret knowledge, another philosophy which absolves him of guilt much as his belief in the unreality of anything outside his mind had done. The Twitch is all. Man is a mechanism reacting involuntarily, as the tic in the man's face did or as a dead frog's muscles do to an electric current. Having discovered this, Jack is at one with the Great Twitch: "Nothing was your fault or anybody's fault; for things are always as[35] they are ... you cannot lose what you have never had ... you are never guilty of the crime which you did not commit" (330/311).

And for a while after the deaths of Willie and Adam, Jack and Anne do not speak of what has happened but maintain the conspiracy of silence which committed Adam and Willie to each other and to their death. Their silence is an evasion of guilt: "If we should ever break the conspiracy of silence we might have to face the fact of that other conspiracy and have to look down and see the blood on our hands" (430/406).

The change in Jack's attitude is effected by a series of events. First Sadie admits her guilt in telling Duffy about Anne, and though Jack does not explicitly take a lesson to himself from her moral courage, he is deeply affected by it. Then he recognizes why Tiny Duffy might well assume that Jack would work for him, as he had for Willie, and sees in Tiny *his* other self. Finally Jack gains a new concept of his mother and regains the past.

Jack's return home, as a truly mature man, is achieved, as Willie's was not. Jack's earlier return, in Chapter Three, one of a series of frustrating episodes, always ending in misunderstanding, was the return of son to mother. His next return, to disclose the truth to Judge Irwin, proved to be the return of son to father. By the Judge's suicide Jack lost his real father and figuratively lost his supposed father, Ellis Burden, but he found a mother who was capable of deep and lasting love.[7] The house to which Jack finally returns is the Judge's, more genuinely his home than his mother's house. When his mother leaves her house to her current husband and gets a divorce, Jack begins for the first time to build a home for himself and Anne; the Judge's house will be taken over by the bank when Jack's book on Cass Mastern is finished, but the physical structure is unimportant. This is the only kind of return possible: return to whatever innocence maturity can regain through admission of guilt. To the innocence of the past and the home of childhood, "you can't go home again."

Similarly Anne gives up her old home, a gift to the ghost of Adam, to become a sanatorium for children. But in the true sense she too has returned home by accepting the past. Her innocence lost by the shattering of her ideals, she had enough courage to act in response to her feelings, but, like Jack's mother, she concealed her actions and by that concealment tried to evade responsibility. Her love for Willie was a guilty secret in a locked-off room in her mind. As Jack's mother doomed Jack by her concealment of her love, so Anne doomed[36] both Willie and Adam by thinking that she could satisfy her love and evade the consequences. Both Anne and Jack's mother are saved by their willingness to feel and to suffer and by their ability to love; together they save Jack.

The doom of Adam is rooted chiefly in his romantic concept of the

---

[7] Robert Slack's interpretation in "The Telemachus Theme," *All the King's Men: A Symposium*, stresses Jack's search for a father but ignores the vital aspect of evasion of guilt and the parallels in the various returns home, as well as the even more significant rôle of the mother.

world and in his refusal to accept the real world in its non-scientific aspects. His idealism clings to the past; Jack's idealism rejects the past. Adam's literal return home, when he and Anne spend the week end in the old mansion, reveals the human side of Adam. But when he learns that his father knew and concealed the Judge's guilt, he rejects his home and the past. When he learns of Anne's guilt, he rejects her, as Valentine rejected Marguerite in Goethe's *Faust,* and like Valentine takes on himself the duty and guilt of attacking the destroyer of his sister's innocence. The destruction of Willie is the final deadly flowering of the romantic idea into act. Adam lives in the past to such an extent that his ideas and action parallel those of Jeremiah Beaumont more than a century earlier (*World Enough and Time*).

The story of Cass Mastern is central to these themes and to the concept of human life and morality which they reflect. Jack's description of human beings applies to all of the characters, including Cass: "the good comes out of bad and the bad out of good" (263/248). Cass won salvation by accepting his guilt and voluntarily expiating his sin. His view of the world prepares the way for Jack's view, a world in which guilt and innocence are inextricably intertwined, in which men must live in the agony of will and not "under the godhead of the Great Twitch" and which is "all of one piece" like a great spider web, and one act can set up in the fabric of the world a vibration that spreads infinitely (200/188–189).

Unlike the image of the spider web, the symbolic significance of most of the profusion of images is left to the reader. The most striking image of innocence is the recurrent memory of Anne: "the image of her face lying in the water, very smooth, with the eyes closed, under the dark greenish purple sky, with the white gull passing over" (126/118). This image is comparable, in its spiritual significance and its poetic quality, with James Joyce's epiphanies. Contrasted with the water images of innocence are other nature images: the scum left on the hard sand when the water has receded (214/201); the two May mornings (281/265; 284/268); the imagined early April scene on the river, when the water will be covered with water hyacinths and nature will teem with coarse, repulsive growth, succeeding the "first heartbreaking misty[37] green, like girlhood dreams" (257–258/243).[8] Chapter Seven, the story of Jack and Anne, is full of water images, the sea being the scene of or the background for most of their activity. Here the epiphany passage appears in its chronological place. There is much swimming and diving, with the kiss under water being a climax in their love. This summer is described in terms of a current or tide carrying them along, an image repeated in the last chapter to suggest the re-

---

8 Norton Girault's analysis of this passage ("The Narrator's Mind as Symbol," pp. 233–234) stresses the "principle of natural change and rebirth" and the combination of the gross and the spiritual.

gaining of the only innocence man can claim, that which he earns by admission of guilt. Jack learns what the tide promised only when he accepts the past. He goes to Anne to tell her that, having regained the past, he can make a future; it is "a very calm, clear night with scarcely a sibilance from the water on the shingle of the beach," and the bay is "bright under the stars" (459/433). The echo of "Dover Beach" is so clear that one almost expects Jack to greet Anne by saying, "Ah, love, let us be true to one another."

Closely related to the themes of guilt and innocence, flight and return, are the themes of regeneration and integration which build for the future by accepting the past. Although these themes involve family relationships more explicitly than do those of guilt and innocence, the two groups are closely interwoven. The polarity of themes contrasts death with regeneration or rebirth, rejection of the past or flight to the past with building the future on the past. The attitude of parents toward children and of children toward parents determines attitudes toward past and future and often toward guilt and innocence.

The basic concept of past and future, as Jack comes to recognize it, is that "we can keep the past only by having the future, for they are forever tied together" (329/311). But we must accept the evil as well as the good of the past, for "this time came out of that time," and if this time is not "so damned fine and beautiful" there must have been "something in that time which wasn't fine and beautiful" (221/207–208). Thus the themes of good or innocence and evil or guilt are virtually inseparable from those of past and future, of death and regeneration.

Because these latter themes involve families and family relationships, the three families and their members must be considered as groups. The first, the Starks, covers four generations, Willie belonging to the second. As a politician Willie clings to the past for its "plain folks" appeal and returns home for publicity purposes. As a son he retains some concern and respect for his father but rejects his father's principles. As a husband he consigns Lucy to the same shelf he has put his father on. As a father Willie rejects his own past as offering[38] any pattern for his son to follow. In bringing Tom up to be a spoiled, conceited young man, devoid of self-discipline and moral principles, Willie dooms him spiritually, not recognizing that his own greatness was nurtured by his struggles. In insisting that Tom be put into the game, Willie directly causes Tom's death. The crushed spinal cord Tom suffers in the game symbolizes the impossibility of regeneration, as the paralysis symbolizes the results of Willie's wrong actions. From Willie's point of view, the injury of Tom destroys the future. Ironically, having destroyed the future in Tom, Willie dies just as he seems on the verge of his own regeneration, which might to some degree restore the future.

Lucy, who has been true to her own past and Willie's, literally and figuratively is the guardian of the future. Whether the child is actually Tom's or not is immaterial; she names it for Willie and will devote to it the care and training which, if she had been allowed her way with Tom, might have saved him. All that really matters is that "it's a little baby, and nothing's its fault" (356/336). Lucy's belief that Willie was a great man, her valiant acceptance of reality, and her capacity for love make her able to build a future on the past.

The Stanton family, as Jack remembers them, present an idyllic picture, the tall man with the little girl at his knee and the fine son, living together in the family mansion, "in the kingdom by the sea." The family mansion is all that remains to Anne and Adam of the past, but a fine chivalric picture of the past lives in Adam's mind and makes him reject the present. When Jack destroys this romantic notion and shatters the father image which dominated it, nothing is left. The father who cherished his son's ideals and illusions more effectively destroys his son than does the father who brings up his son without ideals and illusions, for Adam dies guilty of murder.

In the Stanton family also the future lies in the hands of the woman. At the end Jack's regeneration depends in part on the act of creation involved in his loving and being loved by Anne: "there are two you's, the one you yourself create by loving and the one the beloved creates by loving you" (299/282).

The most complex family relationship is that of the Burdens. In Jack all of these interrelated themes are united. Son, so he thought, of a beautiful but selfish and unloving mother and a weak father, who left the wife he could not hold, Jack adopted a defensive attitude. Having rejected his mother as part of his life, though not as a person, he refuses to follow her wishes in his career. Similarly he rejects the fanaticism of Ellis Burden and rather despises him. Anne protests against his lack of feeling for his parents and says, quite justly, that he does not understand why they acted as they did.[39]

Because he has rejected his personal past and his family, Jack hides from the present and has no future. At first he took refuge from the present in historical research. But even the past offered an incomplete refuge; unable to understand the world of Cass Mastern, Jack gave up his historical research and went into one of the periods called the Great Sleep. This psychological reaction is the converse of his later rebirth: it represents a return to the womb, a deliberate and complete retreat from reality into the security of a dreamless sleep, "like a diver groping downward into dark water feeling for something which may be there and which would glitter if there were any light in the depth, but there isn't any light" (201/189).

Water here is not the image of childhood innocence but of prenatal innocence, of complete absence of consciousness and therefore of light and knowledge. Three times Jack thus retreated from the world and time: when he gave up his historical research; before he left his first wife, Lois; and when he lost his job as journalist, just before he began to work for Willie. In each of the Great Sleeps, he went to the extreme of not-knowing; the image of the inner self as a "sad, clammy little foetus" which "wants to lie in the dark and not know, and be warm in its not-knowing" (11–12/9) is an anticipatory image of Jack when he carries his rejection of past and present as far as he can, short of suicide.

A second flight to the past, this time to his personal past, is Jack's trip West when he discovers that Anne is Willie's mistress. Here also is a water image: it takes him seventy-eight hours to drown in the West; he lies "in the motionless ooze of History" (288/271) in naked innocence on a hotel bed in Long Beach when the family movie of his past has unrolled in his head. His dream of Anne and innocence ended, he has lost what he treasured of the past; evading his responsibility for that loss, he returns from the West with a new innocence, his belief in the Great Twitch absolving him of the crime he did not commit (330/311).

But the Burden family is not what it seems. The suicide of Judge Irwin, announced by the "bright, beautiful, silvery" screams of his mother, reveals to Jack that the Judge, not Ellis Burden, was his father. Jack is not sorry to swap "the good, weak father for the evil, strong one," whom he had always liked and who had been more of a father to him than Ellis Burden had. As Jack discovers, "the truth always kills the father" (375/354). Jack learns that he is the heir of the father he killed; the ice of indifference and rejection breaks as Jack weeps and says: "The poor old bugger, the poor old bugger" (376/354). But it had been a long winter.

It is his mother who gives him back all of the past, which he had[40] rejected because it seemed tainted and horrible (like Hamlet's world in his first soliloquy). When Jack can accept his mother, he can accept his past. She proves capable of love and, like Hamlet's mother, renounces her old life and saves her soul. The truth which had robbed Jack of the past and killed his father finally gives back the past and with it a new life: this is the rebirth of Jack. The symbol and meaning are found in the previous account of Adam's surgical operation, when Jack jestingly refers to baptism of the man with a new personality and seriously raises the question of how a person gets a new set of values "to exercise his personality in terms of" (337/317). Jack has gained the motive for action which he had lacked. He tells Anne, as the prelude to their future together: "if you could not accept the past and its burden there was no future, . . . if you could accept the past you might hope for the future, for only out of the past can you make the future" (461/435). The symbolism of the name "Burden" becomes explicit. Thus the "fact of the past" makes it possible for Jack to "dream the future," to forge the future "Beneath the hammer of truth on the anvil of anguish" (Brother to Dragons, 193–194).

Jack achieves the regeneration and integration which Willie only anticipated in his intention to return to Lucy and thus to his past and his family tradition. Willie was defeated by his own failures; Jack is saved by his "recognition of the common lot of our kind." He has arrived at the recognitions necessary for self-realization, for life as a man of action motivated by ideas, as defined by Warren in *Brother to Dragons:*

> The recognition of complicity is the beginning of innocence.
>
> The recognition of necessity is the beginning of freedom.
>
> The recognition of the direction of fulfillment is the death of the self.
>
> And the death of the self is the beginning of selfhood.
>
> All else is surrogate of hope and destitution of spirit.   (214–215)

Illustrating Warren's belief that "the story of every soul is the story of its self-definition for good or evil, salvation or damnation,"[9] Jack achieves self-definition through his experience with suffering and death: "Reality is not a function of the event as event, but of the relationship of that event to the past, and future, events . . . direction is all. And only as we realize this do we live, for our own identity is dependent upon this principle" (407/*384*). Since past and future are so related, man cannot evade "the responsibility of trying to achieve responsibility" (*Brother to Dragons,* 112) and assuming, with the burden[41] of the past, the burden of the future which will grow out of the past.

Jack's explanation of why his mother and the Judge did not marry when they were free to do so explains both the Judge's inability to go on living and Jack's ability to begin a new life: "by the time we understand . . . the definition we are making for ourselves, it is too late to break out of the box. We can only live in terms of the definition. . . . Yet the definition we have made of ourselves is ourselves. To break out of it we must make a new self" (373/*351*). The power that can create a new self is love, as Jack discovered when he first fell in love with Anne. Years later, his love for his mother results in the regeneration to which Anne also contributes and in which she shares.

The water images symbolizing innocence may signify, when viewed in light of the specific reference to baptism, both original innocence and lost innocence regained by baptism; this interpretation is strengthened by the fact that the water images are associated chiefly with Jack and Anne.

One theme centered in Jack is explicitly stressed from beginning to end: the theme of knowledge or man's search for truth, of man's compulsion to gain knowledge contrasted with his desire to evade it. The telegram-foetus passage shows the conflict between knowing and

---

9 Robert Penn Warren, "Knowledge and the Image of Man," *Sewanee Review,* LXIII (Spring 1955), 183.

not-knowing and concludes with a statement of the theme: "The end of man is knowledge, but there is one thing he can't know. He can't know whether knowledge will save him or kill him. He will be killed, all right, but he can't know whether he is killed because of the knowledge which he has got or because of the knowledge which he hasn't got and which if he had it, would save him. There's the cold in your stomach, but you open the envelope, you have to open the envelope, for the end of man is to know" (12/9). In telling his story, Jack is impelled by the same truth Jeremiah Beaumont learned too late to save himself: "life tells no tales in the end, for all the lies ... will at last speak together in a great chorus of truth in many voices ... that is all we need: knowledge. That is not redemption, but is almost better than redemption" (*World Enough and Time*, 460).

As a historian, Jack sees life and history in terms of Motion toward Knowledge. "For Life is a fire burning along a piece of string ... and the string is what we don't know, our Ignorance, and the trail of ash, which, if a gust of wind does not come, keeps the structure of the string, is History, man's Knowledge, but it is dead, and when the fire has burned up all the string, then man's Knowledge will be equal to God's knowledge and there won't be any fire, which is Life" (160/151). Jack's theme of truth and knowledge is ironically contrasted with[42] Willie's cynical assumption that the truth is always sufficient to damn a person and with his Machiavellian application of the principle that knowledge is power.

Jack's two jobs of historical research are examples of the pursuit of knowledge and the effects of truth. The story of Cass Mastern shows the emptiness of mere facts, without understanding of their significance in terms of human life and spirit. The knowledge Jack gained in this piece of research illuminates his final picture of the world and thus contributes to his rebirth. The second job is the Case of the Upright Judge. Jack takes the job partly because his compulsion to find the truth is strong. That compulsion also makes Jack confront the Judge with the facts; Jack is so deep in the truth that like an undertow or whirlpool it pulls him into "the dizzy whirl and plunge to blackness. For there is a blackness of truth, too" (364/343). The water image, usually associated with light and innocence, identifies darkness with the truth of guilt.

The truth about the Judge does release Jack from vitiating errors, but his knowledge is paid for in blood, as "all knowledge that is worth anything is maybe paid for by blood" (455/429). Jack also has to know the truth about Anne and about who instigated Adam to kill Willie. There is a kind of ironic justice in the relation of the theme of knowledge and truth to Anne: the truth Jack tells her about her father figuratively kills her father by destroying the father-image which had dominated her life.

As the water image above suggests, the images representing ignorance and knowledge may also symbolize guilt and innocence. This double symbolism often invests the light and darkness images John Hart discusses in "Some Major Images in *All the King's Men*" as symbolizing knowledge and ignorance. The blackness over which Jack and Anne maintain a precarious equilibrium is not, as Hart implies, the blackness of ignorance but the blackness of guilt, concerning which they are in a "conspiracy of silence" (429–430/*405*). To slide into the blackness is to be engulfed in guilt and despair. The truth that saves them is their acceptance of "the past and its burden" and their belief in a moral universe, a concept that Hart's "belief in Nature" or the "force in Nature" would convey only to a Wordsworthian.

The epiphany image of Anne is the dominant light symbol of both truth and innocence, signifying that spiritual revelation is one way of attaining truth. The passing of time draws off veils to show the "brightness of the image" and "our conviction increases that the[43] brightness is meaning or the legend of meaning" (126/*119*). The memory of that image reveals to Jack that he is in love, and he experiences a rapturous sense of being "right on the verge of knowing the real and absolute truth about everything" (293/*277*). This concept of love as the way to ultimate truth not only recalls Dante, especially the vision of God at the end of the *Paradiso,* but anticipates the redemptive power of love demonstrated at the end of the novel, which completes the redemption through knowledge.

Jefferson and Warren, as R. P. W., in *Brother to Dragons,* confirm the concept of the cost and power of knowledge:

> All is redeemed,
> In knowledge.
> But knowledge is the most powerful cost.
> It is the bitter bread. (195–196)

> ... if you know,
> Can really know, a thing in all its fullness,
> Then you are different, and if you are different,
> Then everything is different somehow too. (127–128)

The elaborate structure erected on these multiple and contrasted themes, eloquent of the "paradox and doubleness of life" (*World Enough and Time,* 104), gains basic unity and simplicity from the polarity of the design. The two cycles, centered in Willie and Jack, move respectively from kinesis to paralysis and from paralysis to kinesis; from integration to disintegration and from disintegration to integration. The negative movement is determined by lack of balance, initial or developed, between action and idea; by ignorance or misuse of knowledge; by evasion of responsibility; by defective or selfish love. As Willie's death climaxed the negative movement, Jack's rebirth ends the novel with an affirmation: through knowledge and love, Jack achieves self-definition, integration, and motivation for positive action.

The implications of these patterns are clear and are consistent with basic concepts in other works by Robert Penn Warren which have followed *All the King's Men* and which develop some of the same themes.

The concept in *Brother to Dragons* of every act resolving "the essential polarity of possibility" (55) and bearing both the sweetness and the bitterness of its human origin echoes the theme of action and idea. Willie was all of a piece to begin with; his wrong ideas or wrong application of good ideas vitiated his action and destroyed both him and Tom. Adam's wrong ideas cut him off from non-scientific human[44] action because, like Jeremiah Beaumont in *World Enough and Time,* he saw the world as "the enemy of the idea," and he "had lived so long with the idea that that alone seemed real" (207). Like Jeremiah, he "had to create his world or be the victim of a world he did not create"; when he failed to bring forth "out of his emptiness" "whatever fullness might be his" (115), he became a victim of the world. So he destroyed himself, again like Jeremiah, by destroying the corrupter of innocence. "There was the perfect act, outside the world, pure and untarnished ... the perfect justice self-defining, and since defining self, defining all else" (165). The difference between Jack's and Adam's idealism, though both inhibited action, is apparent in the close resemblance between Jeremiah, killing Fort, and Jack, considering bringing about the death of Tiny Duffy. Each saw himself in heroic terms, as no doubt Adam saw himself in terms of fidelity to the tradition of honor. Jeremiah and Adam committed the act, belonging essentially to the same world. But Jack, with Sadie's help, saw himself realistically and saw his act as an evasion of his own complicity; consequently he refrained from wrong action.

Jack's wrong ideas inhibited action or allowed him to be used as a tool without judging the action. He was saved by his unflagging search for truth and self-definition. Warren's belief that "the story of every soul is the story of its self-definition for good or evil, salvation or damnation" is reflected also in the theme of self-definition in *World Enough and Time, Brother to Dragons,* and *Band of Angels.* Like Jeremiah Beaumont, Jack realized "that only when life and death shake hands do we know what is real, and in that acquaintance find our being" (*World Enough and Time,* 375). Thus Jack ceased to believe in the Great Twitch because he had seen "too many people live and die," in ways which "had nothing to do with the Great Twitch" (461/436). When he accepted the burden of guilt and responsibility, including the responsibility of love, he achieved self-definition and regeneration and was ready to act in accordance with his new ideals in a world in which good and evil are mixed and in which the only true innocence is regained through knowledge and admission of guilt. The symbolism of his name, Burden, is reinforced by Warren's use of the word in *Brother to Dragons:*

> If there is glory, the burden, then, is ours.
> If there is virtue, the burden, then, is ours.   (211)

In his own way Jack agreed with Ellis Burden that "the creation of good" is "the index of man's glory and power" (463/*437*).

Thus by a course which suggests the Hindu threefold Way of[45] Activity, Way of Knowledge, and Way of Love, Jack overcomes the division of the age, of the world of "Dover Beach." He sees the reality beneath the dreams; he is ready to participate in the struggle and cease his hopeless flight from the present and its guilt; he exchanges ignorance for knowledge; he is worthy of the love of Anne and shows how love redeems man and points the way to the future. The implication is that the age also could overcome its division if man would change his picture of the world to one based on truth and human reality and would accept the burden of human responsibility.[46]

Robert Penn Warren Chronology

1905 Born in Guthrie, Kentucky, April 24.

1921 Graduated from Clarksville, Tennessee, High School.

1921 Enrolled at Vanderbilt University.

1923–25 A member of the Nashville "Fugitives."

1925 B.A. from Vanderbilt University.

1925–27 Graduate Student at University of California at Berkeley (M.A., 1927).

1927–28 Graduate Student at Yale University.

1928–30 Rhodes Scholar at Oxford (B.Litt., 1930).

1929 *John Brown: The Making of a Martyr.* New York: Payson and Clarke.

1930 "The Briar Patch" in *I'll Take My Stand: The South and the Agrarian Tradition.* New York and London: Harper & Brothers (Harper Torchbook, 1962).

1930 Married Emma Brescia.

1930–31 Assistant Professor of English at Southwestern College, Memphis.

1931–34 Assistant Professor of English at Vanderbilt University.

1934–42 Assistant Professor of English at Louisiana State University; Associate Professor in 1936.

1935 *Thirty-Six Poems.* New York: Alcestis Press.

1935 A founder (with Cleanth Brooks and Charles W. Pipkin) of the *Southern Review.*

1936 *An Approach to Literature* (edited with Cleanth Brooks and John T. Purser). 1st ed., Baton Rouge: Louisiana State University Press; 2nd ed., New York: F. S. Crofts and Co., 1944; 3rd ed., New York: Appleton-Century-Crofts, Inc., 1952; 4th ed., 1964.

1937 Edited *A Southern Harvest: Short Stories by Southern Writers.* Boston: Houghton Mifflin Co.

1938   *Understanding Poetry* (edited with Cleanth Brooks). 1st ed., New York: Henry Holt and Co.; 3rd ed., New York: Holt, Rinehart, and Winston, 1960.

1939   *Night Rider.* Boston: Houghton Mifflin Co.

1939   *Proud Flesh.* (Unpublished play; first performance, 1946.)

1939–40   Guggenheim Fellow.

1942   *Eleven Poems on the Same Theme.* Norfolk, Conn.: New Directions.

1942   Appointed Professor of English at University of Minnesota.

1943   *Understanding Fiction* (edited with Cleanth Brooks). New York: Appleton-Century-Crofts, Inc.; 3rd ed., 1960.

1943   *At Heaven's Gate.* New York: Harcourt, Brace and Co.

1944   *Selected Poems, 1923–1943.* New York: Harcourt, Brace and Co.

1944   Chair of Poetry, Library of Congress.

1946   *All the King's Men.* New York: Harcourt, Brace and Co. Pulitzer Prize.

1946   *Blackberry Winter.* Cummington, Mass.: Cummington Press.

1947–48   Second Guggenheim Fellowship.

1947   *All the King's Men.* (Unpublished play; first performance, 1947.)

1948   *The Circus in the Attic and Other Stories.* New York: Harcourt, Brace and Co.

1949   *Modern Rhetoric* (edited with Cleanth Brooks). 1st ed., New York: Harcourt, Brace and Co.; 2nd ed., 1958.

1950   *World Enough and Time: A Romantic Novel.* New York: Random House.

1950–56   Professor of Playwriting at Yale University.

1951   Divorced Emma Brescia Warren.

1952   Married Eleanor Clark.

1953   *The Southern Review* (edited with Cleanth Brooks). Baton Rouge: Louisiana State University Press.

1953   *Brother to Dragons: A Tale in Verse and Voices.* New York: Random House.

1954   *Short Story Masterpieces* (edited with Albert Erskine). New York: Dell; 2nd ed., 1958.

1955   *Band of Angels.* New York: Random House.

1955   *Six Centuries of Great Poetry* (edited with Albert Erskine). New York: Dell.

1956   *Segregation: The Inner Conflict in the South.* New York: Random House.

1957   *Promises: Poems 1954–1956.* New York: Random House. (Pulitzer Prize, National Book Award, Edna St. Vincent Millay Prize of American Poetry Society.)

1957   *A New Southern Harvest* (edited with Albert Erskine). New York: Bantam.

1958   *Selected Essays.* New York: Random House.

1958   *Remember the Alamo!* New York: Random House. ("Landmark" children's book.)

1959   *The Cave.* New York: Random House.

1959   Elected to the American Academy of Arts and Letters.

1959   *The Gods of Mount Olympus.* New York: Random House. ("Legacy" children's book.)

1960   *You, Emperors, and Other Poems, 1957–1960.* New York: Random House.

1960   *All the King's Men* (play). *Sewanee Review.* (Spring, Vol. 68, No. 2.) (Called *Willie Stark: His Rise and Fall* for first performance in Dallas, Texas, 1958.)

1961   Appointed Professor of English at Yale University.

1961   *The Legacy of the Civil War: Meditations on the Centennial.* New York: Random House.

1961   *Wilderness: A Tale of the Civil War.* New York: Random House.

1964   *Flood.* New York: Random House.

1965   *Who Speaks for the Negro?* New York: Random House.

Suggestions for Study

NOTE: The following topics for discussion and research are intended merely to suggest the kinds of questions a teacher may raise in class discussion or the student choose as subject of an essay. Suggestions marked with an asterisk (*) call for reading of material not included in this book.

PART ONE: THE AUTHOR'S SOURCES AND INTENTIONS

The Huey Long Analogy

1. On the basis of your reading of the first five selections, make a list of the principal similarities and differences between Huey Long and Willie Stark. Do the changes make Willie seem more or less sympathetic than Long? Which of the changes are justified artistically? Can you think of any way in which the novel may be weakened by Warren's retaining some of the true facts about Long?

2. T. Harry Williams says, "In the Long story there is a great tragic query about politics and life itself. Robert Penn Warren poses the question in *All the King's Men*. How much evil may a good man have to do to do good—and how will he be changed by what he does?" Compare the discussions of Huey Long by Williams and Hodding Carter and decide how each would answer the above questions. How would Willie Stark answer them? How would Jack Burden? With whom do you agree?

*3. The life of Huey Long is interesting and significant enough to justify additional research. You may well begin by reading his autobiography, *Every Man a King* (New Orleans: National Book Co., 1933; reissued as a Quadrangle Paperback, 1964), or his "utopian romance," *My First Days in the White House* (Harrisburg, Pennsylvania: The Telegraph Press, 1935). Recommended secondary sources include Hamilton Basso, "The Huey Long Legend," *Life,* XXI (Dec. 9, 1946), 106–121; Carleton Beals, *The Story of Huey P. Long* (Philadelphia: J. B. Lippincott, 1935); Hugh Mercer Blain, ed., *Favorite Huey Long Stories* (Baton Rouge: Otto Claitor, 1937); Forrest Davis, *Huey P. Long: A Candid Biography* (New York: Dodge Publishing Co., 1935); Hermann B. Deutsch, *The Huey Long Murder Case* (Garden City, New York: Doubleday, 1963); Thomas O. Harris, *The Kingfish:*

Huey P. Long, Dictator (New Orleans: Pelican Publishing Co., 1938); Harnett T. Kane, *Louisiana Hayride: The American Rehearsal for Dictatorship* (New York: William Morrow, 1941); A. J. Liebling, *The Earl of Louisiana* (New York: Simon and Schuster, 1961); Thomas Martin, *Dynasty: The Longs of Louisiana* (New York: G. P. Putnam's Sons, 1960); Stan Opotowsky, *The Longs of Louisiana* (New York: E. P. Dutton and Co., 1960); Allan P. Sindler, *Huey Long's Louisiana: State Politics, 1920–1952* (Baltimore: The Johns Hopkins Press, 1956); T. Harry Williams, "The Gentleman from Louisiana: Demagogue or Democrat," *Journal of Southern History*, XXVI (February 1960), 3–21, and "The Longs of Louisiana" in his *Romance and Realism in Southern Politics* (Athens: University of Georgia Press, 1961), pp. 65–84; David H. Zinman, *The Day Huey Long Was Shot: September 8, 1935* (New York: Ivan Obolensky, 1963).

*4. The most complete accounts of the life and career of Dr. Carl Weiss, the presumed assassin of Long, are to be found in the Deutsch and Zinman books listed above. Using these sources, write a comparison of Dr. Weiss and Dr. Adam Stanton.

√   5. In the essay included here, Warren insists on a distinction between the "real" Huey Long and the "mythic" Long. Explain the difference. What, for example, is that "another country" referred to at the end of the essay?

↴   *6. An earlier essay by Warren on the genesis and sources of his novel appeared as "A Note to *All the King's Men*," *Sewanee Review*, LXI (Summer 1953), 476–480, and was reprinted with a few stylistic revisions as the Introduction to the Modern Library edition of the novel in 1953. Read this earlier essay, compare it with the one included here, and decide what effect, if any, ten years have had on Warren's conception of his novel.

*7. Write a comparison of *All the King's Men* with one of the other novels supposedly inspired by Huey Long. In addition to the works discussed by Louis D. Rubin, Jr., Sinclair Lewis's novel *It Can't Happen Here* (1935) is sometimes said to be based on the example of Long.

Three Literary Sources

1. In the earlier essay cited above (#6), Warren says, "Long was but one of the figures that stood in the shadows of imagination behind Willie Stark. Another one of the company was the scholarly and benign figure of William James." Compare the extract from James's *Pragmatism* with the philosophy expressed by Willie Stark.

2. Warren says that at the time he wrote *All the King's Men* he was "deep in Machiavelli and Dante. Machiavelli appears once in the meditations of Jack Burden, and a passage from the *Divine Comedy*

provided the epigraph of the novel." Can you find other influences of Dante and Machiavelli in the novel?

3. In addition to the literary sources acknowledged by Warren, the influence of other writers may be found in *All the King's Men*. These include John Milton, William Blake, Matthew Arnold, Nathaniel Hawthorne, Herman Melville, Joseph Conrad, William Faulkner, Ernest Hemingway, and F. Scott Fitzgerald. Make a study of the literary allusions in *All the King's Men* or trace the influence of one of the above writers.

Touchstones

1. Select one of the extracts from Warren's criticism and use it as a touchstone for the analysis or evaluation of *All the King's Men*.

2. In the Modern Library Introduction to *All the King's Men*, Warren says that his writing of the novel was interrupted "by the study for and writing of a long essay on Coleridge." Judging from the extracts from that essay reprinted here, would you say that Warren was not only writing a critique of *The Ancient Mariner* but also setting down guidelines for himself that may be applied to *All the King's Men*? Could we go so far as to say that the essay is, in a sense, *about* the novel?

*3. Several of the critics in Part Two make passing allusions to *The Ancient Mariner* in describing Jack Burden, but they do not develop the analogy. After you have read *The Rime of the Ancient Mariner*, find other specific influences of the poem on the novel.

4. Warren's "Knowledge and the Image of Man" is a direct statement of his personal creed. Granted that his philosophy of life may have changed somewhat between 1946 and 1954, how does the essay help to illuminate some of the main themes of the novel? Warren is here speaking in his own voice. How does that voice differ from Jack Burden's?

5. In the *Paris Review* interview, Warren says, "It turned out, in a way, that what he [Jack Burden] thought about the story was more important than the story itself." Do you agree with Warren? Piece together in detail what you consider (a) the story and (b) Jack Burden's thoughts and reactions to the story. Which seems more significant, and why?

6. Show some of the specific ways in which the dramatic versions of *All the King's Men* discussed by William Schutte help to clarify Warren's intentions. Judging from the later versions, what changes in the novel might Warren make if he were writing the novel today?

*7. Of the three dramatic versions discussed by Schutte, only the second ("*All the King's Men*: A Play," *Sewanee Review*, LXVIII

[Spring 1960], 177–239) is readily available for study. Read that version and make a detailed comparison of the novel and the play.

PART TWO: THE CRITICS' RESPONSE

First Analyses

1. The essays by Heilman, Baker, and Girault were published in 1947, the year after the novel first appeared; and, though the three critics had an opportunity to see numerous short reviews of the novel, it is unlikely that they read one another before writing their essays. Whereas each critic has tried to provide a "first" full-scale analysis of the novel, their basic approaches differ. Discuss these differences. Which approach seems to be most valid? How would each critic defend his approach as superior to that of the others? On the basis of your reading of Part One, decide which approach Warren himself would probably prefer.

2. Because the approaches of the three critics differ, they sometimes reach opposing conclusions regarding key aspects of the novel. Find an example of such disagreement as a possible subject for an essay. On the basis of evidence provided by the novel itself and by the critical selections that follow, attempt to arbitrate the dispute.

*3. The three critics refer to reviews of *All the King's Men* published in newspapers and journals. Using the references provided, *The Book Review Digest,* and other sources, make your own comparative study of as many reviews as you can find.

*4. Heilman sees *All the King's Men* as a tragedy, but develops his thesis in rather general terms. An exception is his statement "Then there are the ironic intra-family confrontations and injuries, the repercussions of generation upon generation, as with Hamlet and Orestes—a type of situation which, it may be observed in passing, Aristotle praises." Compare *All the King's Men* with a classical or Shakespearean tragedy on the basis of Aristotle's theory of tragedy or any single part of it, such as the nature of the tragic hero or the concepts of recognition and reversal or catharsis.

5. Heilman says that Warren in *All the King's Men* "begins with history and politics, but the real subject is the nature of man: Warren is no more discussing American politics than *Hamlet* is discussing Danish politics." Do you agree? What would you say if the latter part of the statement read "Warren is no more discussing American politics than *Julius Caesar* is discussing Roman politics?"

*6. Baker places considerable emphasis on the definition of "irony" in Brooks and Warren's *Understanding Fiction.* Using another term selected from the glossary-index of that textbook as a basis of your discussion, write an analysis of the novel. To what extent does *All the King's Men* illustrate the term you have chosen?

7. Judging from the tone of his essay, Baker has strong personal reservations about the so-called "New Criticism." Using much the same evidence that Baker has gathered, but writing from the viewpoint of an imaginary New Critic, write a reply to Baker in which what he sees as a primary limitation of the novel becomes its chief virtue.

8. Heilman writes in passing, "The fall in the old rhyme [Humpty Dumpty] becomes a version of The Fall," and Girault says parenthetically, "There can be a pun in Warren's father-symbolism that equates man's knowledge of his temporal father with his knowledge of the Heavenly Father." Can you find other such analogies with Christianity? If so, you may wish to write a paper on the religious level of meaning in *All the King's Men*.

9. In the second part of his essay, Girault discusses the minor characters of the novel as representing aspects of Willie Stark. Choose any one of the "king's men" or women and develop the relationship at some length.

10. Girault concludes his essay with a close analysis of a single descriptive passage and says, "One could probe the passage further and discover new connotations which function to point up the total meaning of the novel." Test this statement by probing further into the passage discussed by Girault. Then make a similar analysis of another passage in the novel. Close study of the opening description of Highway 58 may be especially rewarding.

Varied Approaches

1. The essays in this section are all primarily concerned with the meaning of *All the King's Men,* but the critics use different concepts and ideas in approaching the novel. Identify these different "tools" of investigation. Which are most convincing? Taken together, do these essays illustrate Warren's general remarks on criticism in Part One?

2. The social-historical approach used by Malcolm Sillars provides useful information about the background of *All the King's Men,* but as a critical approach is open to the charge that it confuses literature with life. For instance, would you agree that "the gap can be bridged either by a Populist who climbs up or an aristocrat who bends down. This is the essential lesson of *All the King's Men* and perhaps of America"? In what ways, however, can the kind of information provided by Sillars be made relevant to literary criticism? Provide examples.

3. Newton Stallknecht's remarks on the novel were contributed to a rather informal symposium and thus constitute more an "impression" than the product of a close critical investigation. On the basis

of your reading of the novel and the other selections in this handbook, would you qualify or support his view of Warren as a Christian nihilist or an existentialist? Is it possible that some of Stallknecht's conclusions may be correct even if he has based his reading on such false premises as this: "Nothing is then left of human nature, as Mr. Warren sees it, but The Great Twitch"?

4. Both Stallknecht and Norman Kelvin use the term "nihilist" in discussing Warren. Do they use it in the same way? To what extent is Seymour Gross's "reply" to Kelvin also a reply to Stallknecht? If you were Kelvin or Stallknecht, what rejoinder could you make to Gross?

5. The selection from Joseph Frank is only the introduction of an essay-review on Warren's *World Enough and Time*, but it could serve also as the introduction to a full-scale analysis of the romantic-realistic duality in *All the King's Men*. Attempt such an analysis, finding evidence from the novel, discussing the role of the minor characters, and reaching a conclusion regarding Warren's attitude toward Romanticism.

6. From Eisinger's discussion of *All the King's Men* (an extract from a longer study), try to decide what he means by "conservative." Does his analysis of the characters in terms of Hegelian dialectic support his reading of the novel as "a book that speaks so eloquently with a conservative voice"? Are there ways in which the novel could be considered "liberal" rather than "conservative"?

Three Recent Assessments

1. Compare John Hardy's discussion of the Humpty Dumpty theme in the novel with that by James Ruoff. Can Willie Stark be both Humpty and the king? See the remarks on this subject in the Preface to this handbook.

2. Hardy refers to "the 'burden' of Jack Burden." Pursue the implications of this idea. Can you find other examples of name symbolism in the novel?

3. Hardy (page 592 of the original) parenthetically suggests the subject of "another essay." Write that essay.

4. Roger Sale remarks, "If Jack is just as much a smart aleck in 1939 as he was in 1922, the whole dramatic point of the novel is evaded and finally blurred." Is this a valid criticism? The "discrepancy between tone and moral position" which Sale finds in the novel probably derives from the difference between Jack-past and Jack-present. In investigating this subject, you may well begin by writing a historical chronology of all the events in the novel that can be dated.

5. Do you agree with Sale's view that "To delete the network of symbols and the discourses on metaphysics would be to make the book

much better and not necessarily lesser"? If you do not, write a reply to Sale in the manner of Gross's reply to Kelvin. This is more difficult than it may seem, for you must not only be sure that you understand Sale's premises (what does he mean by "better" and "lesser"?) but that your own standards of evaluation are defensible.

6. Choose any one of the themes discussed by Elizabeth Kerr and see whether you can find additional evidence in the novel to support or qualify her reading. Do you feel that she has the "last word" on *All the King's Men,* or does her essay, like those which precede it, demonstrate the validity of Warren's analogy of criticism to "the monstrous Orillo": "when the sword lops off any member of the monster, that member is immediately rejoined to the body, and the monster is as formidable as ever"?

Selected Bibliography

NOTE: The following bibliography is limited to some of the more important additional criticism of *All the King's Men*. Studies included in this handbook are not listed. Although the principal books by Warren are identified in the Chronology above, students will find a more complete bibliography of Warren's own writings in Leonard Casper's *Robert Penn Warren: The Dark and Bloody Ground*, cited below. The most complete bibliography of secondary writings on Warren is Maurice Beebe and Erin Marcus, "Criticism of Robert Penn Warren: A Selected Checklist," *Modern Fiction Studies*, VI (Spring 1960), 83–88.

Allen, Charles A. "Robert Penn Warren: The Psychology of Self-Knowledge." *Literature and Psychology*, VIII (Winter 1958), 21–25. Sees *AKM* as the best of Warren's novels and argues that Warren's own vision is more important in this novel than myth, legend, and history.

Anderson, Charles R. "Violence and Order in the Novels of Robert Penn Warren." [*Hopkins Review*, 1953.] In Louis D. Rubin, Jr., and Robert Jacobs, eds., *Southern Renascence: The Literature of the Modern South*. Baltimore: Johns Hopkins University Press, 1953. Pp. 207–224. On *AKM*, pp. 215–219.

Baumbach, Jonathan. "The Metaphysics of Demagoguery: *All the King's Men* by Robert Penn Warren." In his *The Landscape of Nightmare: Studies in the Contemporary Novel*. New York: New York University Press, 1965. Pp. 16–34. A close analysis of various interlocking themes in the novel—"While Willie and Adam die unfulfilled, Jack completes the spiritual voyage; he moves, an exemplary sleepwalker, from sin to recognition and guilt to redemption and rebirth."

Bentley, Eric. "*All the King's Men*." *Theatre Arts*, XXXI (November 1947), 72–73. A review of the play *Proud Flesh*. "Warren, potentially at least, is as much a playwright as he is poet and novelist. As a *first* play it is astonishing."

————. "The Meaning of Robert Penn Warren's Novels." [*Kenyon Review*, 1948.] In William Van O'Connor, ed., *Forms of Modern Fiction: Essays Collected in Honor of Joseph Warren Beach*. Minneapolis: University of Minnesota Press, 1948. Pp. 269–286. On *AKM*, pp. 275–282.

Bohner, Charles H. *Robert Penn Warren*. Twayne's United States Authors Series, No. 69. New York: Twayne, 1964. This introduction to Warren's work "aims at providing an overview of Warren's literary career, an analysis of the themes which have preoccupied him, and an account of the development of his art as it has deepened and matured." On *AKM*, pp. 83–98 and *passim*.

Bradbury, John M. *The Fugitives: A Critical Account.* Chapel Hill: University of North Carolina Press, 1958. On *AKM,* pp. 209–212, 229.

Brantley, Frederick. "The Achievement of Robert Penn Warren." In B. Rajan, ed., *Modern American Poetry.* London: Dennis Dobson Ltd., 1951. Pp. 66–80. Published as Volume V of *Focus.* On *AKM,* pp. 67–72.

Cargill, Oscar. "Anatomist of Monsters." *College English,* IX (October 1947), 1–8. On *AKM,* pp. 6–8.

Carter, Everett. "The 'Little Myth' of Robert Penn Warren." *Modern Fiction Studies,* VI (Spring 1960), 3–12. On *AKM,* pp. 8–10.

Casper, Leonard. "Mirror for Mobs: The Willie Stark Stories." *Drama Critique,* II (November 1959), 120–124. A discussion of the changes appearing in the various play versions, the movie, and the novel itself.

————. *Robert Penn Warren: The Dark and Bloody Ground.* Seattle: University of Washington Press, 1960. The first full-length study of Warren. The book opens with an extensive survey of the past criticism on Warren, summarizes major plots, analyzes principal themes, and closes with a rather comprehensive checklist of writings by and about Warren. For Casper, Warren's chief concern is "the human condition" and how it has been affected by the past. On *AKM,* pp. 121–132 and *passim.*

Cottrell, Beekman W. "Cass Mastern and the Awful Responsibility of Time." In *All the King's Men: A Symposium.* Carnegie Series in English, No. 3. Pittsburgh: Carnegie Institute of Technology, 1957. Pp. 39–49.

Davis, Joe. "Robert Penn Warren and the Journey to the West." *Modern Fiction Studies,* VI (Spring 1960), 73–82. Discusses the journey-west motif in five of Warren's major narratives, including *AKM.*

Fergusson, Francis. "Three Novels." *Perspectives U.S.A.,* No. 6 (Winter 1954), pp. 30–44. With *AKM* Mr. Fergusson discusses James Gould Cozzens' *Guard of Honor* (1948) and Lionel Trilling's *The Middle of the Journey* (1948). He says "they are examples of the best our American fiction can show. Each of them has a high intelligence and art; they all have interesting and serious themes. . . . The three of them suggest the unmapped complexity of the United States in our time."

Flint, F. Cudworth. "Robert Penn Warren." *The American Oxonian,* XXXIV (April 1947), 65–79. On *AKM,* 65–75.

Frank, William. "Warren's Achievement." *College English,* XIX (May 1958), 366. A brief rebuttal of the essay by Norman Kelvin partly included in this handbook.

Fuchs, Carolyn. "Words, Action, and the Modern Novel." *Kerygma,* IV (Winter 1964), 3–11. A major theme in modern novels is man's need to bridge his words and deeds. The characters in many contemporary novels fail in this task, but Jack Burden of *AKM* succeeds.

Gossett, Louise Y. "Violence and the Integrity of the Self: Robert Penn Warren." In her *Violence in Recent Southern Fiction.* Durham, North Carolina: Duke University Press, 1965. Pp. 52–75.

Gross, Seymour L. "Conrad and *All the King's Men.*" *Twentieth Century Literature,* III (April 1957), 27–32.

————. "Robert Penn Warren." *Critic,* XVIII (August–September 1959), 11–13, 80–82. A close scrutiny of *AKM* that expands upon his "The Achievement of Robert Penn Warren," included here.

Hart, John A. "Some Major Images in *All the King's Men.*" In *All the King's Men: A Symposium.* Carnegie Series in English, No. 3. Pittsburgh: Carnegie Institute of Technology, 1957. Pp. 63–74. "In *All the King's Men,* characters seem to be motivated by three main sources of power: the life that has private meaning, the force that lives within Willie Stark, and the vitality of Nature. These sources of power are identifiable primarily, if not solely, through the image patterns found in the novel."

Heseltine, H. P. "The Deep, Twisting Strain of Life: The Novels of Robert Penn Warren." *Melbourne Critical Review,* No. 5 (1962), pp. 76–89.

Humboldt, Charles. "The Lost Cause of Robert Penn Warren." *Masses and Midstream,* I (July 1948), 8–20. On *AKM,* pp. 15–18.

Humphrey, Robert. *Stream of Consciousness in the Modern Novel.* Berkeley: University of California Press, 1954. Pp. 114–116.

Hynes, Sam. "Robert Penn Warren: The Symbolic Journey." *University of Kansas City Review,* XVII (Summer 1951), 279–285. On *AKM,* pp. 282–283 and *passim.*

Kaplan, Charles. "Jack Burden: Modern Ishmael." *College English,* XXII (October 1960), 19–24. Sees a strong parallel between Ishmael of Melville's *Moby-Dick* and Jack Burden: "The fate of the Ishmael-outcast who picks up his burden of human responsibility and re-enters the magnetic field is rebirth, love, and life."

Kerr, Dell. "An Exercise on Robert Penn Warren's *All the King's Men.*" *Exercise Exchange,* V (October 1957), 8–9.

King, Roma A., Jr. "Time and Structure in the Early Novels of Robert Penn Warren." *South Atlantic Quarterly,* LVI (Autumn 1957), 486–493. On *AKM,* pp. 489–493.

Longley, John L., Jr., ed. *Robert Penn Warren: A Collection of Critical Essays.* New York University Press, 1965. Includes seventeen selections on Warren's major themes, his individual novels, and his poetry. Most of the material on *AKM* is included in this handbook.

Phillips, William L. "Study Guides: Robert Penn Warren's *All the King's Men.*" *Exercise Exchange,* I, No. 1 (no date), 6–7.

Prescott, Orville. "The Political Novel: Warren, Orwell, Koestler." In his *In My Opinion.* Indianapolis and New York: Bobbs-Merrill, 1952. Pp. 24–27.

Ransom, John Crowe, and others. "*All the King's Men: A Symposium.*" *Folio,* XV (May 1950), 2–22. Ransom opens with a biographical sketch of Warren; George Gerhard discusses the structure of the novel; Richard B. Hudson points out "a few possible directions of inquiry"; Joseph Raben proposes to deal with "the essential argument" of the novel; and, finally, Newton P. Stallknecht (whose contribution is reprinted in this handbook) suggests certain philosophical implications in *AKM.*

Ray, Robert J. and Ann. "Time in *All the King's Men:* A Stylistic Analysis." *Texas Studies in Literature and Language,* V (Autumn 1963), 452–457.

Rubin, Louis D., Jr. "Burden's Landing: *All the King's Men* and the Modern South." In his *The Faraway Country: Writers of the Modern South.* Seattle: University of Washington Press, 1963. Pp. 105–130. *AKM* concerns the "dichotomy between moral absolutes and practical necessity, as dramatized in the lives of some human beings who must try to define themselves by conflicting standards."

Satterwhite, Joseph H. "Robert Penn Warren and Emily Dickinson." *Modern Language Notes,* LXXI (May 1956), 347–349.

Slack, Robert C. "The Telemachus Theme." In *All the King's Men: A Symposium.* Carnegie Series in English, No. 3. Pittsburgh: Carnegie Institute of Technology, 1957. Pp. 29–38. In Jack Burden "Warren, like so many other twentieth-century writers, has portrayed the wasteland wanderings of a modern Telemachus. But he has also done a rarer thing: he has brought his Telemachus home."

Sochatoff, A. Fred. "Some Treatments of the Huey Long Theme." In *All the King's Men: A Symposium.* Carnegie Series in English, No. 3. Pittsburgh: Carnegie Institute of Technology, 1957. Pp. 3–15. Compares *AKM* with several other novels based on the Huey Long analogy.

Steinberg, Erwin R. "The Enigma of Willie Stark." In *All the King's Men: A Symposium.* Carnegie Series in English, No. 3. Pittsburgh: Carnegie Institute of Technology, 1957. Pp. 17–28. Argues that Willie Stark is not as fully developed a character as Jack Burden; the many-sided Willie is a defect in the novel.

Stewart, James T. "Two Uses of Maupassant by Robert Penn Warren." *Modern Language Notes,* LXXX (April 1955), 279–280.

Stewart, John L. "The Achievement of Robert Penn Warren." *South Atlantic Quarterly,* XLVII (October 1948), 562–579. On *AKM,* pp. 574–578.

——— "Robert Penn Warren and the Knot of History." *ELH,* XXVI (March 1959), 102–136. On *AKM,* pp. 108–109, 113–115.

———. *The Burden of Time: The Fugitives and Agrarians/The Nashville Groups of the 1920's and 1930's, and the Writings of John Crowe Ransom, Allen Tate, and Robert Penn Warren.* Princeton: Princeton University Press, 1965. This substantial volume includes no separate discussion of *AKM,* but there are more than 100 pages on Warren's work in general, and the whole book is extremely valuable for an understanding of his intellectual background.

Strugnell, John R. "Robert Penn Warren and the Uses of the Past." *Review of English Literature,* IV (October 1963), 93–102.

Tyler, Parker. "Novel into Film: *All the King's Men.*" In John Crowe Ransom, ed., *The Kenyon Critics: Studies in Modern Literature.* Cleveland and New York: World Publishing Co., 1951. Pp. 225–232.

———. "An American Theater Motif: The Psychodrama." *American Quarterly,* XV (Summer 1963), 140–151.

Weissbuch, Ted N. "Jack Burden: Call Me Carraway." *College English,* XXII (February 1961), 361. In partial answer to Kaplan (see above), this critic sees more of a parallel between Jack Burden and Nick Carraway of F. Scott Fitzgerald's *The Great Gatsby* than between Burden and Ishmael.

West, Paul. *Robert Penn Warren*. University of Minnesota Pamphlets on American Writers, No. 44. Minneapolis: University of Minnesota Press, 1964. A brief survey of Warren's thought and art.

White, Robert. "Robert Penn Warren and the Myth of the Garden." *Faulkner Studies*, III (Winter 1954), 59–67. On *AKM,* pp. 61–64.

Woodruff, Neal, Jr. "The Technique of *All the King's Men.*" In *All the King's Men: A Symposium.* Carnegie Series in English, No. 3. Pittsburgh: Carnegie Institute of Technology, 1957. Pp. 51–62. Develops the idea that "the texture of the novel . . . depends directly upon the quality of the mind of [Jack Burden]. . . . Burden's mind, with its individual capacities and limitations, is a basic element in the technique of the novel."